IMAGES
of America

HILTONS

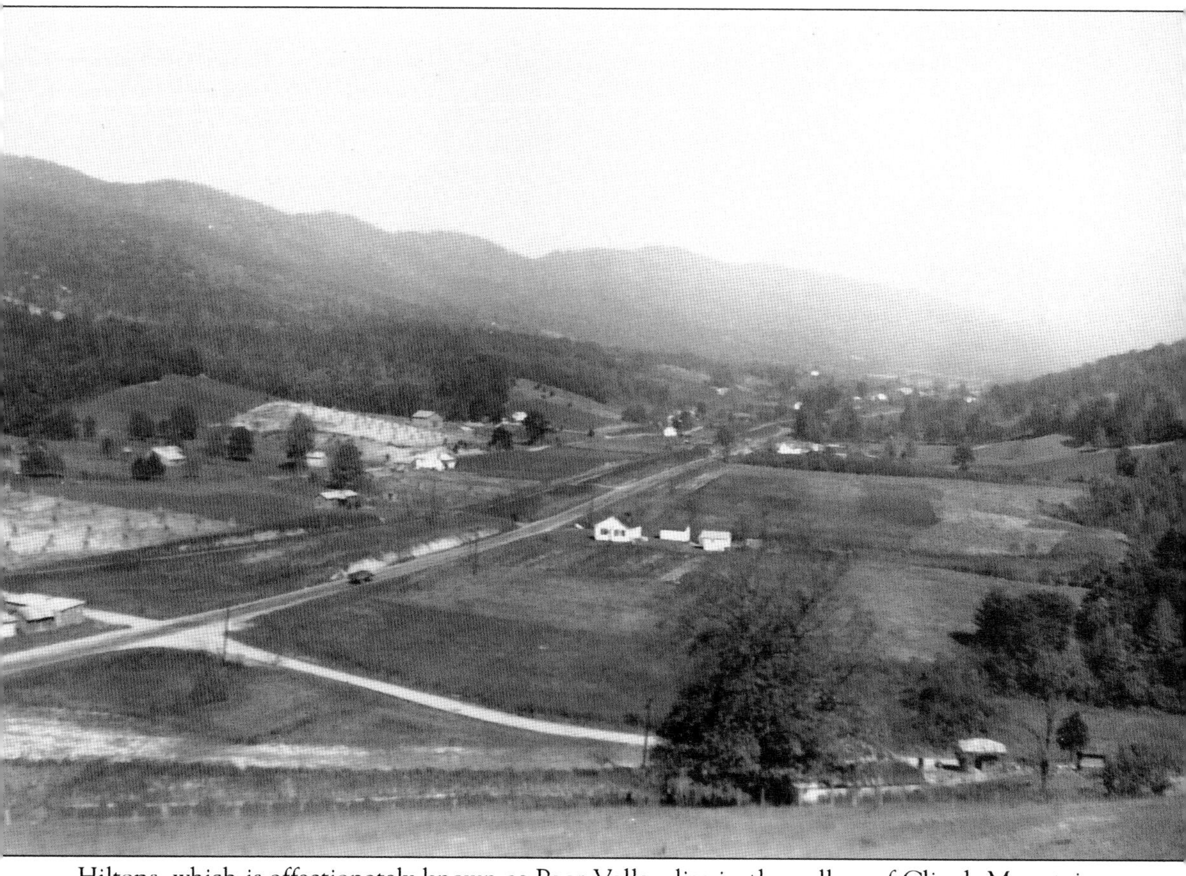

Hiltons, which is affectionately known as Poor Valley, lies in the valleys of Clinch Mountain. This picture shows "Brickyard Gap," an area to the right where the mountains open up into a gap that leads to the Holston River. At the river, there was a functioning brickyard. There is now a Brickyard Road in Hiltons to commemorate the spot. (Courtesy of Elsie Derting.)

On the Cover: Pictured in 1924 at the home of William and Rachel Parker are, from left to right, Earl Derting, Carl Derting, Homer Derting, Nevada Parker Derting, Joe Derting, Salome Parker, Rachel Parker, and William Parker. Nevada married Martin Luther Derting, and they had six sons. (Courtesy of Elsie Derting.)

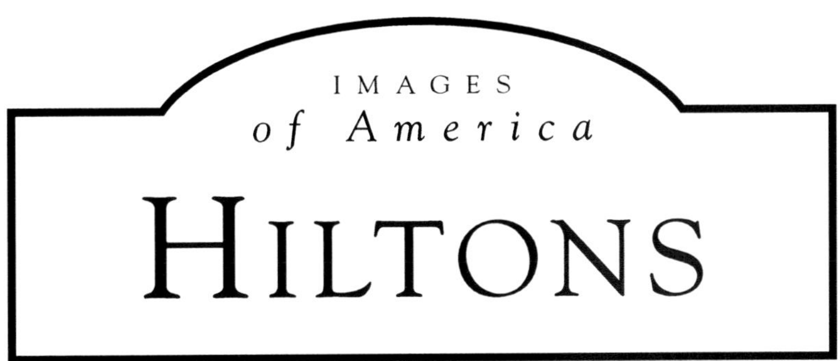

Daphne and Ronnie Matthews

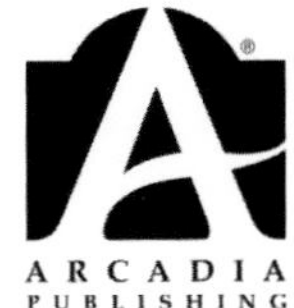

ISBN 978-0-7385-5423-5

Published by Arcadia Publishing
Charleston SC, Chicago IL, Portsmouth NH, San Francisco CA

Printed in the United States of America

Library of Congress Catalog Card Number: 2008922737

For all general information contact Arcadia Publishing at:
Telephone 843-853-2070
Fax 843-853-0044
E-mail sales@arcadiapublishing.com
For customer service and orders:
Toll-Free 1-888-313-2665

Visit us on the Internet at www.arcadiapublishing.com

To those who have gone before us and walked the final walk, may this book help to ensure you are never forgotten.

Contents

Acknowledgments

First, we would like to thank the people of Hiltons. Without them, this would not be possible. More specifically, we would like to thank Elsie Derting, Marianna Gardner, Elsie Gardner, Mary Owens, Stanley and Lennea Hickam, and Elzoria Hickam. We would like to thank Lois Grey, Betty McNutt, and Muriel Matthews. We would also like to give a special thank-you to Rita Jett Forrester, who helped tremendously with the Carter family information. Ann Goode Cooper was also a great help. She not only gave us a historical picture of her family, but she also gave us a "look" into her next book. Don't worry, Ann; we won't tell. Of course, we would like to thank God. With him, all things are possible. During the writing of this book, one thing after another kept getting in the way. We just took it in stride and knew that God would provide the resources and the time. He has, and this is our contribution to him. Without our editor at Arcadia Publishing, Brooksi Hudson, we would not have produced such a fine product. She has been a great help in this endeavor. In fact, the entire Arcadia staff is irreplaceable. Thanks to you all.

Last, but certainly not least, we would like to thank Pat Williams, who stepped in during Daphne's illness and typed. Without her, this book would not have been finished on time.

INTRODUCTION

Hiltons, Virginia, is an agricultural area that is located in the southwestern corner of Virginia. Hiltons derives its name from the Reverend Samuel Hilton. Reverend Hilton had relocated to the area from North Carolina. In 1795, he constructed a log cabin on the banks of the Holston River, and the area, which would become known as Hiltons, came into existence.

In the early days, transportation was limited to the use of horses and wagons. Roads were rough and amounted to little more than bumpy paths, which were often impassable during inclement weather. Travel from one location to another was difficult and time consuming. Fording the river to reach points beyond it was a dangerous option and unpleasant during cold weather. With the construction of the railroad in the 1880s, transportation became more manageable, and Hiltons began to grow as an important transportation center, becoming known as Hiltons Station. The railroad was also used as a mail carrier, enabling people to send and receive mail much faster than before. Arrival of the mail train was a big event in those simple times. And thanks to the railroad, visitors from the world outside could more easily reach Hiltons.

The railroad brought both commerce and transportation. Goods could be ordered to furnish homes and could be produced for export. The timber industry was important to Hiltons, as indeed it was for all of southwest Virginia. Logging companies and support industries sprang up and provided much needed cash and helped to support local businesses. Animal hides, mainly rabbit furs, and herbs were also important sources of money. These items were sent by rail to faraway places, such as New York City. A number of stores where goods could be bought or exchanged sprang up throughout the community, contributing to the economy.

In 1917, a passenger train wreck occurred in front of the R. L. Curtis home, causing quite a commotion in the sleepy little town. Two train cars had partly overturned as a result of an extreme cold spell, which had left ice upon the tracks. There were no reported injuries, and the good people of Hiltons provided food and shelter to the passengers until the wreck was cleared up and the trains were running again. As the years passed and automobiles became the dominant source of transportation, the "station" part was dropped, and the area became known simply as Hiltons. In 1933, Highway 58 was completed, running eastward to the Virginia coast. This state route enabled Hiltons to remain an important transportation route until the construction of Interstate 81, which bypasses the Hiltons area.

As in most small communities in America, religion plays an important role in the lives of people in Hiltons. Small churches dot the landscape, among them Darthula, New Hurland, Chestnut Flats, Browder's Chapel, and Stoney Point. Baptism and revivals were important religious ceremonies, as well as social gatherings. Many of the residents of Hiltons would walk for miles to hear sermons, and the churches would become so crowded that folks would stand outside and even into the road. Such preachers as Pruner Hart and John Robert Gardner would preach sermons that were renowned throughout the region. None were as well known as the Reverend T. R. Carter. Known as "Big Tom," his speaking ability, keen wit, and knowledge of mountain medicine endeared him to the residents of Hiltons and cemented his place as a local legend.

The once-thriving tobacco industry played an important role in the economy of Hiltons and the surrounding communities. For years, the tobacco plant provided a source of income for many of the families in the area. Indeed it was a rarity not to have raised the plant or at the very least helped a neighbor prepare the plant for market in some fashion. Money from the sale of tobacco provided a means of purchasing such items as vehicles, homes, Christmas presents, and luxuries, such as washing machines. The changing of times and attitudes toward tobacco products, once a lucrative enterprise, caused a reduction in its usage. Many small-time tobacco farmers have given up planting the crop, but the unique musky smell of Burley tobacco still lingers in now empty barns.

The Hiltons area has produced many fine soldiers who have served their country admirably. Among these are the six Derting brothers, the sons of Martin Luther and Nevada Parker Derting, all of whom served in the armed forces during World War II. Military service is still seen as a source of great pride and honor.

Music also plays an important role in Hiltons' society today, just as it did in years gone by. Hiltons is home to the Carter Store and Fold, owned by the descendants of A. P., Sara, and Maybelle Carter, the original Carter family, who were pioneers in the country music business. A. P. roamed the countryside memorizing lyrics and tunes to songs he had heard, as well as composing music of his own. On August 3, 1927, history was made in Bristol, Tennessee, at what has become known as the "Bristol Sessions." The Carter Family, along with other musical acts, recorded their songs for Ralph Peer, a record company executive, and country music was born. Though the original members of the Carter Family are long dead, their musical tradition lives on at the Carter Fold. Each Saturday evening, old-time country and bluegrass music is still performed there. Audiences of all ages and from various places still enjoy the distinct sound of old-time music played just as it was so many years ago. The original store, which was operated by A. P. Carter, is now a museum, along with the cabin that he was born in. The Fold, as it is known, is a part of the Crooked Road, a venture to help preserve the musical heritage of Virginia.

Hiltons is also home to author Ann Goode Cooper, who still lives in the old family home. Cooper has written 13 books and is currently working another that will be based on true events in the life of her uncle Will.

Many historic homes and farms have been passed down from generation to generation and are still worked today. As it is in many small Appalachian towns, there is a strong connection to the land and also to family. There are some who live there who would never dream of moving from the area because their loved ones are buried there, and they cannot fathom the thought of leaving their fond memories behind. This is a testament of the depth of feeling and family connection that can still be found in Hiltons today.

One

LANDMARKS

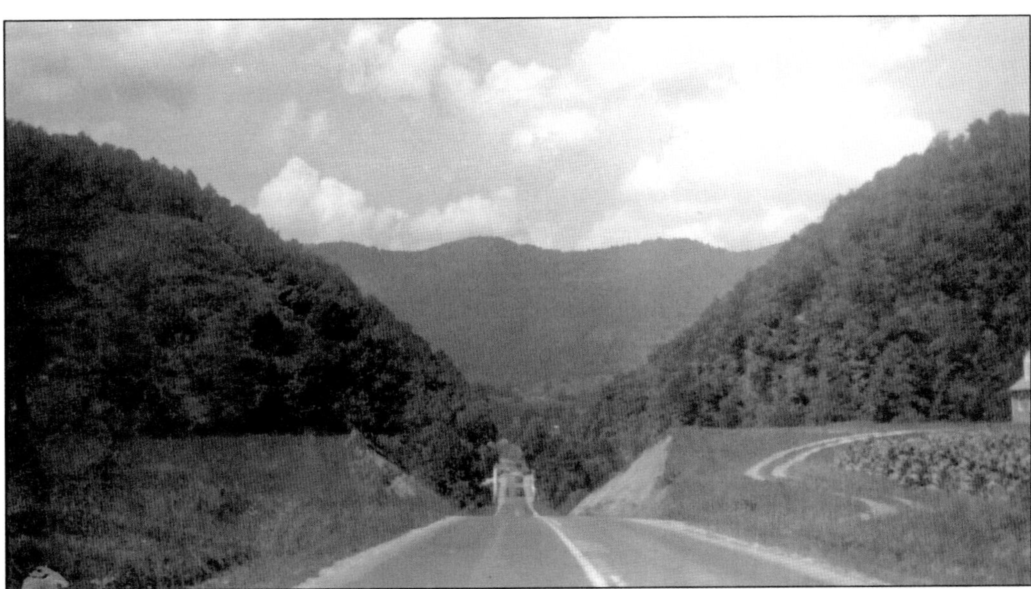

This is where the Holston River Bridge enters into Hiltons from Bristol. This valley down to the bridge is a sure sign for many travelers that they are home. Highway 58 was a major route to the Bristol area in the early days. Many celebrations were held for the opening of this passageway. (Courtesy of Elsie Derting.)

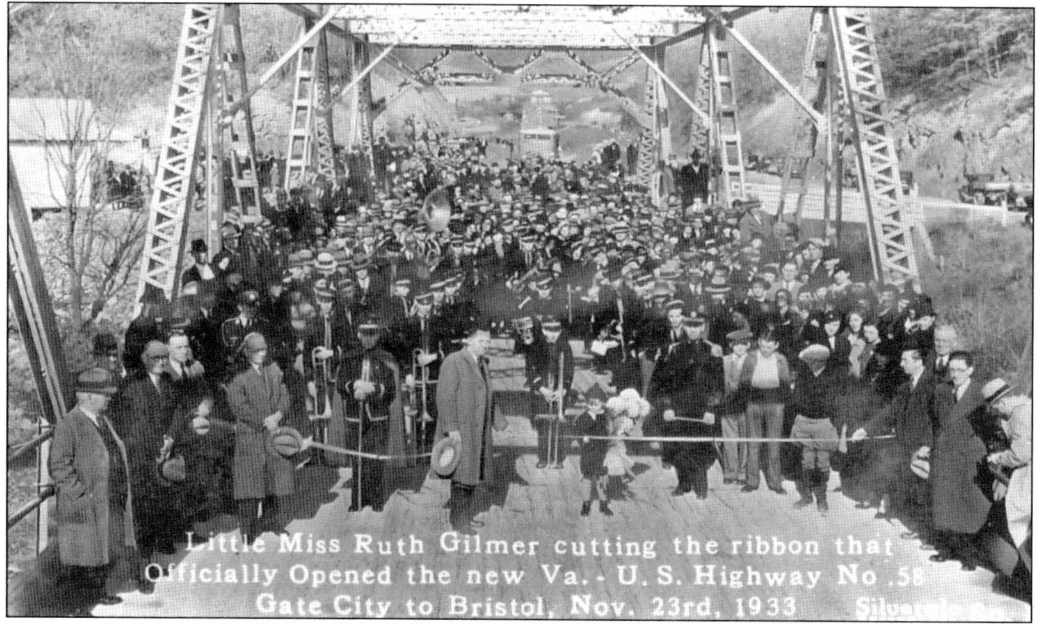

This postcard is a souvenir of the actual opening of the bridge in the early 1930s. Highway 58 was completed in 1933 and became a major route for transportation. This highway cut out much of the need for the railroad in Hiltons. (Courtesy of Elsie Gardner.)

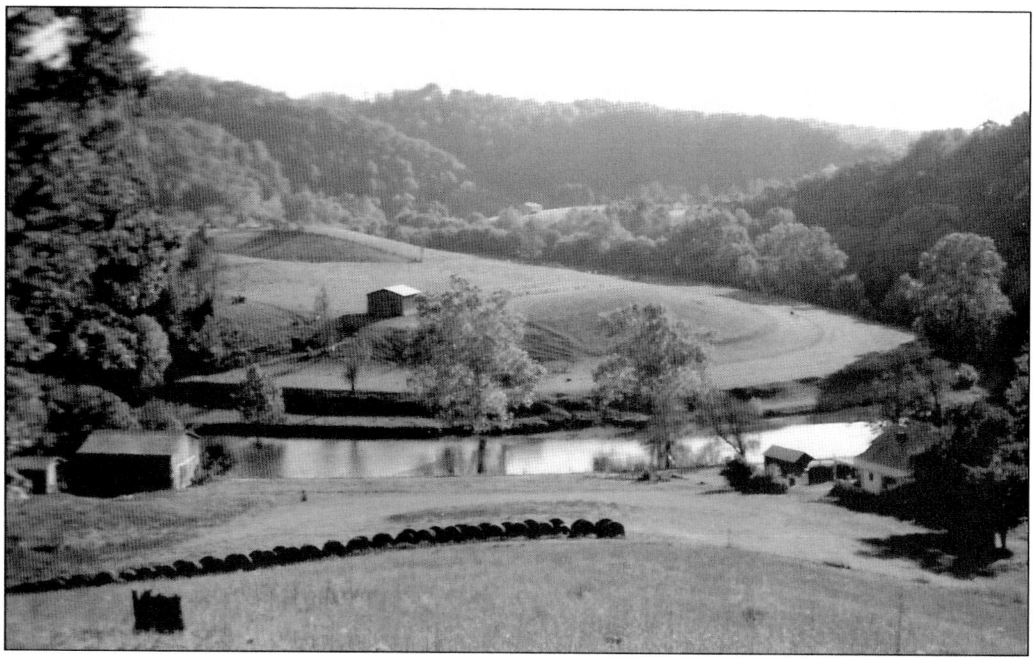

Pictured here is the beautiful Clyde Gardner farm, which is now farmed by Marvin and Marianna Gardner. Marvin, a direct descendent of Clyde Gardner, is carrying on the family tradition. In the year 2012, the Gardner family will have farmed this same land for 100 years. (Courtesy of Marianna Gardner.)

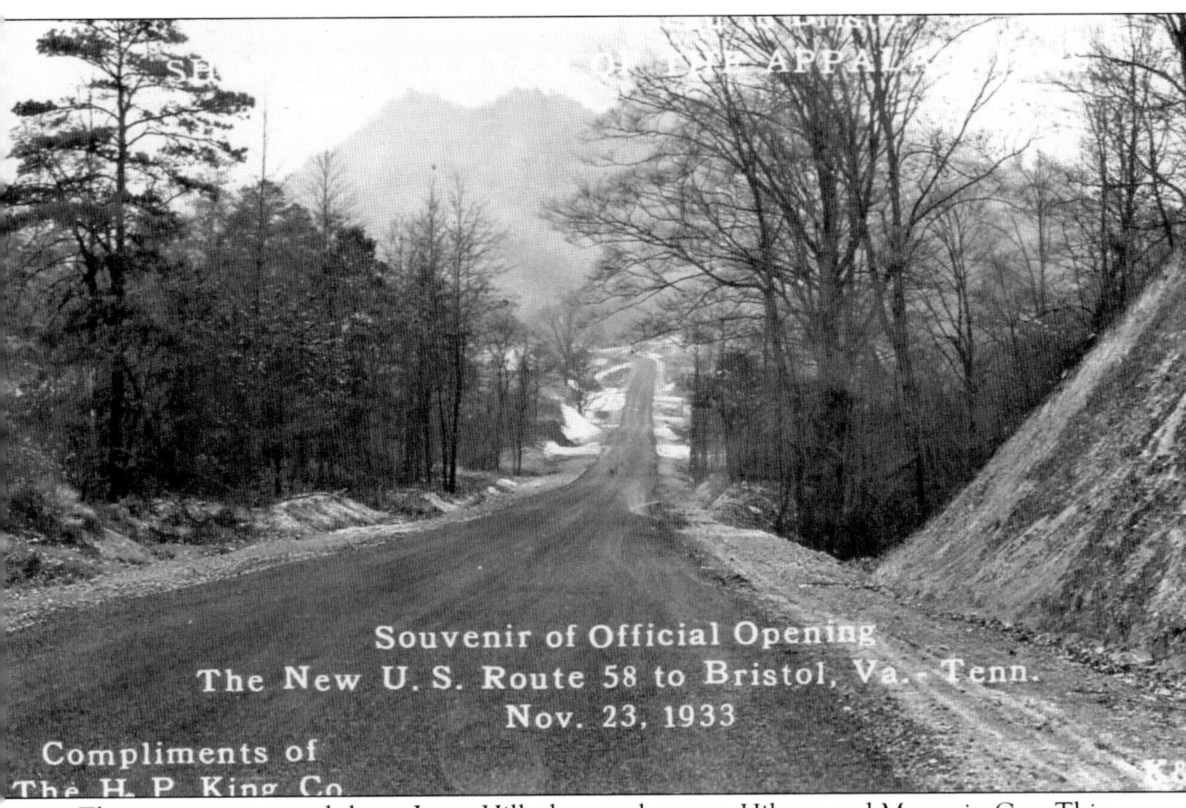

This souvenir postcard shows Jayne Hill, the area between Hiltons and Moccasin Gap. This series of postcards was given out by the H. P. King Company as a souvenir of the official opening of Route 58 to Bristol on November 23, 1933. This card could be exchanged for a free soda. (Courtesy of Marianna Gardner.)

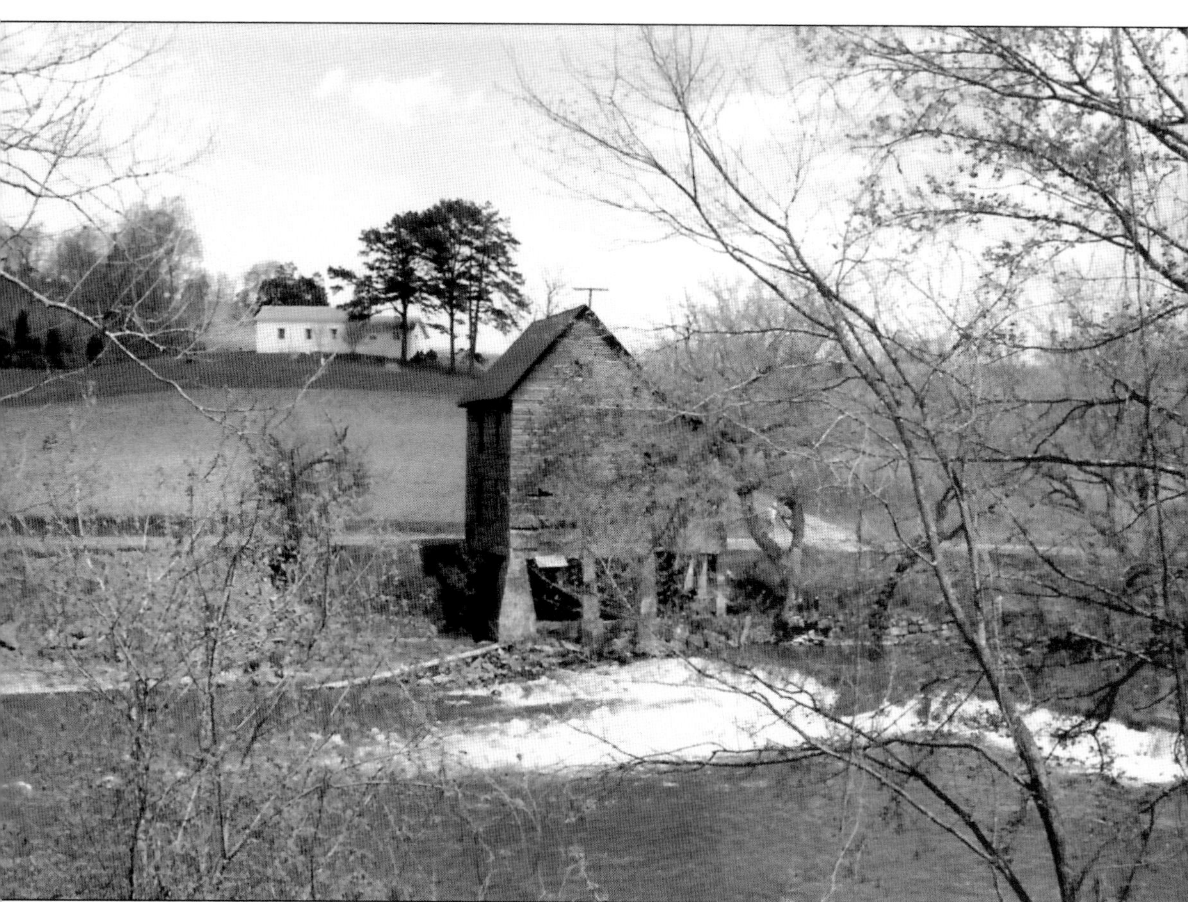

Folks from miles around would bring corn and grains to be ground into meal at the historic Lunsford's Mill. The mill has fallen into a state of disrepair, and attempts to restore it have not yet come to fruition. On the hill behind the mill, the Darthula Church is visible. The church was named for Darthula J. Strong, who first envisioned a small community school in the area and took the steps to help it become a reality. (Courtesy of Marianna Gardner.)

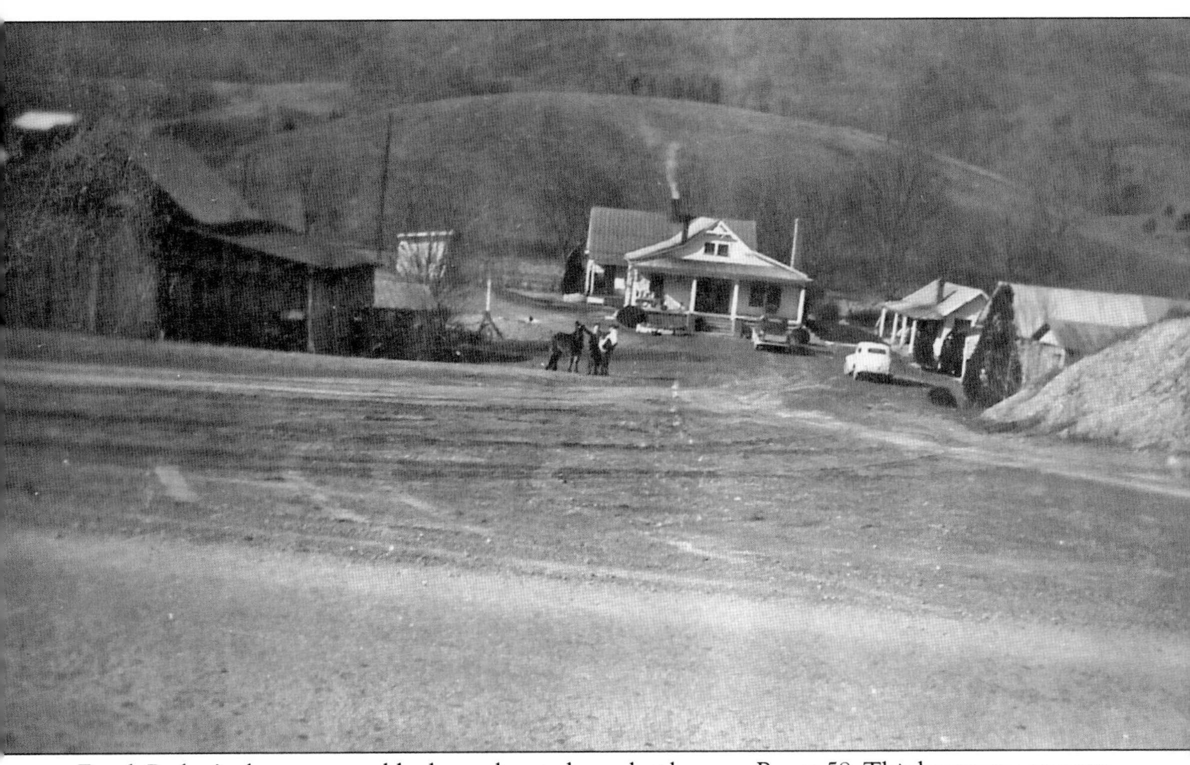

Frank Parker's place was an older home located on what became Route 58. This house was present in the early 1930s, when much of Hiltons was being built. Parker, who lived from 1883 to 1966, was born in Hiltons and married Goldie Foster. He was a mail carrier for many years, beginning his career with horseback postal delivery. (Courtesy of Elzoria Hickam.)

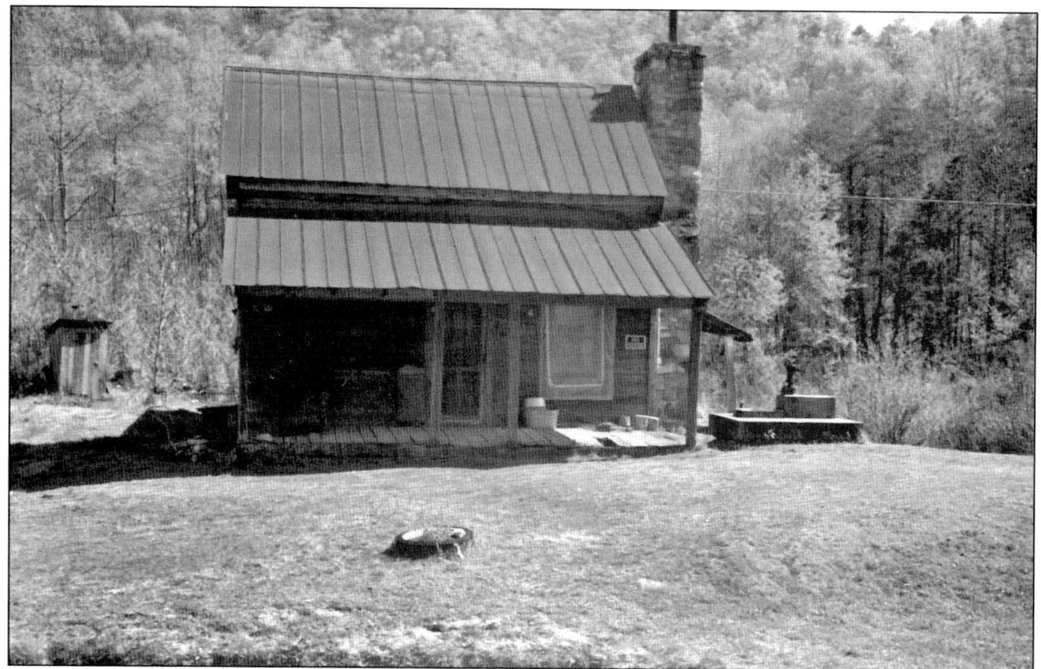

This is the Mary Ann Cookenhour home. In 1850, Isaac Cookenhour built this house as a log cabin near Brickyard Gap. His daughter, Mary Ann Cookenhour, lived in the home until her death in 1939. Isaac Cookenhour was postmaster of the Laura community beginning in 1874 for several years. He ran the post office from his home. (Courtesy of Elzoria Hickam.)

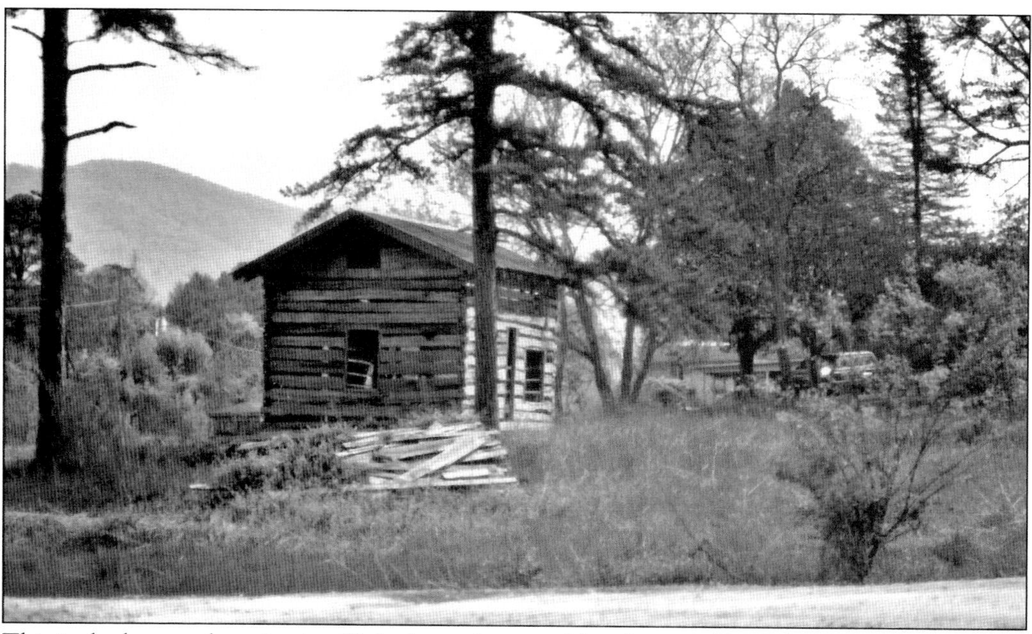

This is the house where Lucian Blalock was born and lived most of his life. The house has been relocated from its original site to its present location just off of Route 58. Blalock was born in 1881 and died in 1947. He was a merchant in Scott County, Virginia, and a foreman on the Land N Railroad. (Courtesy of Elzoria Hickam.)

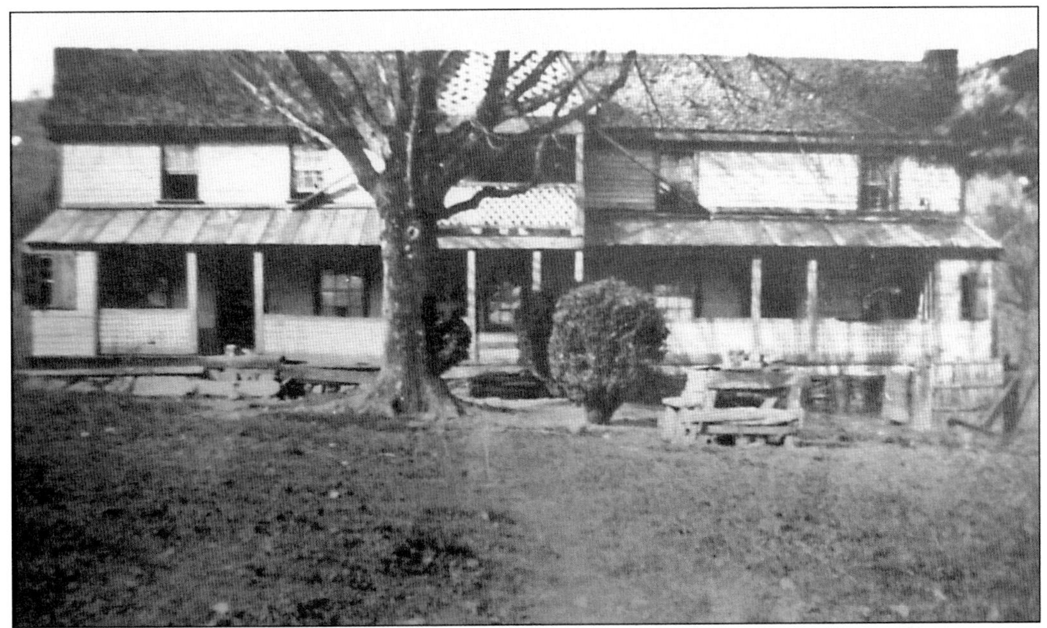

The former home of Emanuel J. Hickham is located close to what is now the "Bud" Derting property. The vintage image above shows the Hickam House at 614 Maces Spring Road, and below is the structure in more recent days. Construction of the home began before the Civil War; however, it was not finished until afterwards because of hard times during the war. Dr. Hilton's office was on the far left side of the house, and the post office was on the far right side. Hilton also served as postmaster for a while, but then his brother took over those duties. This house was an important piece of history for Hiltons for many years. (Courtesy of Elzoria Hickam.)

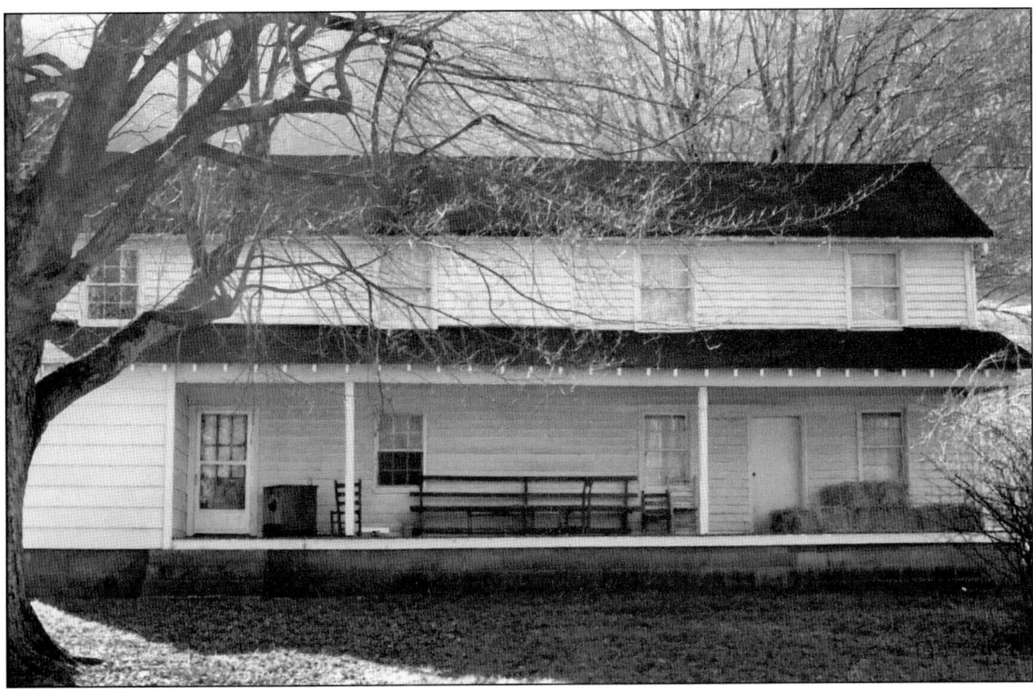

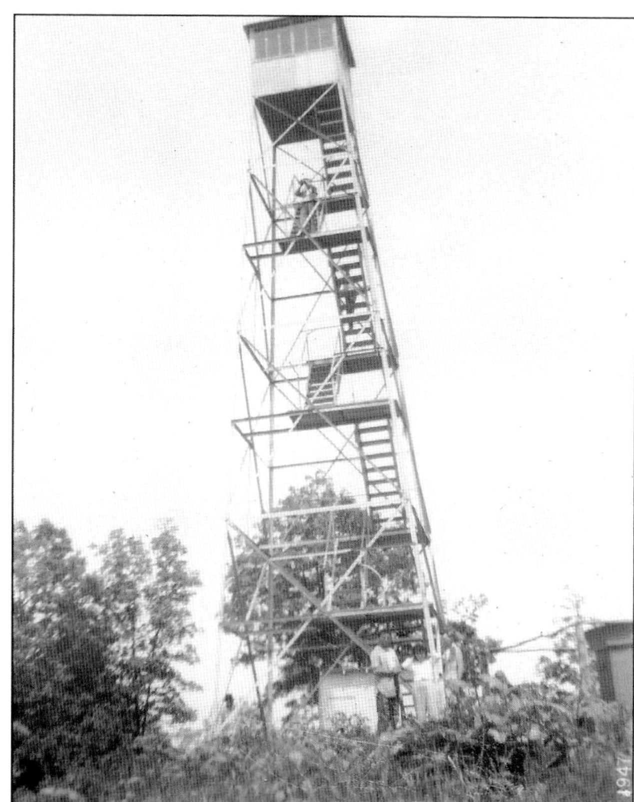

This fire tower was an important asset to the community. From its height, the forests around Hiltons could be easily observed. If smoke was seen, the location was noted and a team of volunteers could then put out the fire before it spread. Many volunteered to man the fire tower, including A. P. Carter. Note the children climbing the tower. (Courtesy of Elsie Derting.)

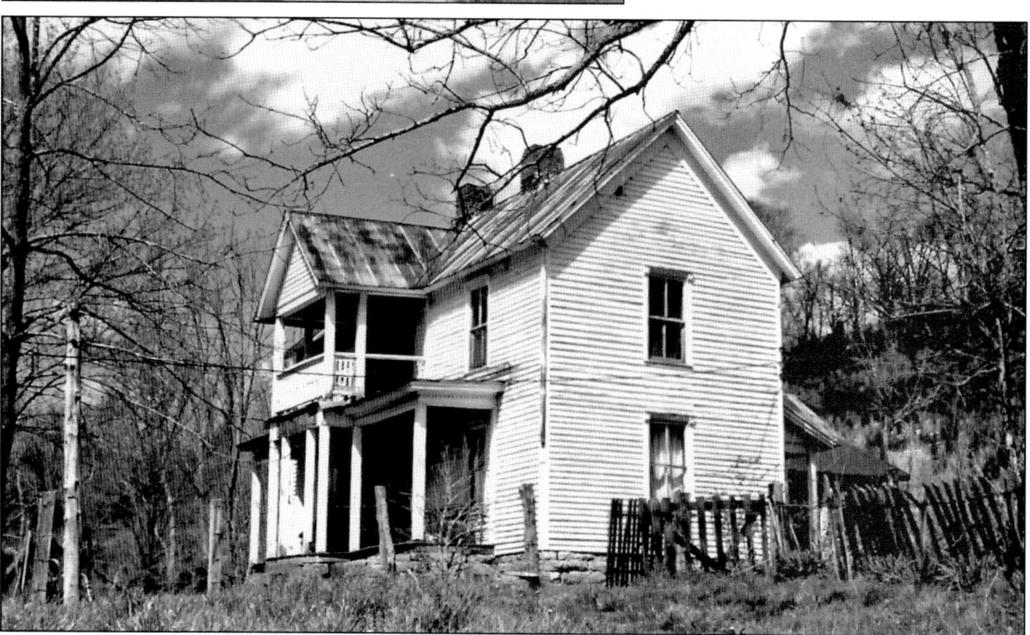

This is the home place of Elsie Gardner. It was built around 1905 by Hiram Gardner Sr. Gardner was a farmer and a logger. His mother was Margaret Barnhart, and he married Matilda Smith. Elsie Gardner married Clyde Gardner and now lives on the farm he worked all his life. (Courtesy of Elsie Gardner.)

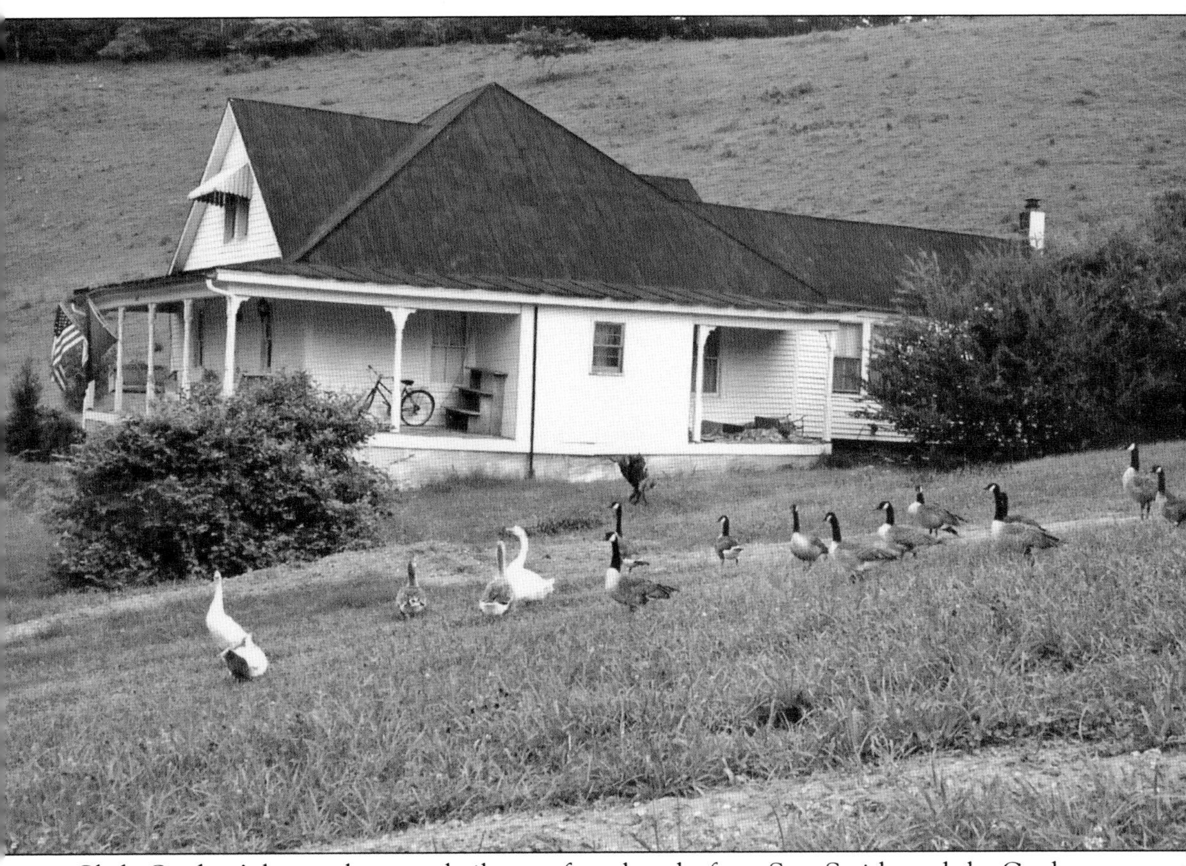

Clyde Gardner's home place was built on a farm bought from Sam Smith, and the Gardners moved into it in February 1912. This farm is now home to its third generation of Gardners, who work the fields just as proudly as their ancestors did at the turn of the 20th century. (Courtesy of Marianna Gardner.)

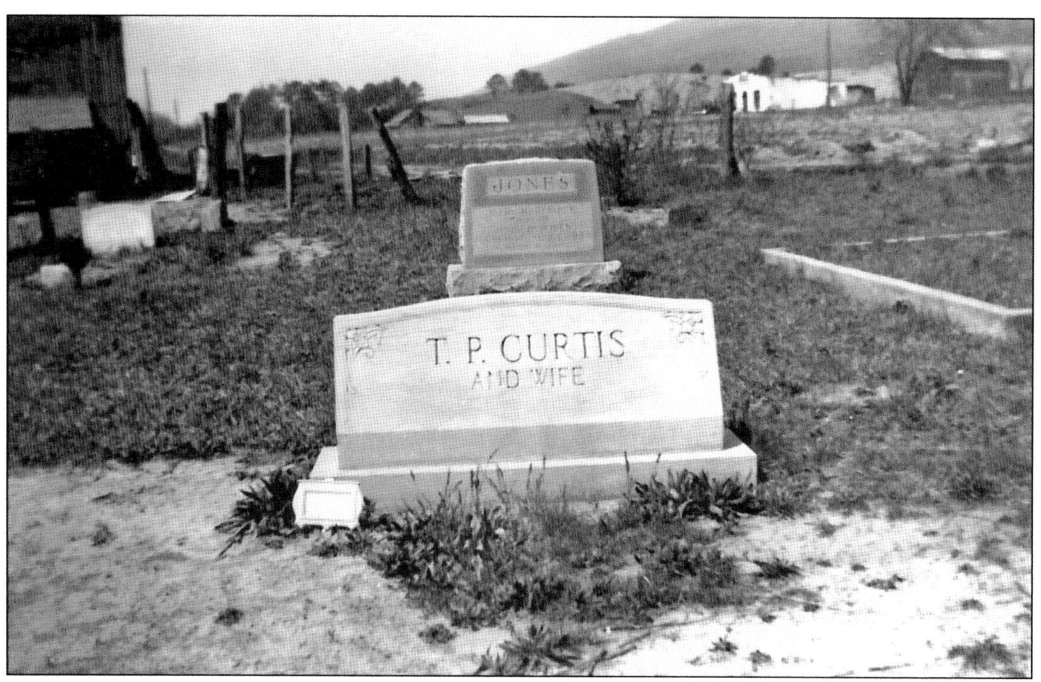

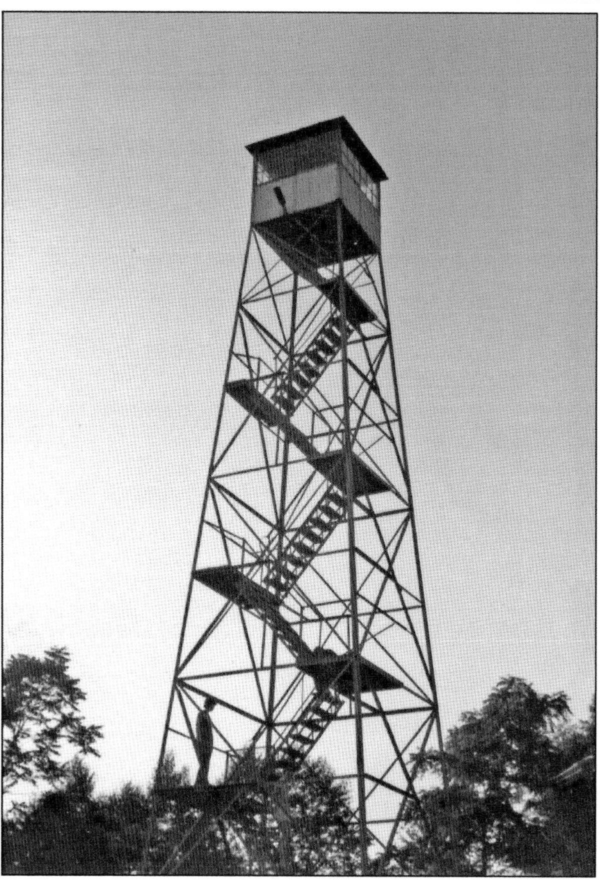

Above is the Old Hiltons Community Cemetery, which is near the old depot. The Corbett Derting Store is visible in the far right back. The cemetery has been there for many years, and its fading memorials have been cataloged. Below is one of the fire towers in Hiltons. This is Big Knob Tower on Clinch Mountain. During the dry summers, there was an increased risk of forest fire. These fires could burn rapidly, and there was great danger that fire would spread to homes and barns throughout the community if it got out of control. Standing fire watch at the tower was an important job. (Courtesy of Marianna Gardner.)

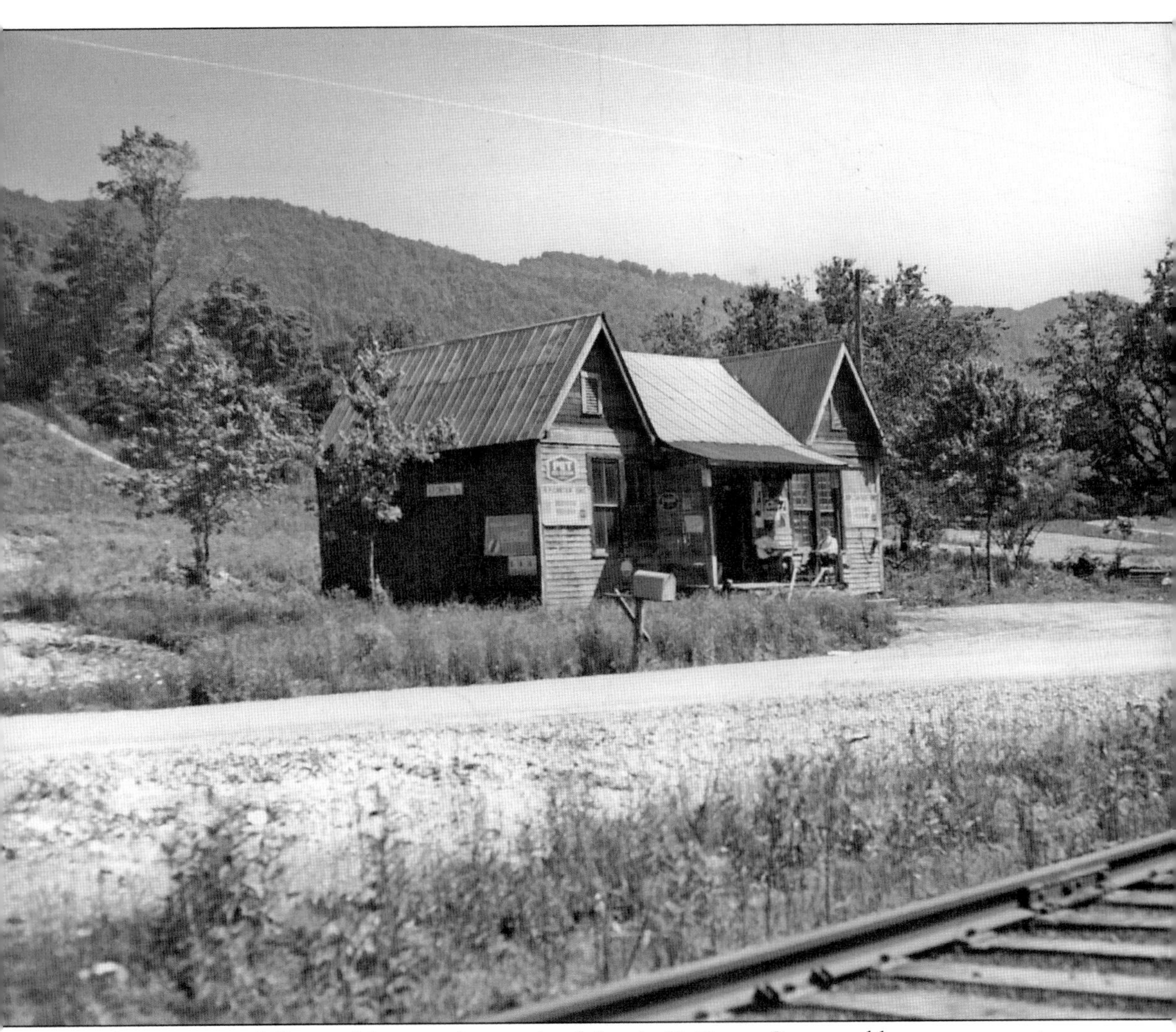

In the evenings, folks would sit on the porch of the A. P. Carter Store and have conversations, as well as play their varied musical instruments. In those simpler times, outlets for entertainment were not as accessible as they are today. These impromptu musical sessions provided a source of recreation and enjoyment. After a hard day's work, especially during the summertime, residents of the area could go and listen to the music or join in if they wanted. The store was refurbished and is now a museum that is part of the A. P. Carter Store and Fold complex. It can be visited on Saturday evenings before the festivities at the Fold begin. (Courtesy of Rita Jett Forrester.)

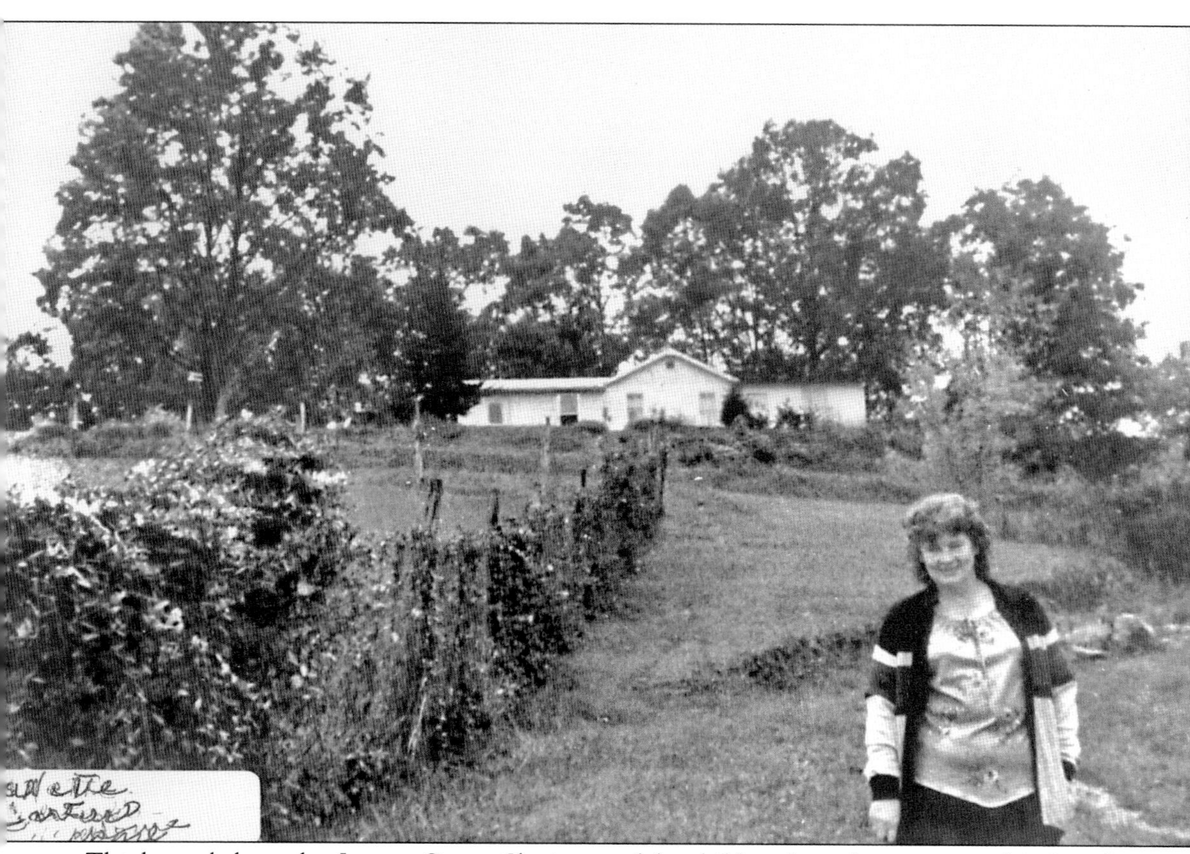

This house belonged to Janette Carter. She is one of the children from the marriage of A. P. and Sara Carter. Janette lived in Hiltons her entire life and, in the early 1970s, began having music at the A. P. Carter Store and Fold in an effort to preserve the original music of the Carter family. The Carter Music Center is one of the venues on what is known as the "Crooked Road." The Crooked Road is the state of Virginia's musical heritage trail, which spans 250 miles through 10 counties. Some of the venues are the Birthplace of Country Music Alliance, the Blue Ridge Institute and Museum, the Blue Ridge Music Center, the Carter Fold, Country Cabin, the Ralph Stanley Museum, the Rex Theater, the Old Fiddler's Convention, and the Floyd Country Store and County Sales. (Courtesy of Rita Jett Forrester.)

Two

CHURCHES

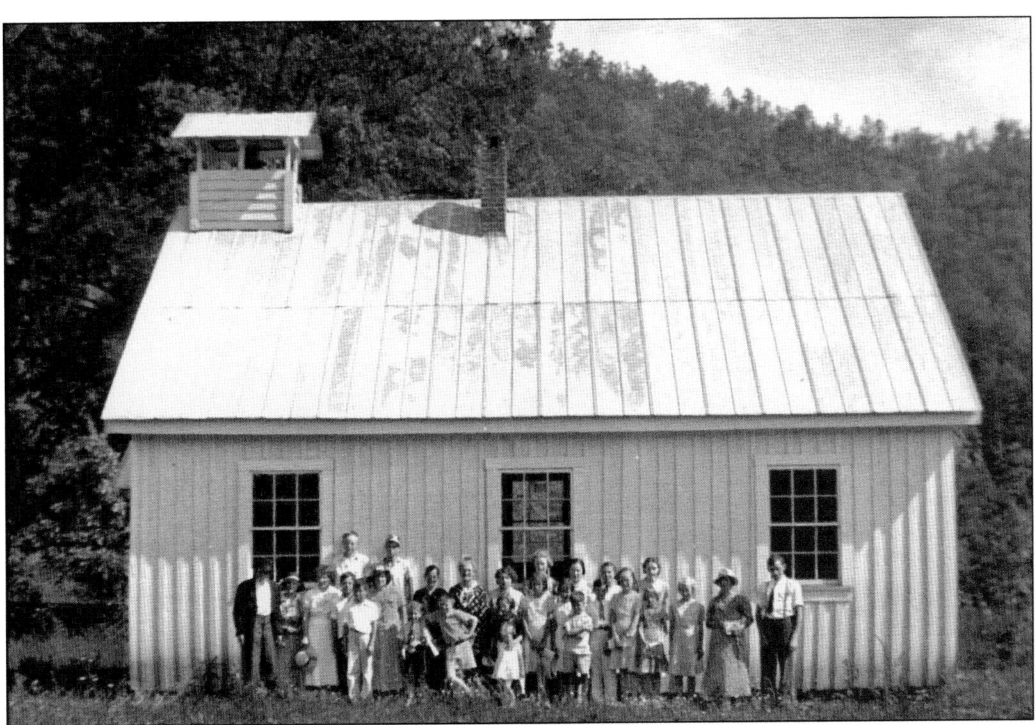

Members of the Parker's Chapel Church congregation include William Parker, Salome Parker, Florida Parker Baker, David Cochran, Roy Derting, ? Cochran, Ted Harris, Joe Derting, Lionel Johnson, Josephine Felty, Lee Baker, Addie Dixon, Wilma Sue Maddux, Nora Smith, Georgie Gardner, Loraine Smith, Juanita Maddux, Lawrence Baker, Mary Ella Felty, Ralph Derting, Madge Gardner, Audaleen Harris, Clara Faye Maddux, Elsie Maddux, Mae Litton, Nevada Derting, and Eugene Parker. Homer Derting took the picture. (Courtesy of Elsie Derting.)

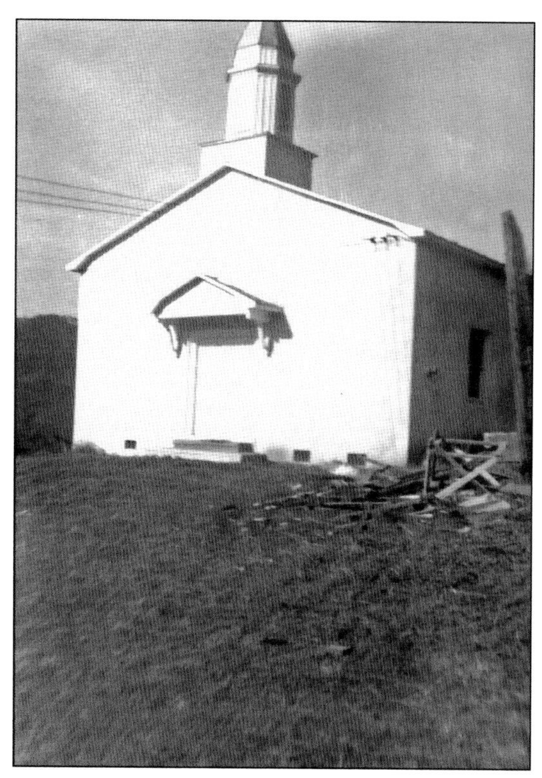

Darthula Baptist Church and School, established in 1882, was a sided building (left) constructed by John H. Hilton. Darthula J. Strong investigated having the school. Hilton gave the land. Darthula meant to give money for the school, but she died before the project began, and a relative claimed her money before it could be used. Therefore, Hilton also gave money to start the school. Members of the congregation pictured below are, from left to right, as follows: (first row) Ezra Addington; (second row) Barbara Parnell, Patsy Mason, Doris Parnell, Frankie Hodge, and Peggy Sampson; (third row) Lelia Hilton Neal, Jessie Hilton Addington, and Faye Hilton Larkey. This picture was taken in 1949. Rev. William Hilton presided in the 1880s.

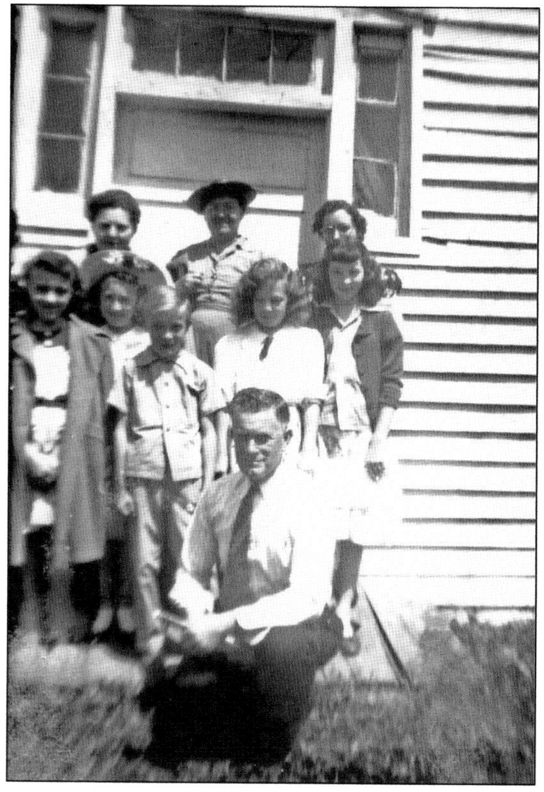

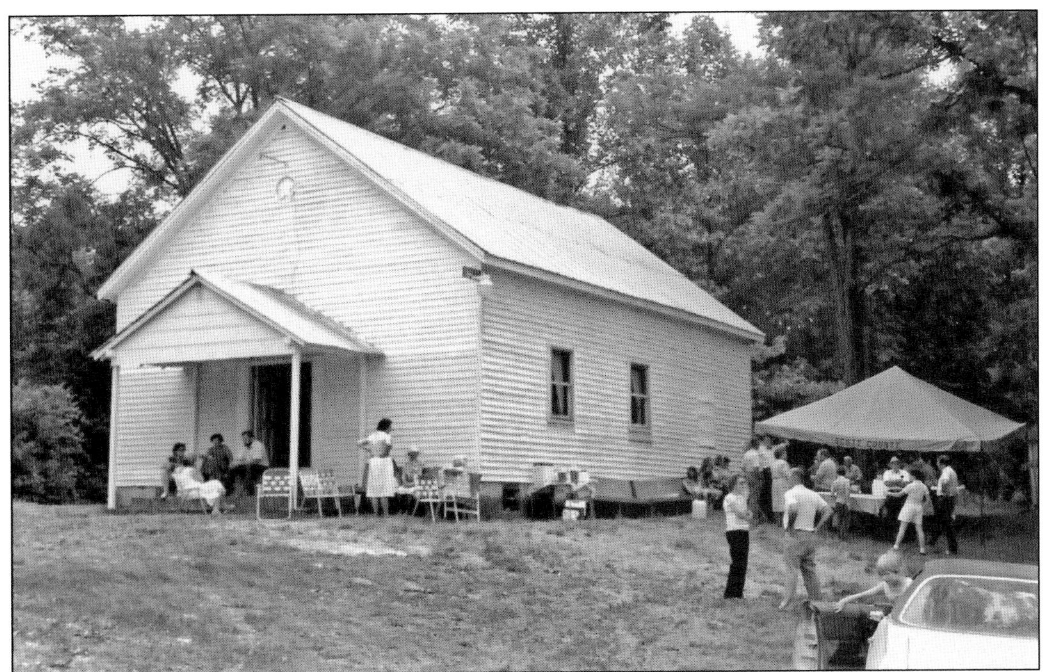

The Stoney Point School and Church was used simultaneously. Built in the late 1860s, it is still used as church today. Preacher King was a circuit minister that went to Beech Grove Church and Stoney Point Church. The building was last used as a school in the early 1930s. (Courtesy of Marianna Gardner.)

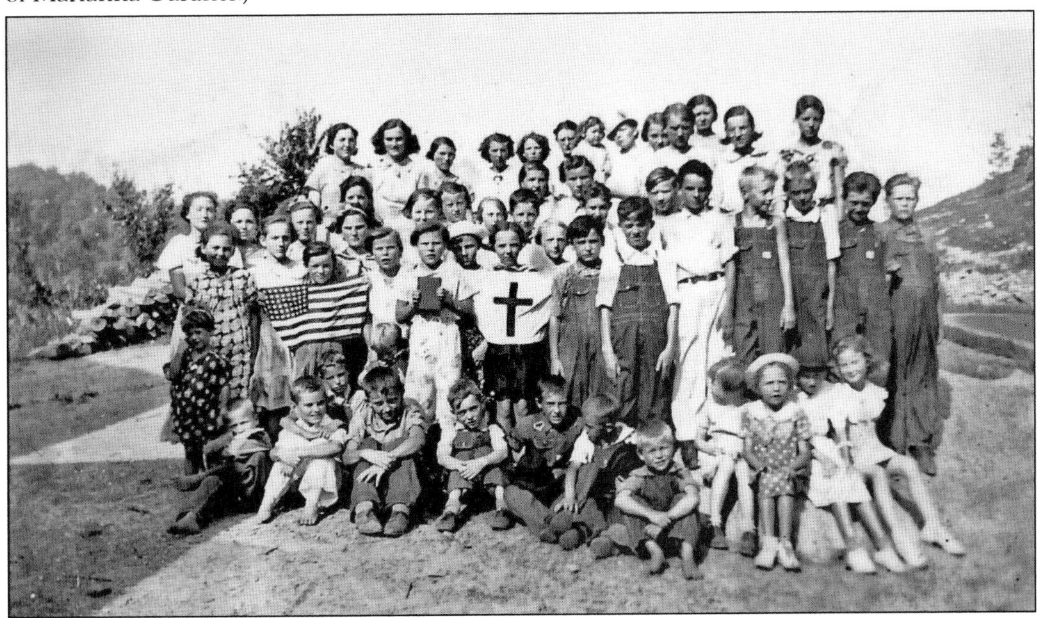

The Beech Grove Church congregation is pictured here. This is a Sunday school picture that includes Earlie Hunsucker Good. This church was formerly known as Blue Springs. It is a Primitive Baptist Church located on Highway 58 toward Bristol. The Primitive Baptist denomination stressed simplicity in their services, which consisted of preaching, praying, and singing. (Courtesy of Marianna Gardner.)

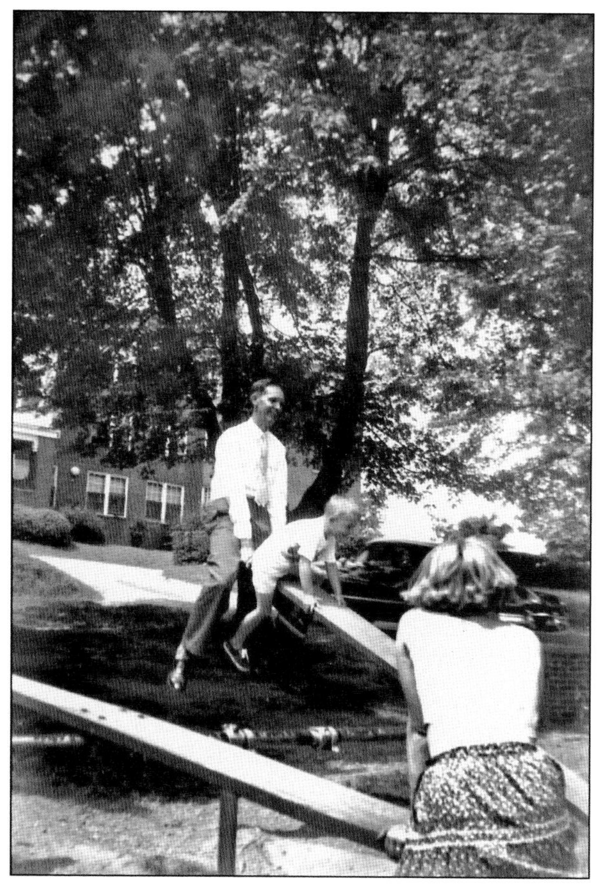

These two pictures show parts of the congregation of the United Methodist Church of Hiltons. During the 1950s, members of the congregation visited the Holston Home for Children in Greeneville, Tennessee. On the footbridge pictured below, from left to right, are Phyllis Blalock, Francis Sims, Yvonne Hensley, and Robert Morehouse Jr. At left, the preacher, J. W. Gott, is on the see-saw with the children who lived at the children's home. Gott lead the United Methodist Church for many years.

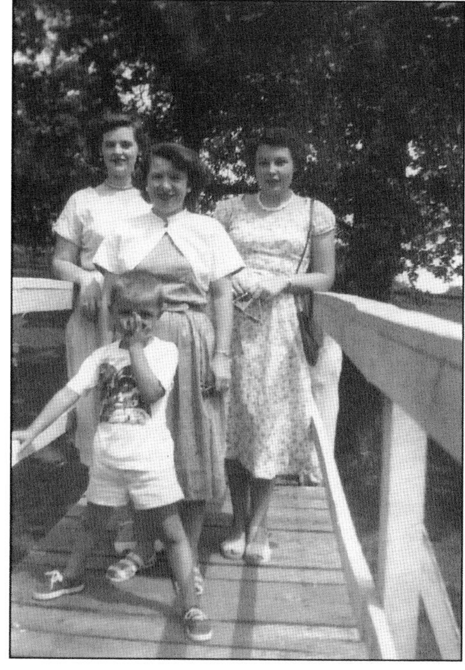

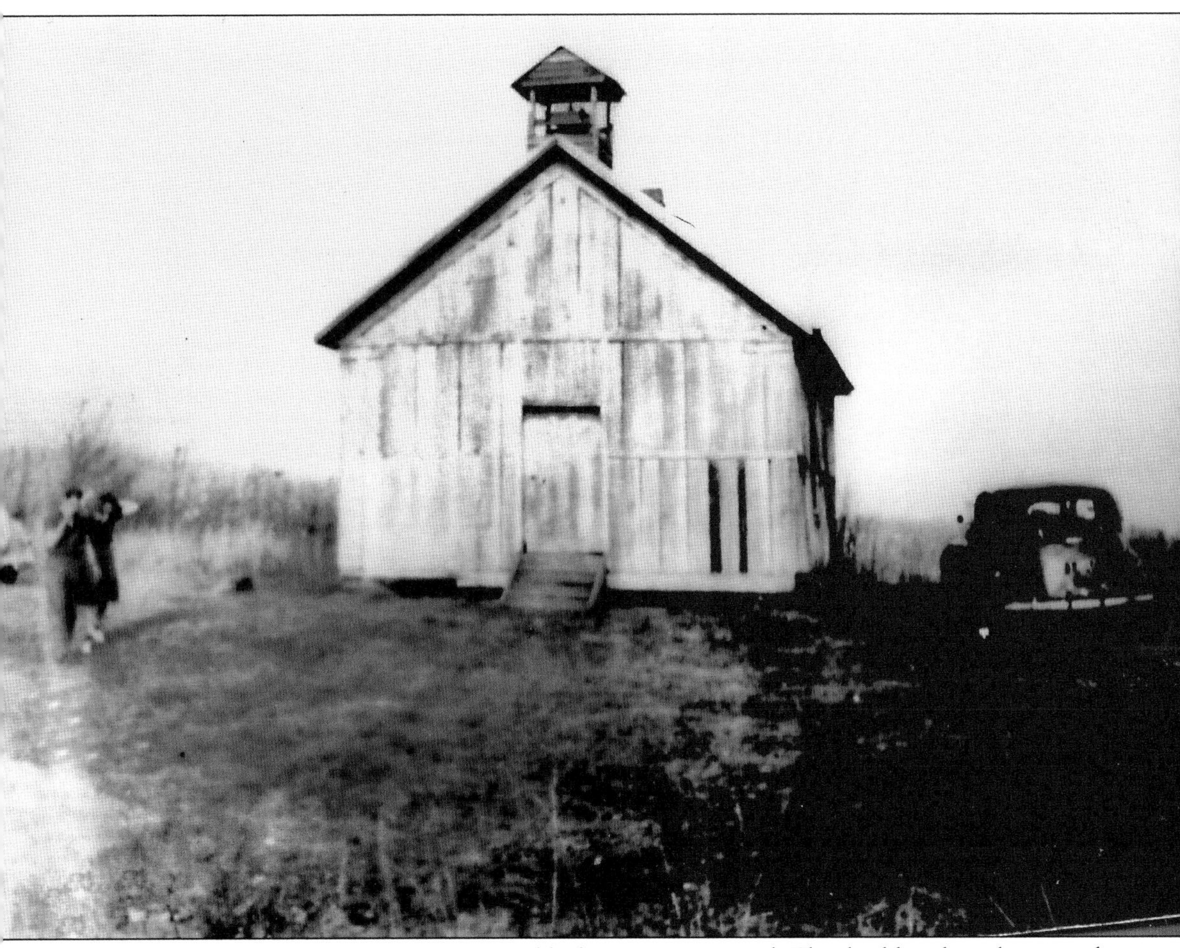

The Old Chestnut Flats Church is pictured before it was restored. This building has also served as one of the many schools scattered across Hiltons. The church still has services once a month during the summer. There have been several pastors at this church, and at one time, great revivals were held there. Each September, members and their families meet there to have a church service and dinner together. (Courtesy of Opal McMurray.)

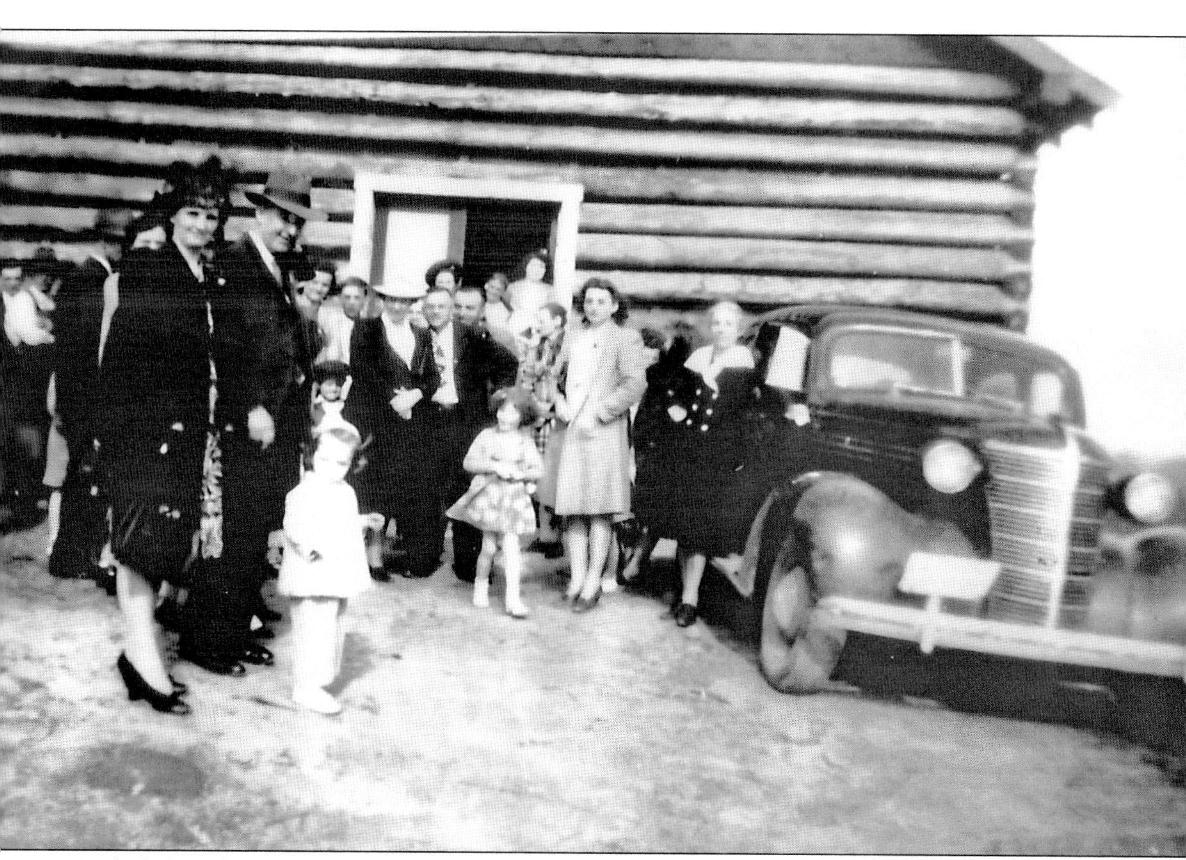

Included in this group of people in front of the old Chestnut Flats Church are Mattie ?; Odie Godsey McMurray; Bob Carter and his wife, Towns Godsey; Charlie Godsey; ? Hensley; and Madge Hensley. Mattie is leaning against Lloyd Matthew's 1951 Ford. (Courtesy of Opal McMurray.)

Three

SCHOOLS

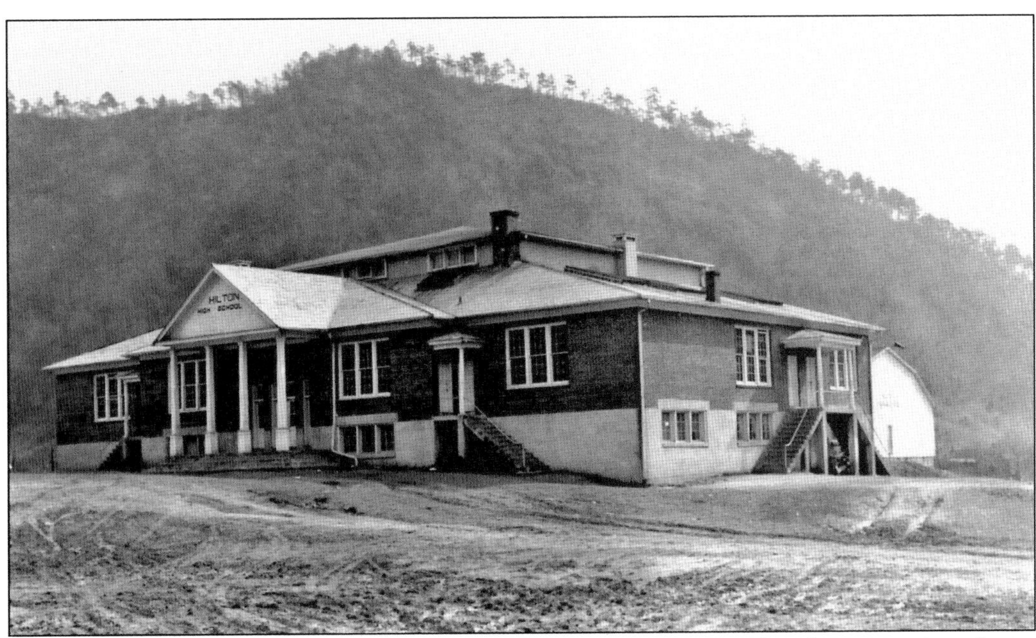

The new Hiltons High School opened in October 1921. It was considered quite modern for its day. There was a lab for chemistry and equipment for a biology lab, which for rural Virginia at the time was considered progressive. The school had a successful sports program and various types of clubs for enrichment. The structure ceased being a high school with the construction of Gate City High School in 1956. (Courtesy of Elsie Derting.)

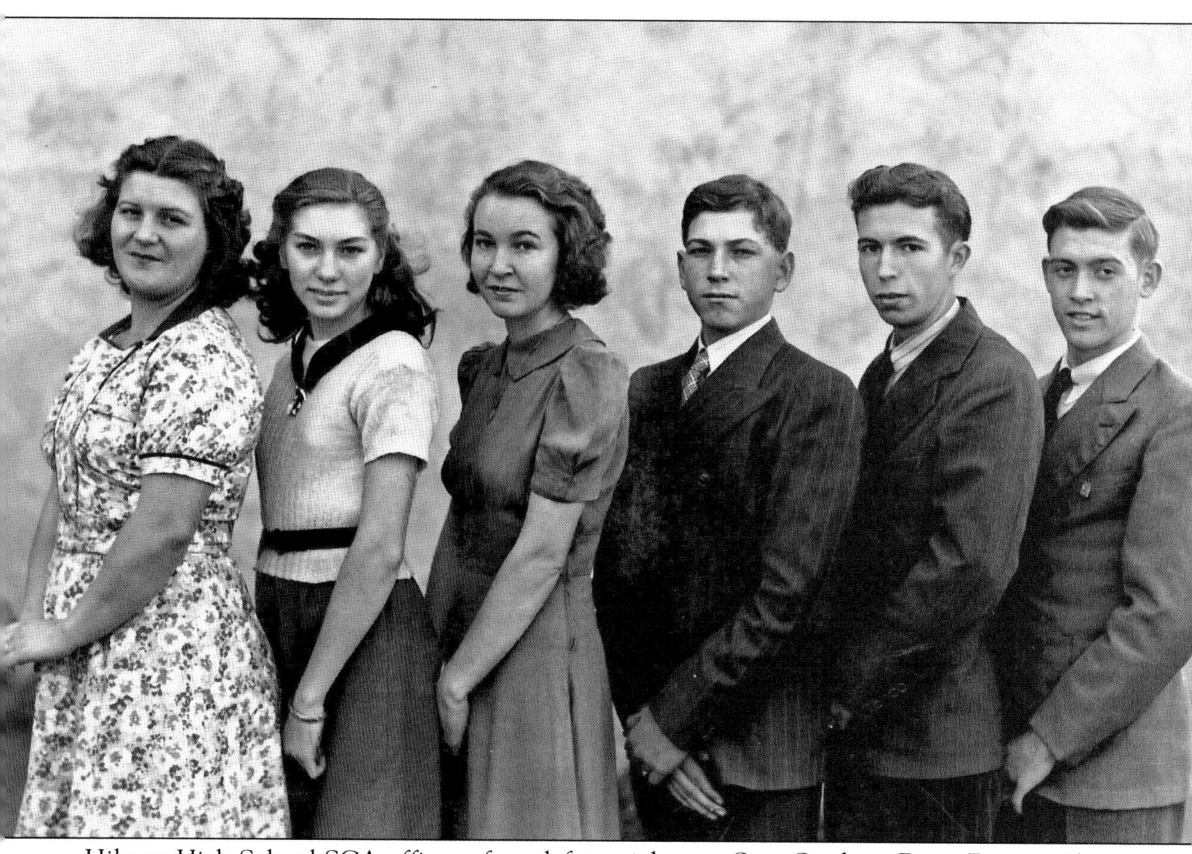

Hiltons High School SCA officers, from left to right, are Sara Gardner, Doris Farmer, Elsie Maddux, Bill Miller, S. W. Baker, and Warren Baker. This was one of the many clubs offered at the school in the 1920s and 1930s. (Courtesy of Elsie Derting.)

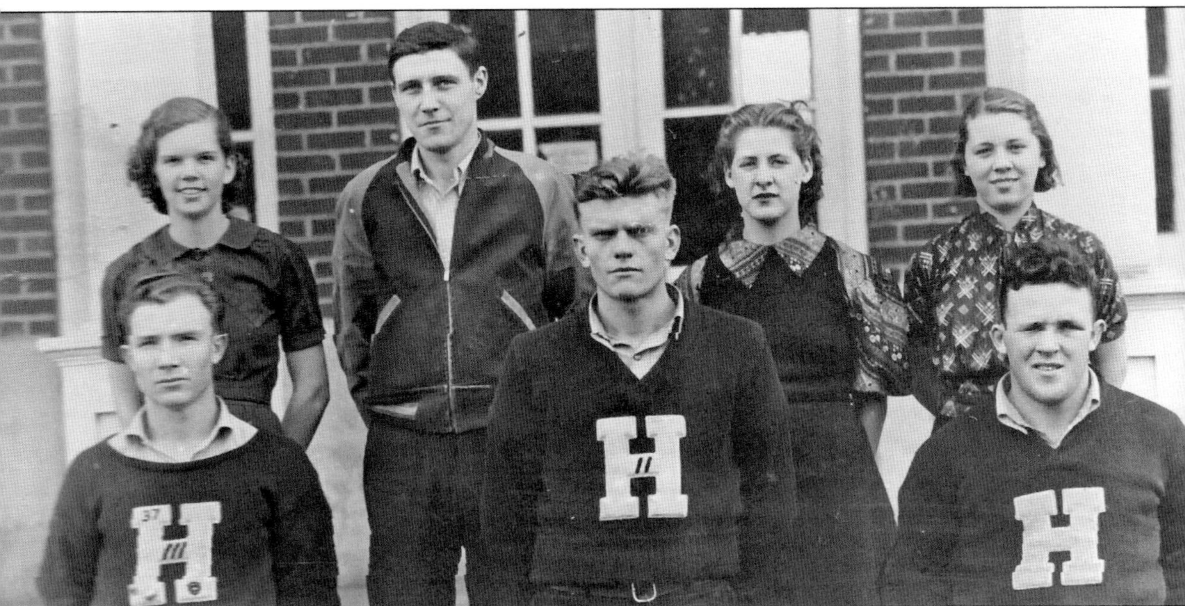

The Monogram Club had several members, including (shown here, in no particular order) Charlie Jett, president; Beatrice Gardner, vice president; Joe Carter, secretary; and Waldemar Gardner, treasurer. Other members were Willie Mae Moore, Oliver Bays, and Elizabeth Metcalfe. (Courtesy of Elsie Gardner.)

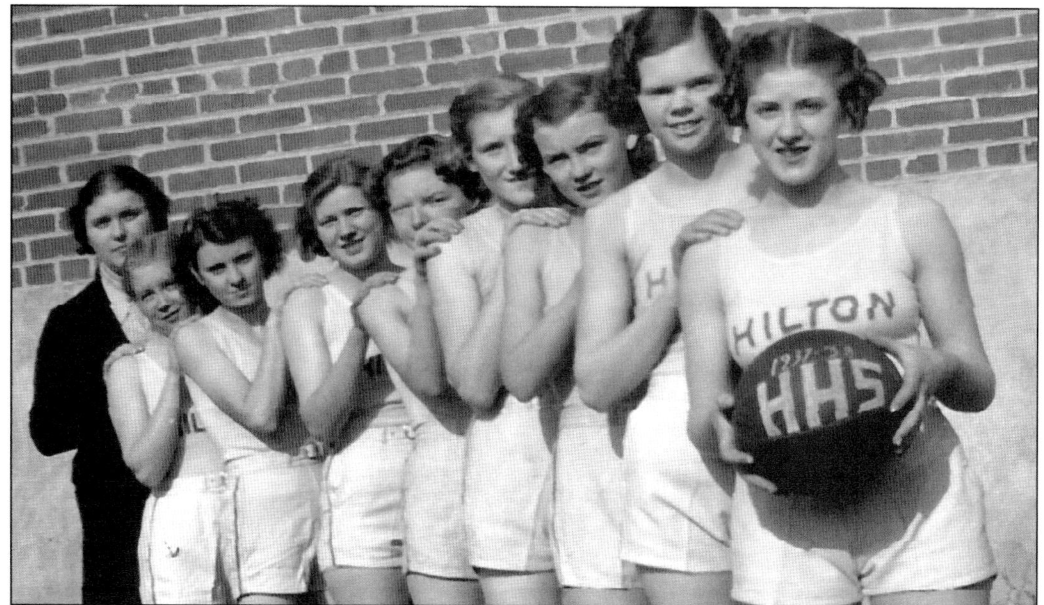

Members of the Hiltons High School girls basketball team, pictured from left to right, are Georgia Ison, coach; Hazel Dixon, guard; Lois Carter, forward; Edna Hammond, forward; Lucille Camper, guard; Barbara Blackburn, forward; Jeanette Carter, guard; Willie Mae Moore, forward; and Elizabeth Metcalfe, guard. (Courtesy of Elsie Derting.)

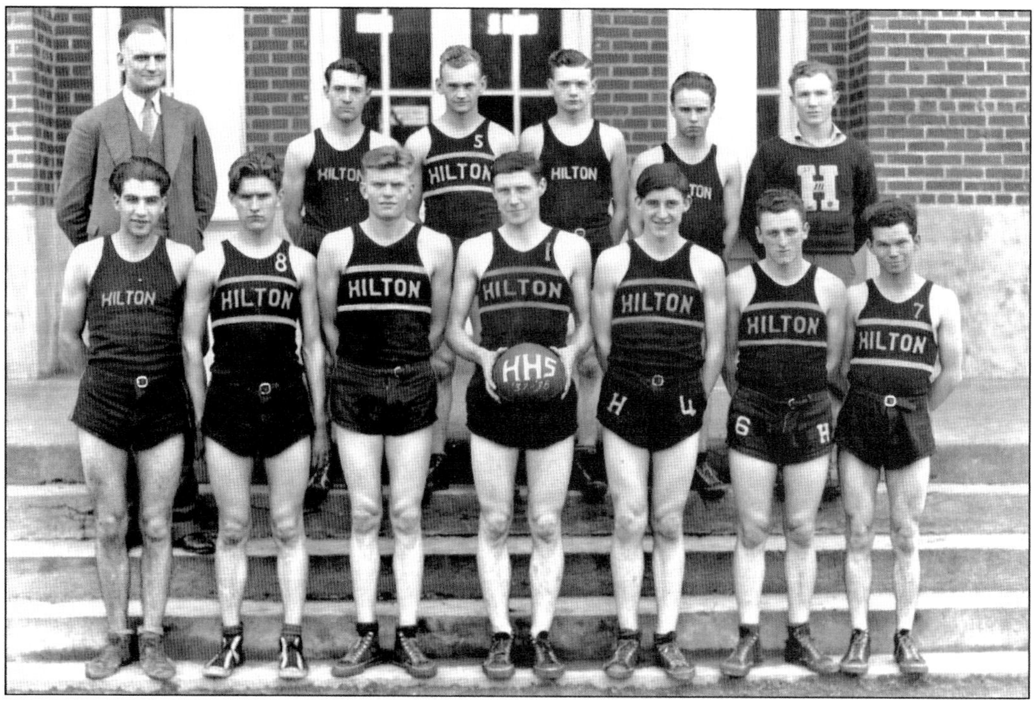

Pictured around 1929, from left to right, are the following members of the Hiltons High School boys basketball team: (first row) Charley Shaffer, Jack Carter, Joe Carter, Oliver Bays, F. M. Bays, "Bug" Addington, and Homer Derting; (second row) G. D. Grove, Sylvester Harper, Cecil Hensley, Fred Hensley, Jamie Carroll, and Charley Jett. (Courtesy of Elsie Derting.)

This is one of the first school buses used in Hiltons. O. S. Miller is pictured here with his daughter Maxie and his son Jimmy. He drove the school bus and later went on to do further work in the Scott County School System. Having a school bus in the area gave many of the children of Hiltons, who otherwise would not have been so fortunate, an opportunity to attend school. (Courtesy of Elsie Derting.)

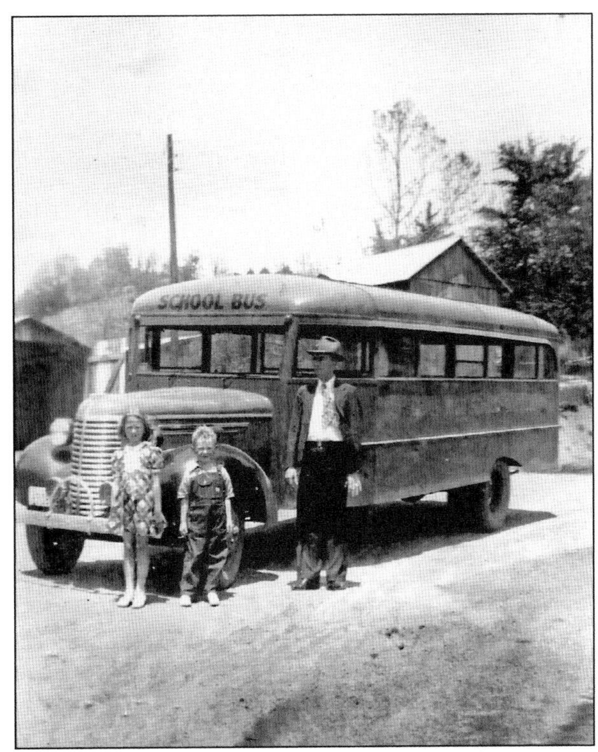

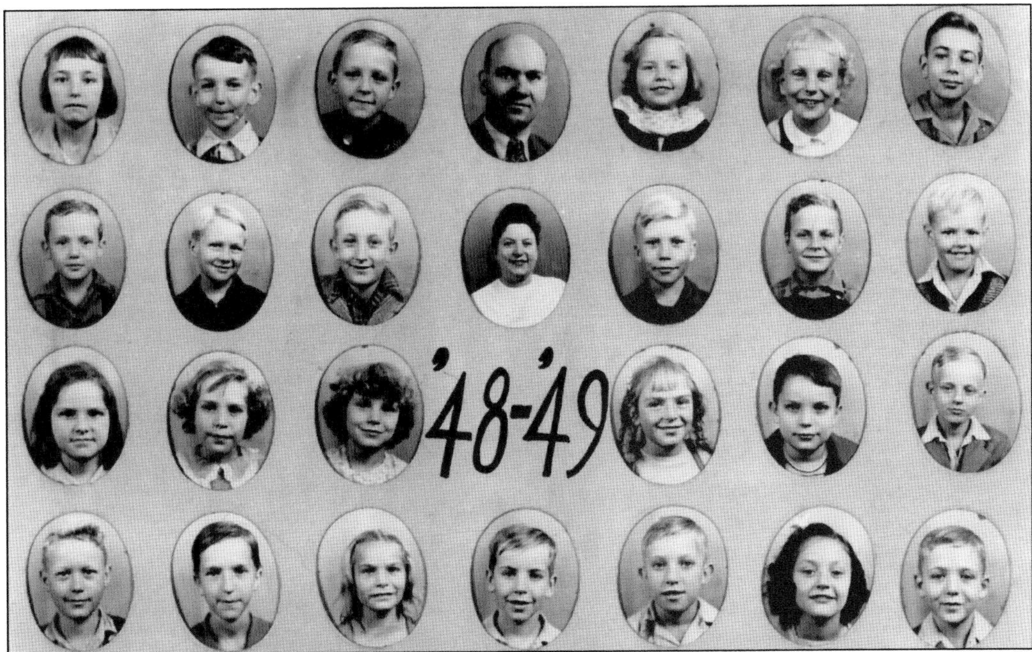

The Hiltons Elementary 1948–1949 second grade class includes, in no particular order, Mary Ann Salyer, Cecil McMurray, J. D. McMurray, Mr. Flanary (principal), Frances Lumpkins, Brenda Lou Maddux, Roger Reedy, Bobby Tipton, Harry Mann, Wayne Thompson, Mrs. Hilton (teacher), Donald Oaks, Claude Salyer, Lester Safreit, Myrtle Wolfe, Freddie McMurray, Joan Quillin, James Owens, Floyd Quillin, Sula Larkey, and Norma Pierson. (Courtesy of Mary Owens.)

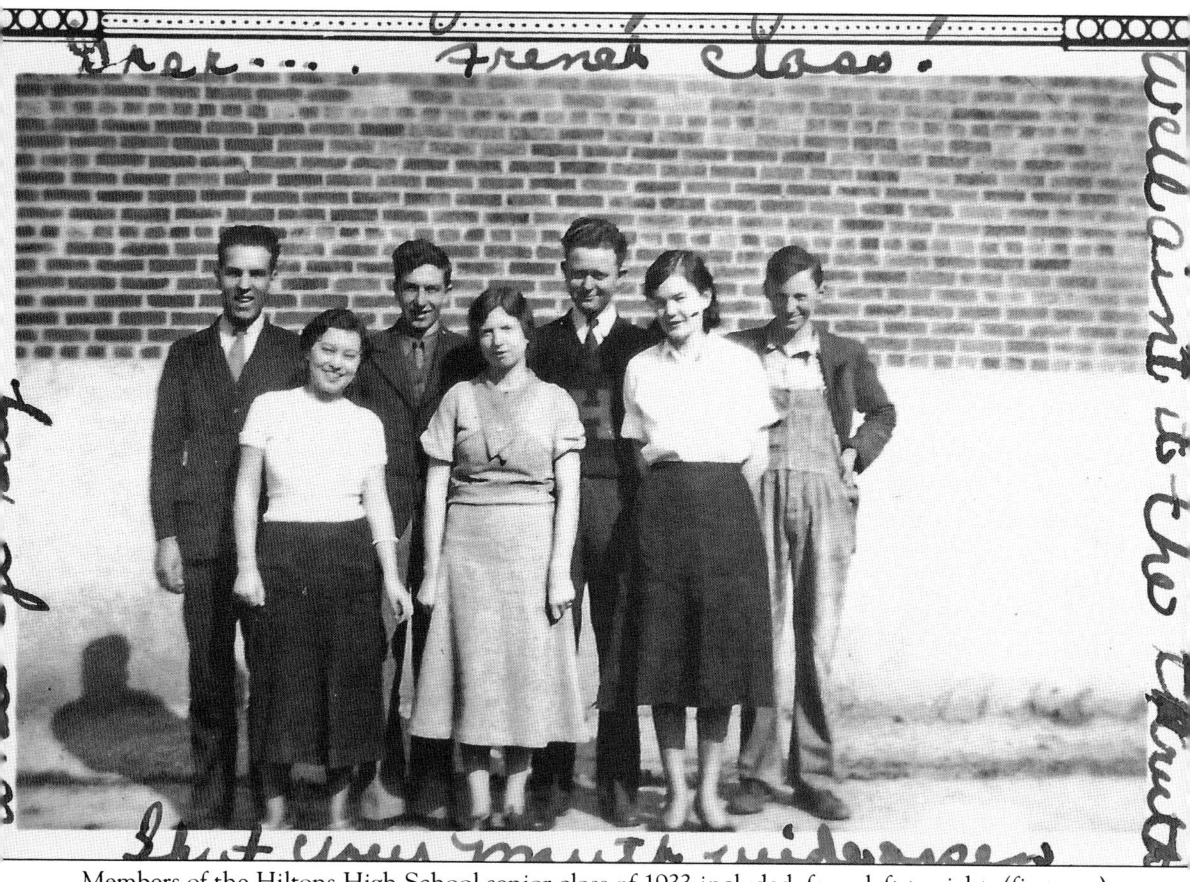

Members of the Hiltons High School senior class of 1933 included, from left to right, (first row) Suella "Steam shovel" Quillen, Lotus "Sis" Curtis, and Uva Maddux; (second row) Claude "Windy" McMurray, Cecil "Senator" Daugherty, Johnnie "Sport" Miller, and F. M. "Peg" Parker Jr. (Courtesy of Lotus Brooks.)

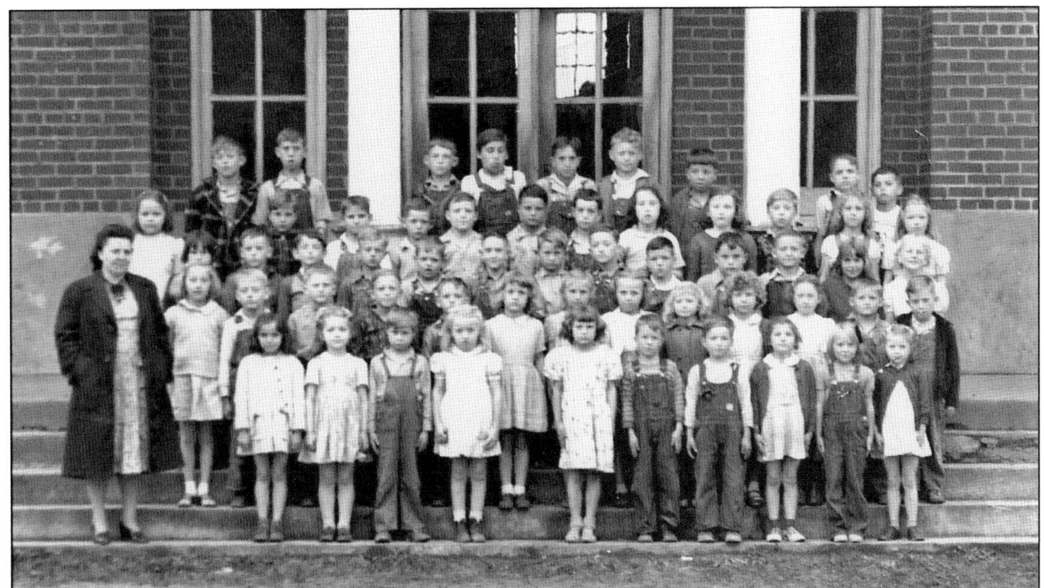

Pictured is the first grade class at Hiltons High School in 1947. Hiltons High School included grades first through twelfth until 1956, when the high school students were moved to the new Gate City High School. Lela Hilton was the teacher, and she had 57 students. This group of students went on to become the last freshman class at Hiltons High School. (Courtesy of Marianna Gardner.)

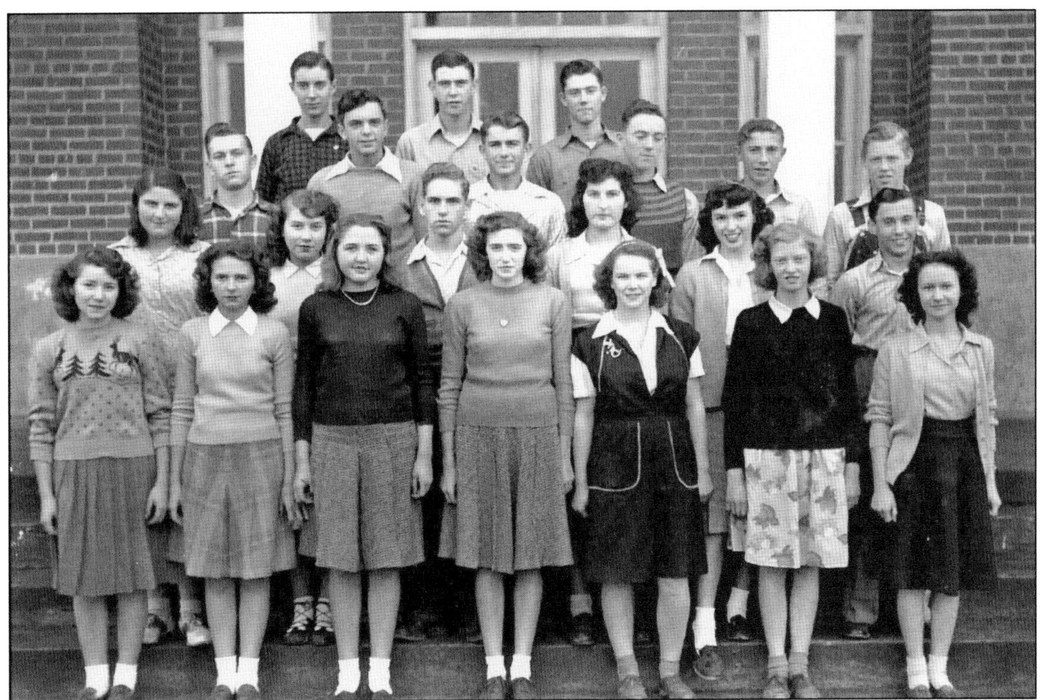

The Hiltons High School graduating class of 1948 poses proudly. In the early years of Hiltons High School, there was no way of producing modern-day style annuals. Therefore, each picture was printed and then pasted onto typed pages to make professional-looking and long-lasting memory books for the students. (Courtesy of Marianna Gardner.)

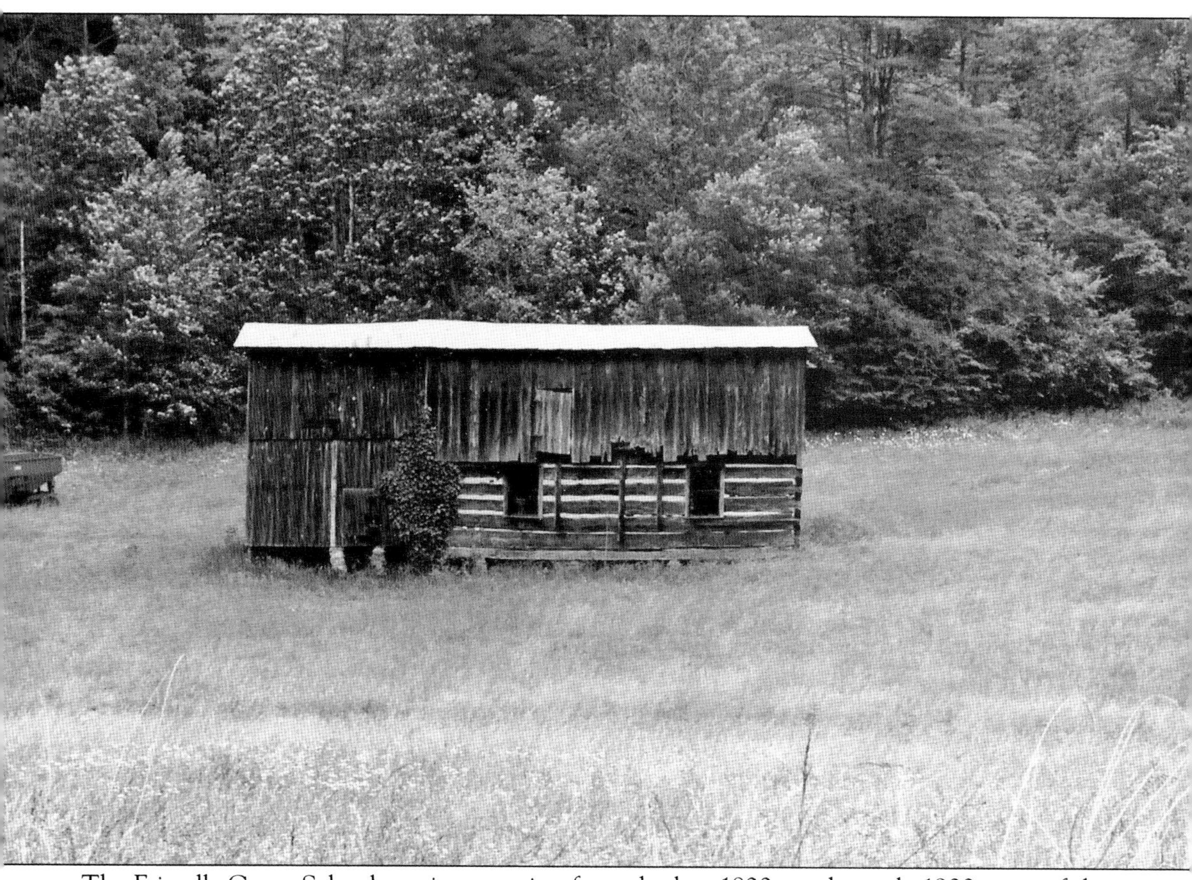

The Friendly Grove School was in operation from the late 1800s to the early 1900s, one of the many small schools that were scattered throughout the Hiltons area. The building still stands today, in use as a barn. (Courtesy of Carmen Good.)

Four

MILITARY

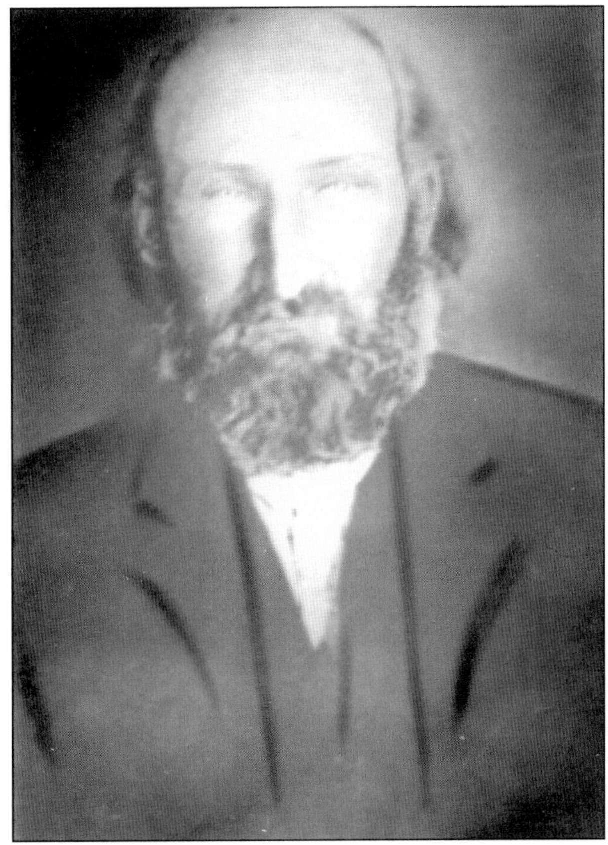

Pictured is Isaac Hickam, who served in the Confederacy during the Civil War. His brother, Emanuel, enlisted in the Confederate Army in August 1862 but was AWOL a month later. The next mention of Emanuel shows that he was a private in the Union army. The reason for his change of service is not known. He died as a scout in Kentucky of typhoid fever. They had two other brothers who fought in the Confederacy. (Courtesy of Stanley and Lennea Hickam.)

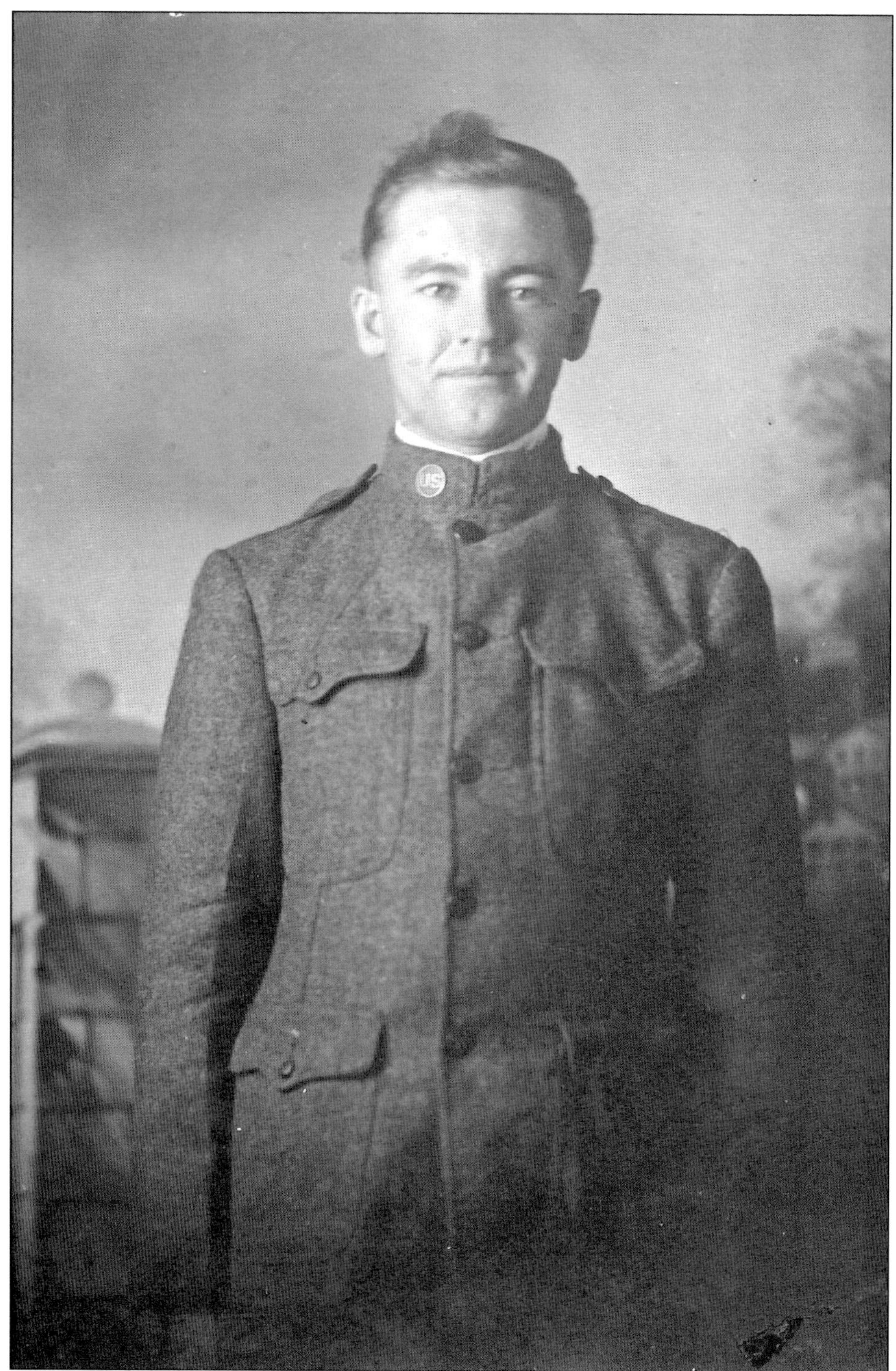

James C. Good, who served in World War I, had three sons, Dan, Elmer, and Charles, and one daughter, Carmen. World War I was known for trench warfare and the use of mustard gas, and was known as "The war to end all wars." For America, the war lasted from 1917 until November 1918. (Courtesy of Carmen Good.)

In the 1940s, James Addington was drafted into the army with a mandatory one year of service. He quickly made sergeant and fought in France with General Patton during World War II. He was reported MIA but had really been burned and temporally blinded. Addington returned to service in time for the Battle of the Bulge. He was awarded the Bronze Star, the Silver Star, the Purple Heart, and other medals. (Courtesy of Stanley and Lennea Hickam.)

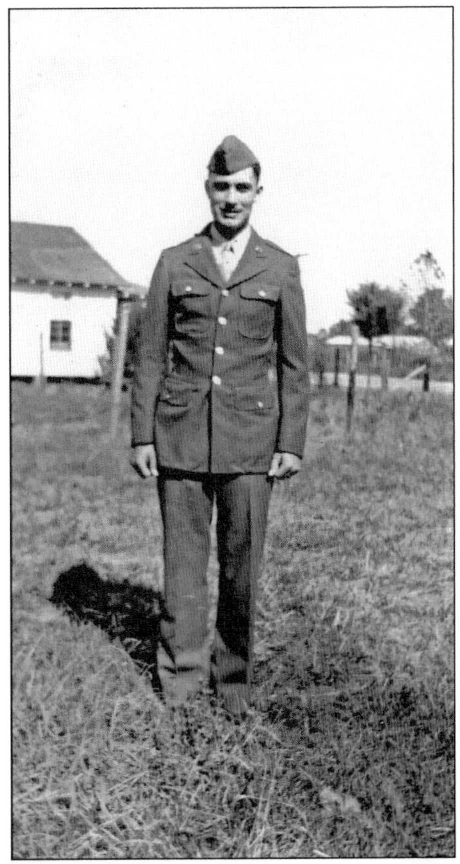

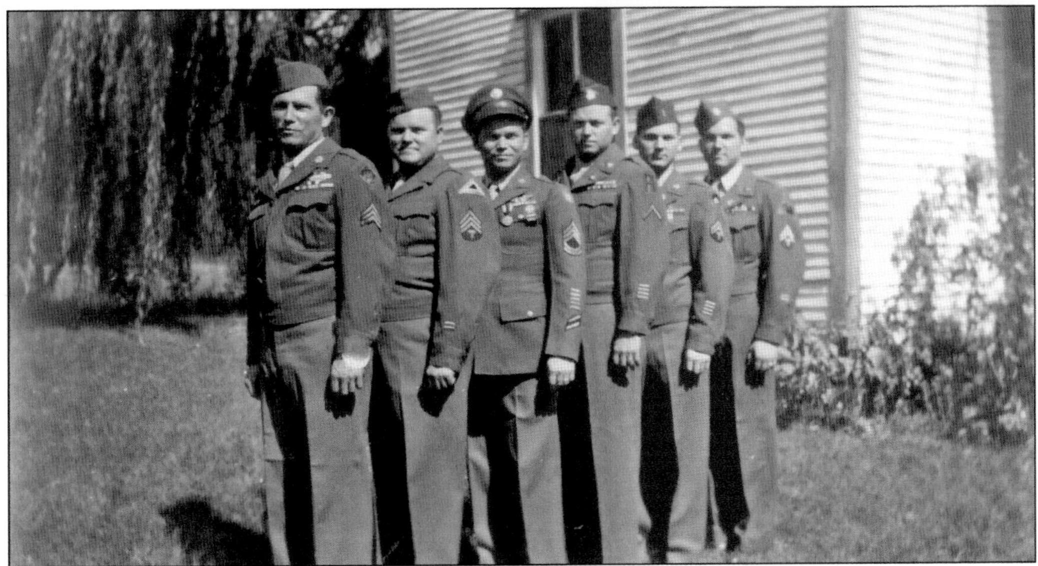

These are the Derting brothers, sons of Martin Luther and Nevada Parker Derting. All six sons served in World War II and returned home safely. Pictured from left to right are Earl, Carl, Homer, Joe, Ralph, and Roy. The first five were drafted into the army, and Roy, the youngest, joined voluntarily, but by that time, the fighting had stopped. (Courtesy of Stanley and Lennea Hickam.)

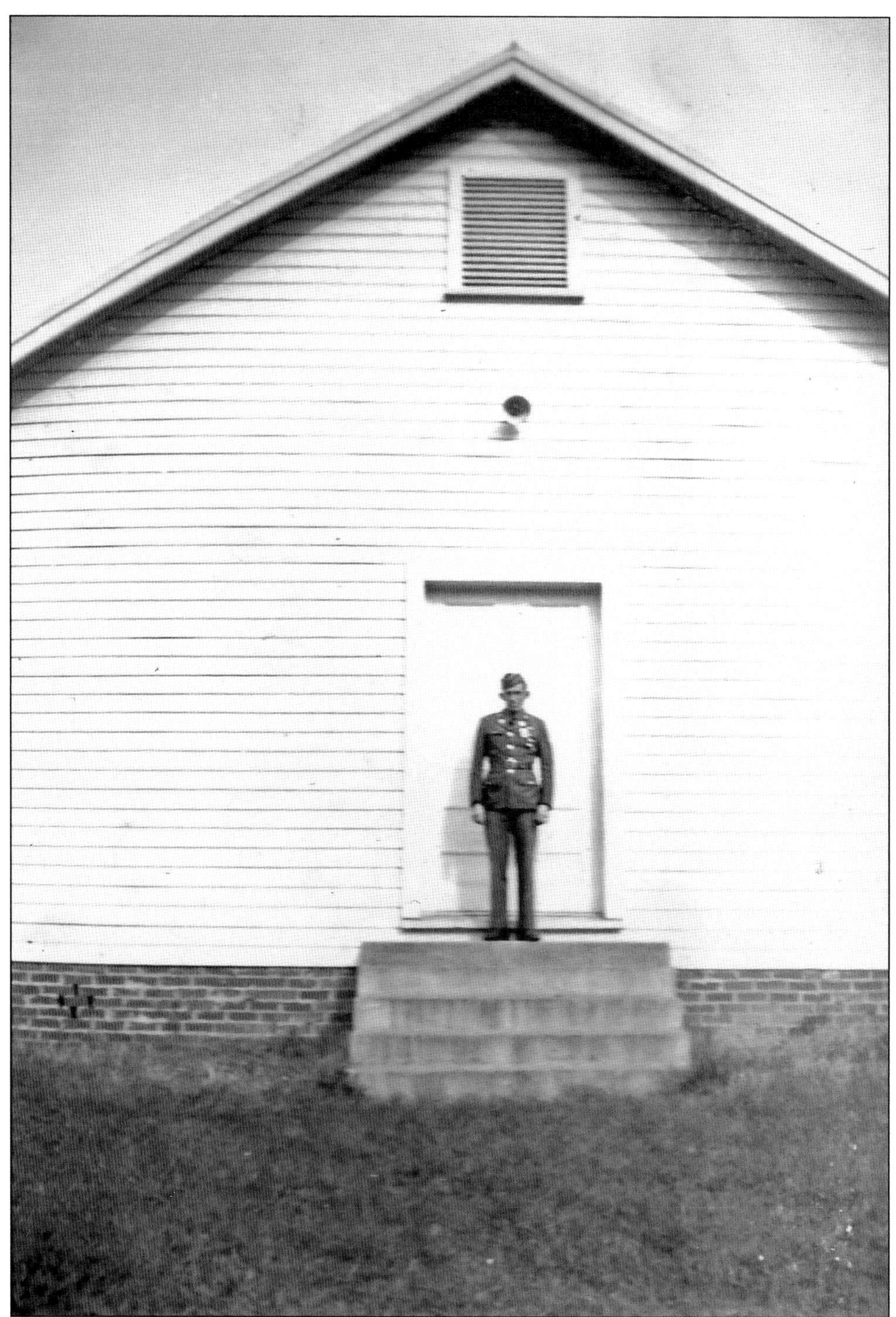

Charles Cochran poses in uniform in front of Missionary Baptist Church in the early 1940s. His father, the Reverend J. R. Cochran, was pastor of this church in October 1937. World War II began for the United States on December 7, 1941, with the bombing of Pearl Harbor. It lasted until the formal surrender on September 2, 1945. (Courtesy of Elsie Derting.)

Pictured at right is Charles Thomas Good, who served in World War II. Below is his brother, Elmer Good, who also served during that war. They are two of the sons of James C. Good and Earlie Hartsock Good. James served in World War I and is pictured on page 36. Military service is often a family tradition, as was the case with the Good family. They had a sister named Carmen. (Courtesy of Carmen Good.)

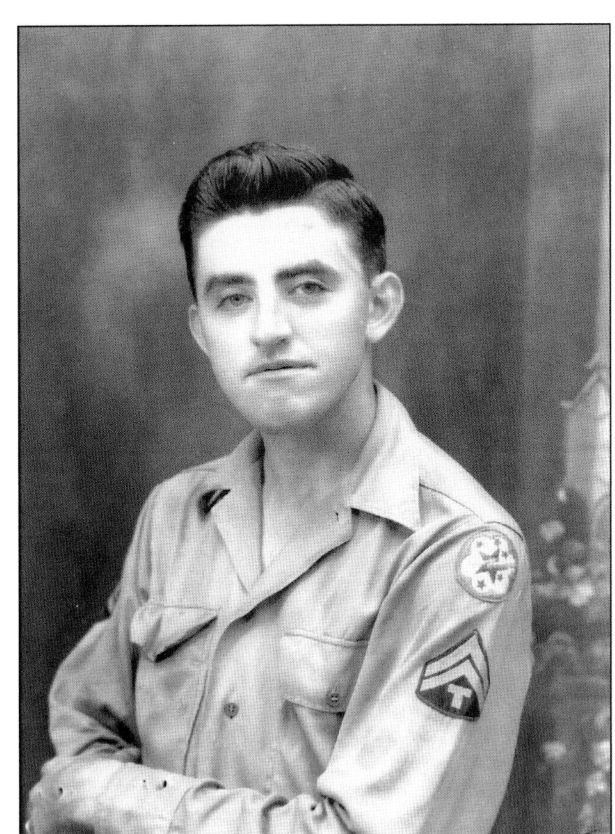

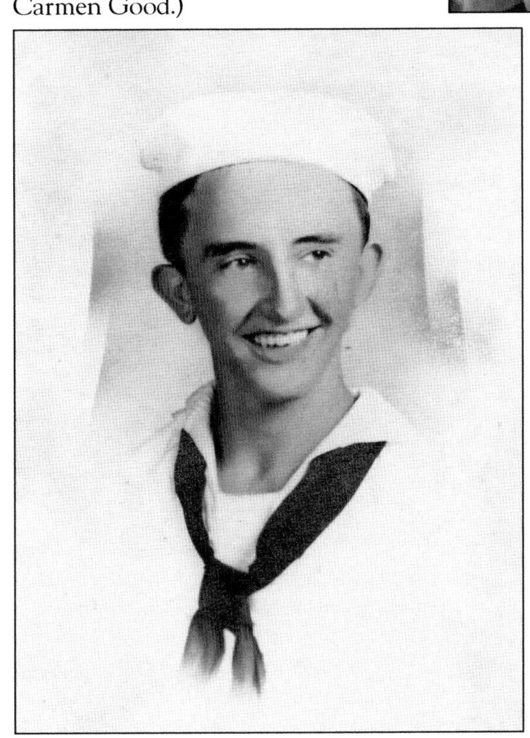

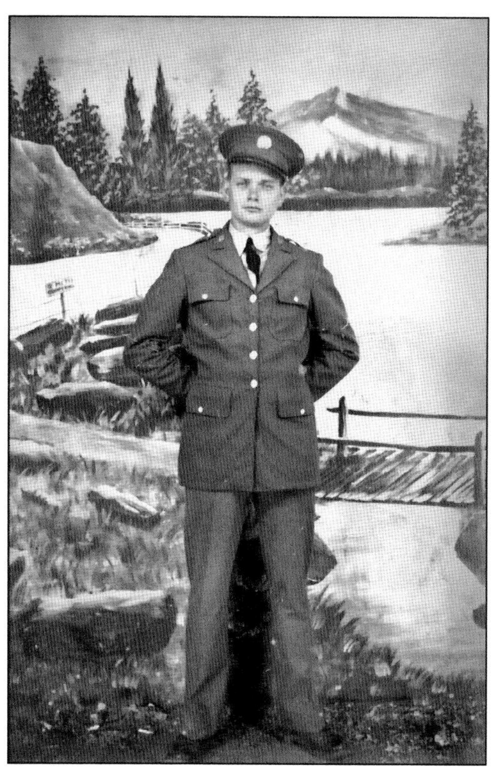

Fred Hensley poses around 1941 in his service uniform. Hensley is the son of Steve and Myrtle Hensley. Fred had two sons, Gary and Ralph Hensley. (Courtesy of Marianna Gardner.)

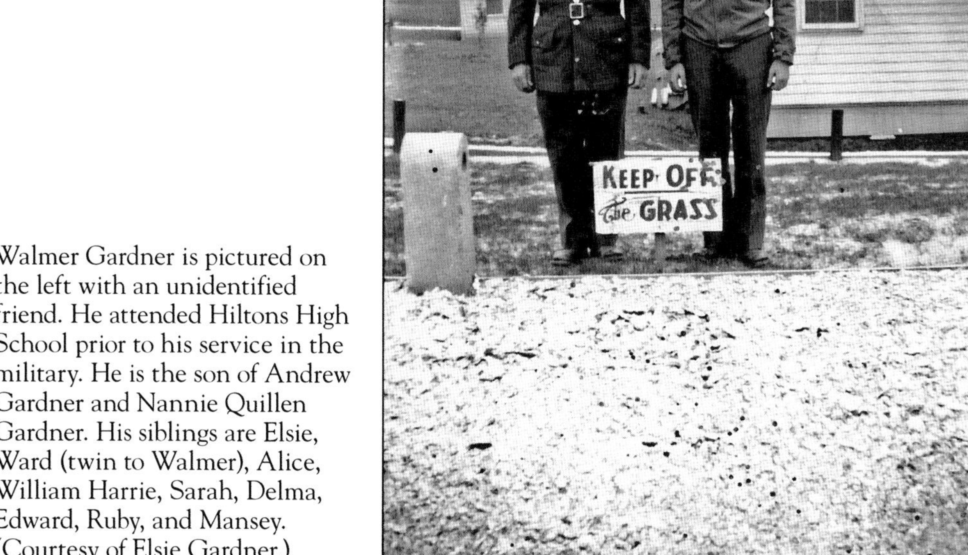

Walmer Gardner is pictured on the left with an unidentified friend. He attended Hiltons High School prior to his service in the military. He is the son of Andrew Gardner and Nannie Quillen Gardner. His siblings are Elsie, Ward (twin to Walmer), Alice, William Harrie, Sarah, Delma, Edward, Ruby, and Mansey. (Courtesy of Elsie Gardner.)

Jay Peters and Joe Weatherly are enjoying a beautiful Hiltons day. Joe was a sergeant in the U.S. Army when this picture was taken. His job was in communications, and he earned the Purple Heart and the Bronze Star during his tour of duty. (Courtesy of Marianna Gardner.)

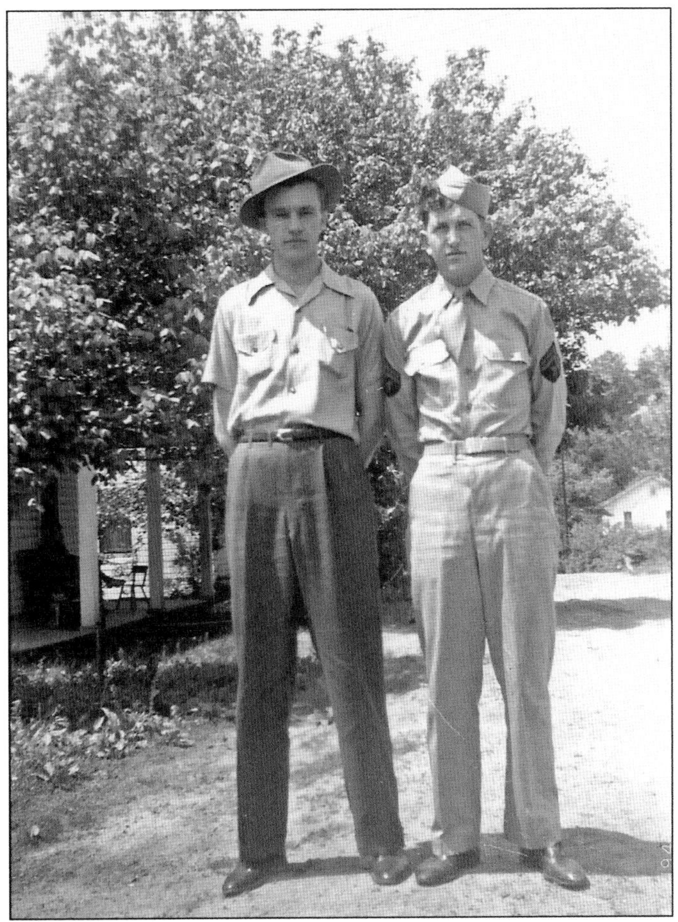

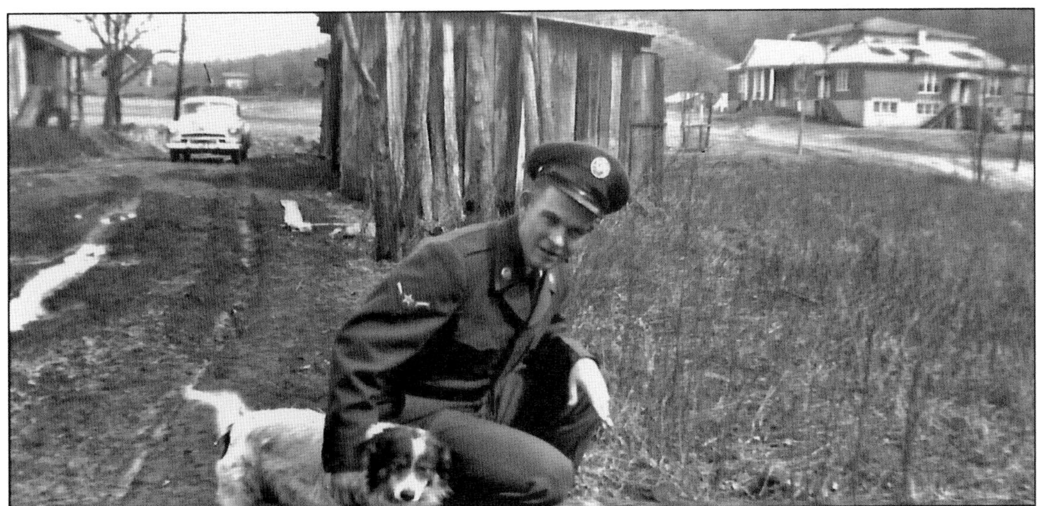

Bobby Blaylock was the son of Charles and Minnie Blaylock of Hiltons. His brothers were Grady, Carl, Herman, and Raymond. He retired from the military and lived for a number of years in Florida. Bobby was known for his sense of humor and good nature. (Courtesy of Marianna Gardner.)

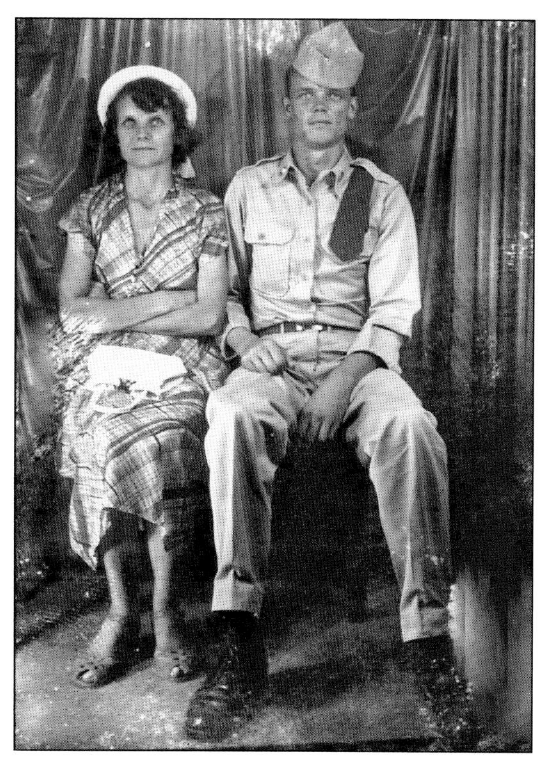

Odie L. Godsey McMurray and her son Doug McMurray sat for this photograph in the early 1950s, before Doug went overseas to serve in Germany during the Korean Conflict. Doug is pictured below in full uniform during his time in service. Doug was born on February 11, 1931, and died on September 6, 2005. He retired from the Tennessee Valley Authority and was a farmer and a part-time landscaper. He was married to Opal Sellers, and they are the parents of Gail and Doyle, both of whom served in the U.S. Army, and Neil and Michael, who are talented musicians. Doug is buried at Mountain Home Cemetery. (Courtesy of Opal McMurray.)

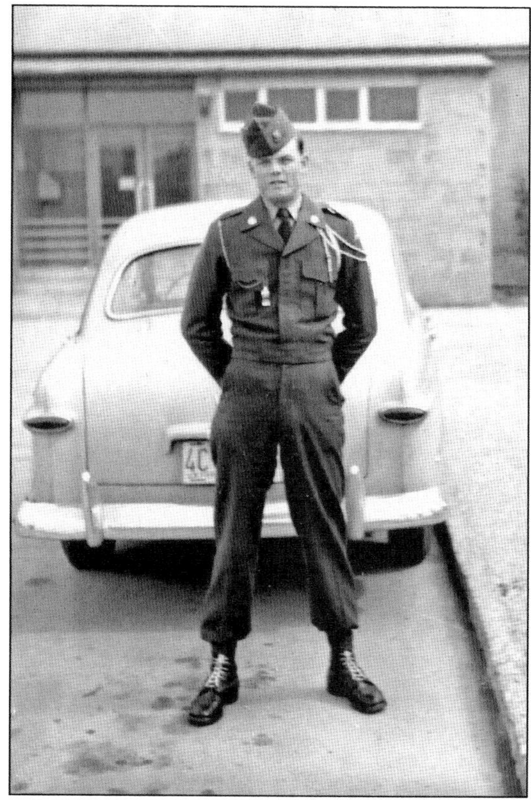

Five

PEOPLE

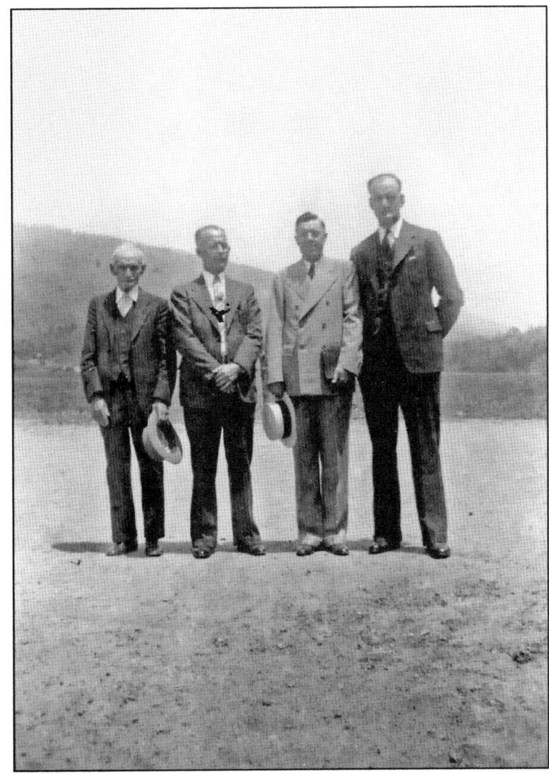

These four men were speakers at a local function in Hiltons on May 19, 1940. Pictured from left to right are C. L. Poulston, J. l. Cochran, unidentified, and G. D. Grove, who was the principal of Hiltons High School from the late 1930s to the early 1940s. The other three men were preachers from the Bristol area. (Courtesy of Elsie Derting.)

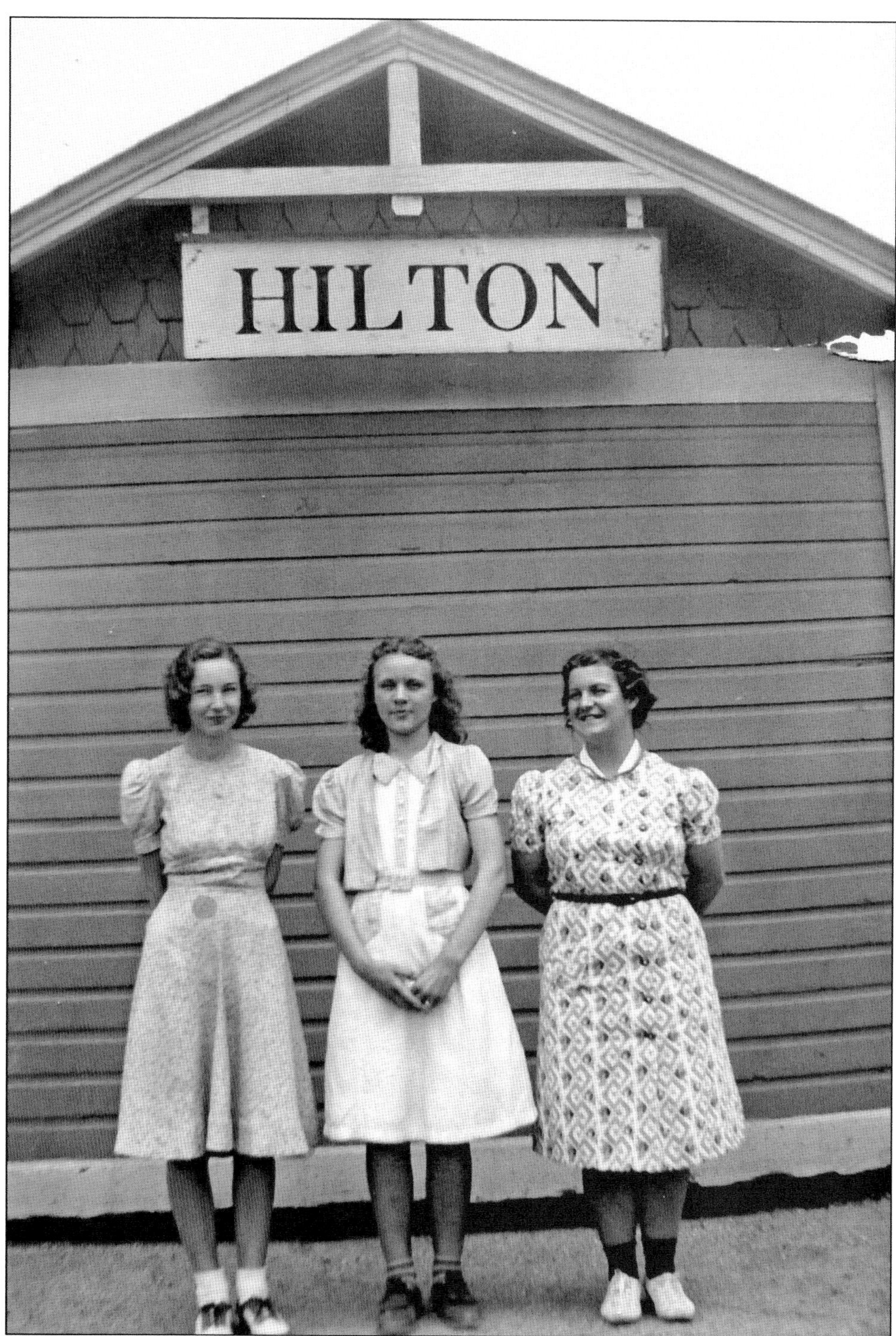

Elsie Maddux, Lucille Fugate, and Sara Gardner are pictured on May 20, 1940. Fugate is a direct descendent of James W. Carter and Nancy Bays Carter of the Lunsfords Mill Dam area of Hiltons. The Carters are buried in the Blue Springs Cemetery. Their children were William Dulaney, Matilda, Rebecca, Sarah, and Thomas Jefferson Carter. (Courtesy of Elsie Derting.)

Oliver Burl and Molly Anne Elizabeth (known as Maude) McNutt Sanders are the parents of Edward, Elsie, Roy, and Elzoria Sanders Hickam. This picture of the couple was taken in 1918. Oliver worked in many different jobs, including construction, and helped build the Hiltons High School. (Courtesy of Elzoria Hickam.)

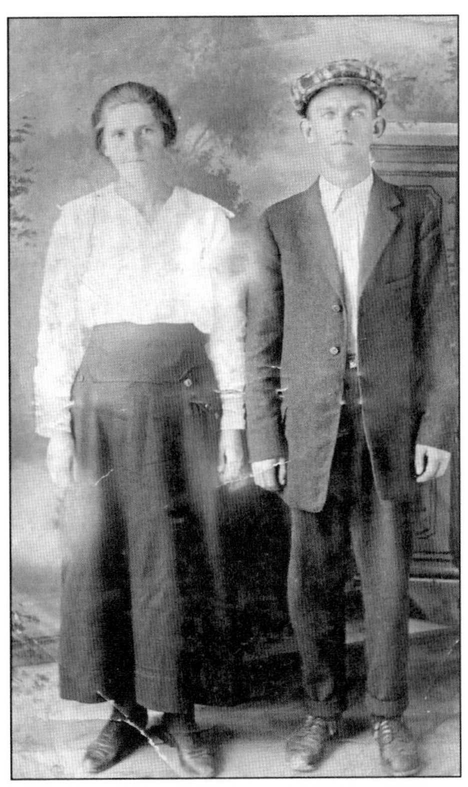

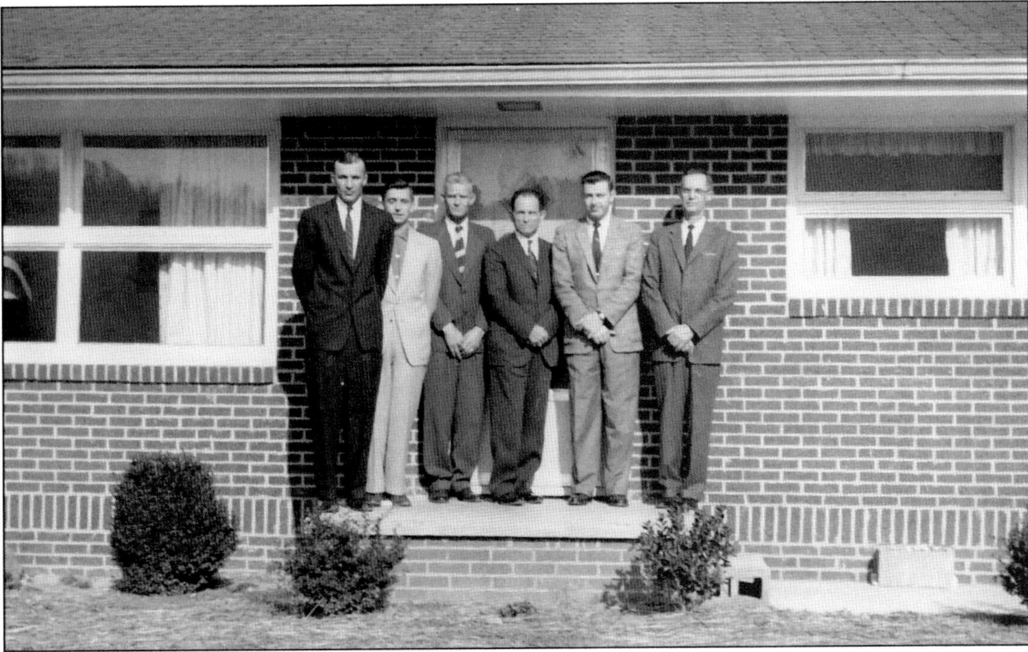

This is the building committee created to build the parsonage for Hiltons United Methodist Church. Standing in front of the new Hiltons Methodist parsonage, from left to right, are J. W. Peters, Sam Hobbs, Earl Hickam, Earl Derting, Gaylord Davis, and Rev. J. W. Gott. (Courtesy of Mary Owens.)

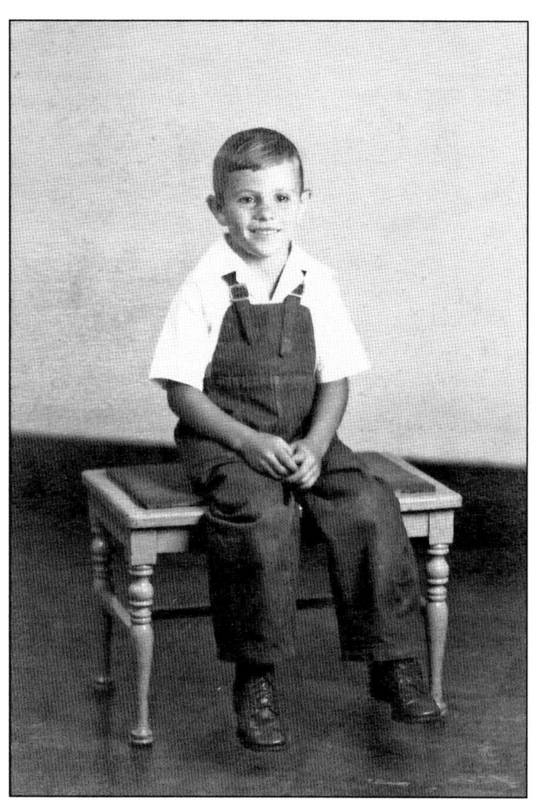

Ronald Derting is the only child of Ruth Gardner Derting and Garn Derting. Ronald and his wife, Velma, had two children named Misty and Brandon. (Courtesy of Marianna Gardner.)

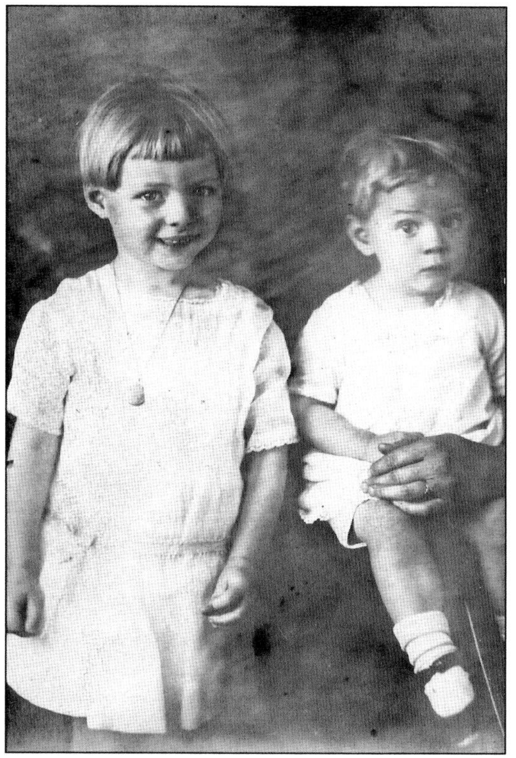

Pictured here are Virginia (left) and Beatrice Gardner, daughters of Hiram and Rosa Salley Gardner. (Courtesy of Elsie Gardner.)

Clyde Taft Gardner and his sister Ruth Gardner Derting are the children of William Dale Gardner and Martha Washington Larkey Gardner. Other siblings are Bertha Virginia, Blanch Ora, Albert Vance, and Clara Hester. Clyde married Elsie Gardner, and they moved to California, where Clyde worked in the logging industry before returning to their home on the North Fork of the Holston River in Hiltons. (Courtesy of Elsie Gardner.)

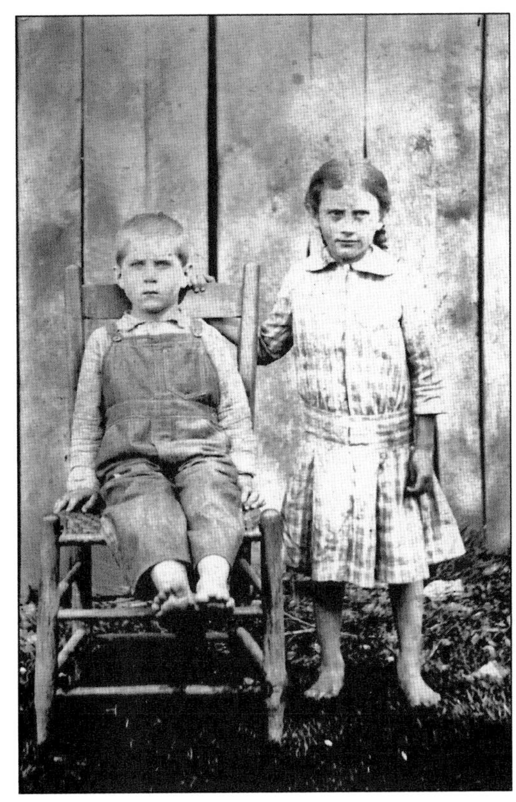

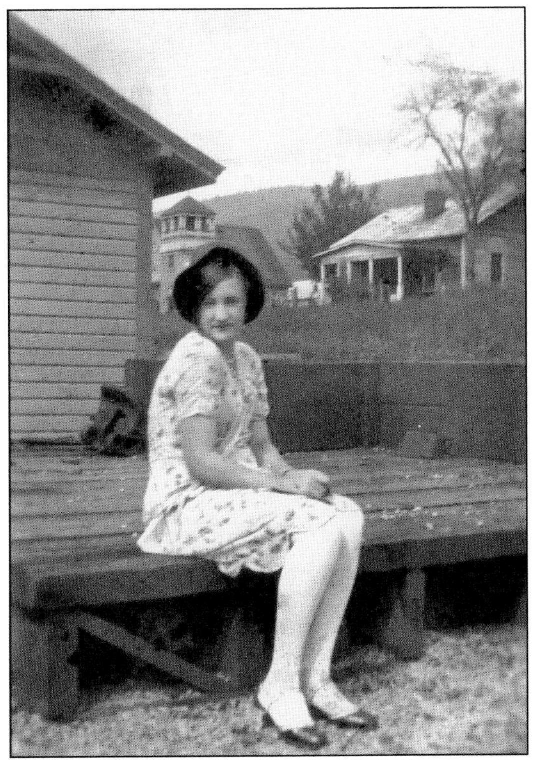

Roe Darnell is pictured at the old Hiltons train depot. She was raised by John Darnell and his wife. Roe married Bob Wilhelm. The Hiltons train depot was an important stop when the railroad ran through town. After the train stopped running, the depot stood for some time, and people still loved to visit it. (Courtesy of Marianna Gardner.)

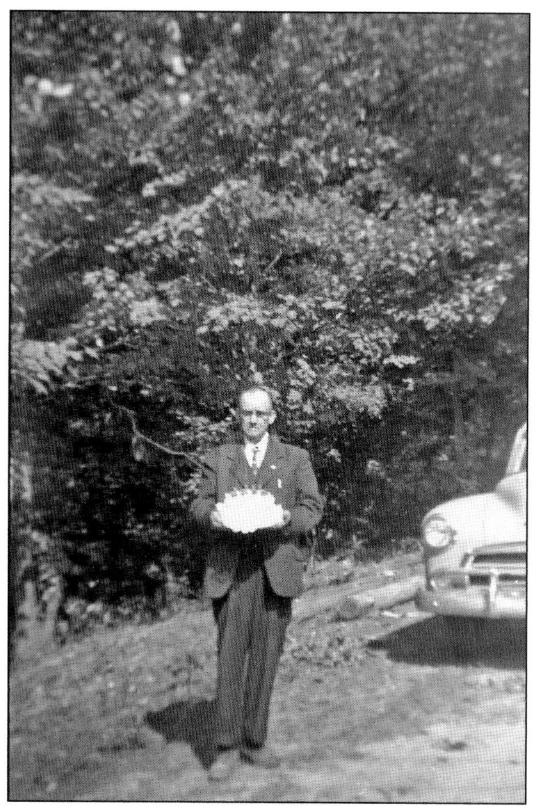

Mel Hensley holds his birthday cake in March 1958 at his 75th birthday party. Mel built his country store in Hiltons across from the Hiltons High School in 1928. The children in Hiltons would often buy their school supplies and a Coca-Cola at his store. Mel died in 1965 and is buried in the Hensley Cemetery. (Courtesy of Marianna Gardner.)

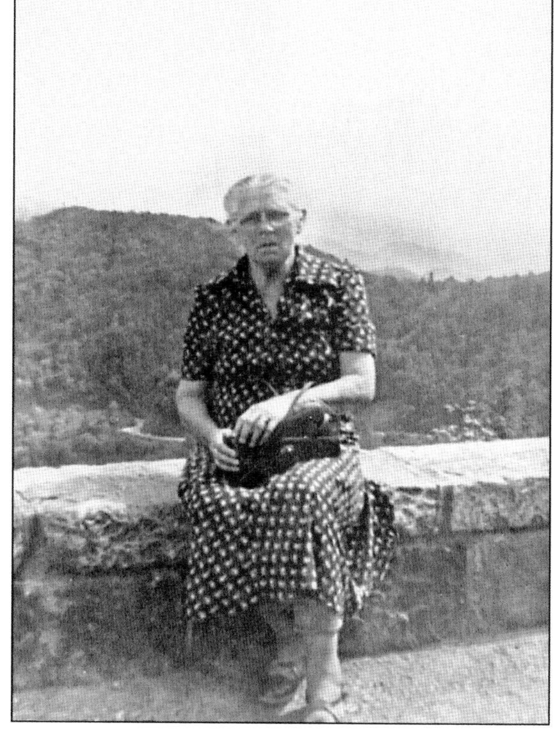

Della Ramey McMurray Johnson, pictured around 1956, was married to Noah McMurray. Their children are William Harley, Leland, Willard, Florance, Mable, Nelsie, Genevieve, Ruth, Lola, and Effie. Della later married Robie Johnson. (Courtesy of Opal McMurray.)

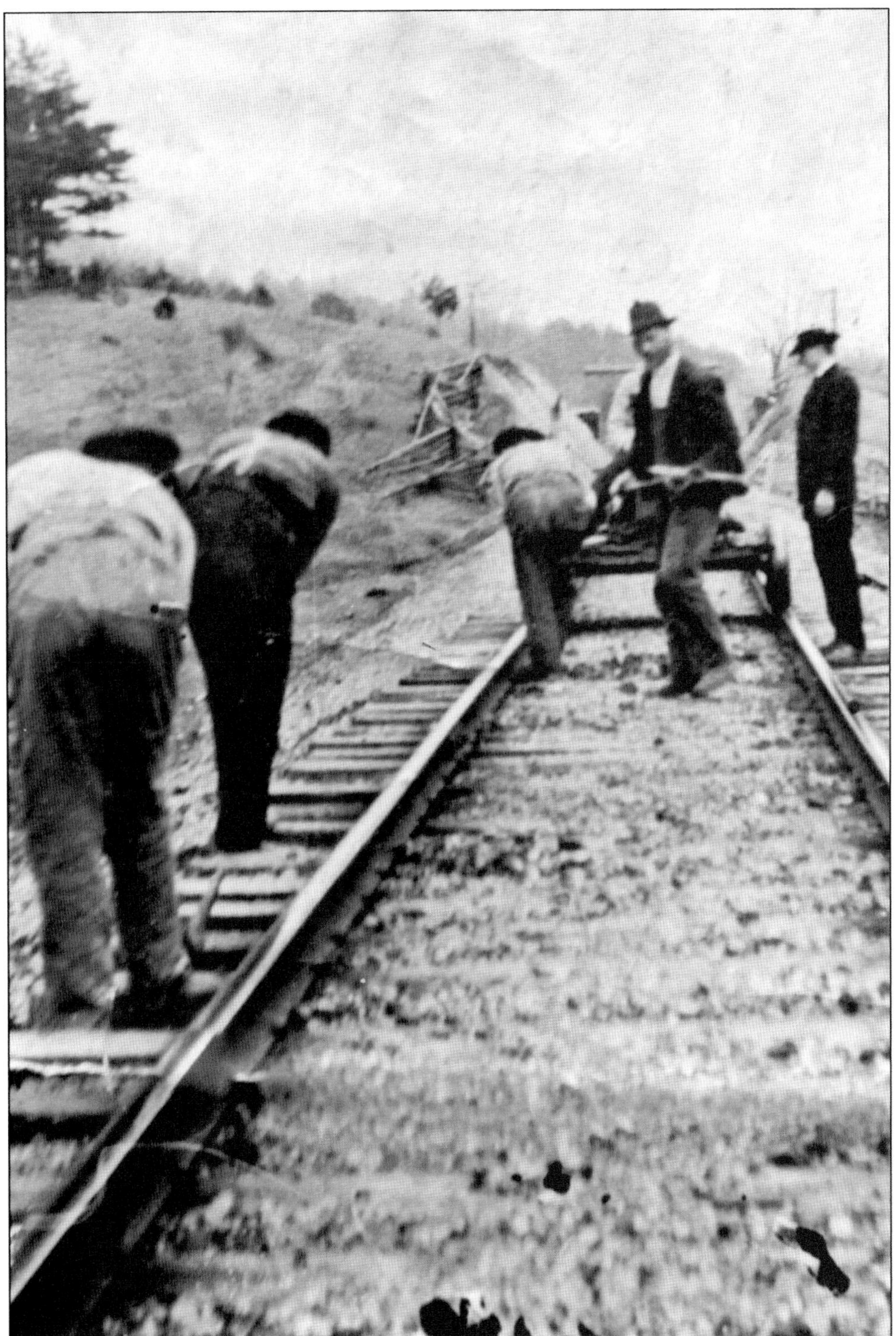

These men helped build the first railroad in Hiltons. From left to right, the first three men are unidentified, and the last two are Luke Peters and Gay Baker. The railroad brought much to the Hiltons area in the way of commerce. People could receive goods from other states and send produce and furs to all parts of the country. It also carried the mail. (Courtesy of Elsie Derting.)

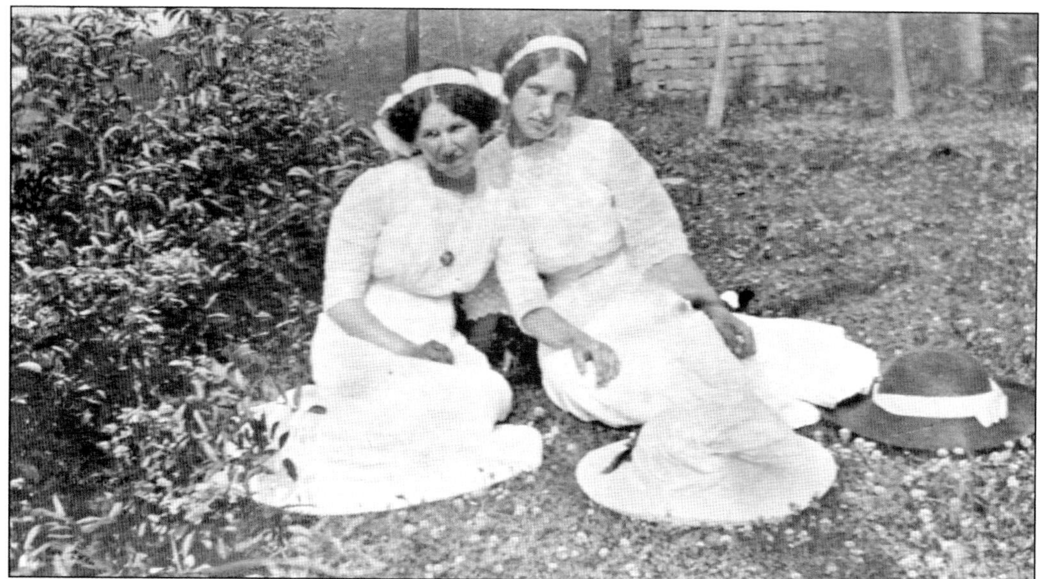

The two lovely ladies in this picture from June 25, 1913, are Nevada Parker Derting (left) and Della Maddux Henry. Nevada Parker and Martin L. Derting were married June 25, 1912. (Courtesy of Elsie Derting.)

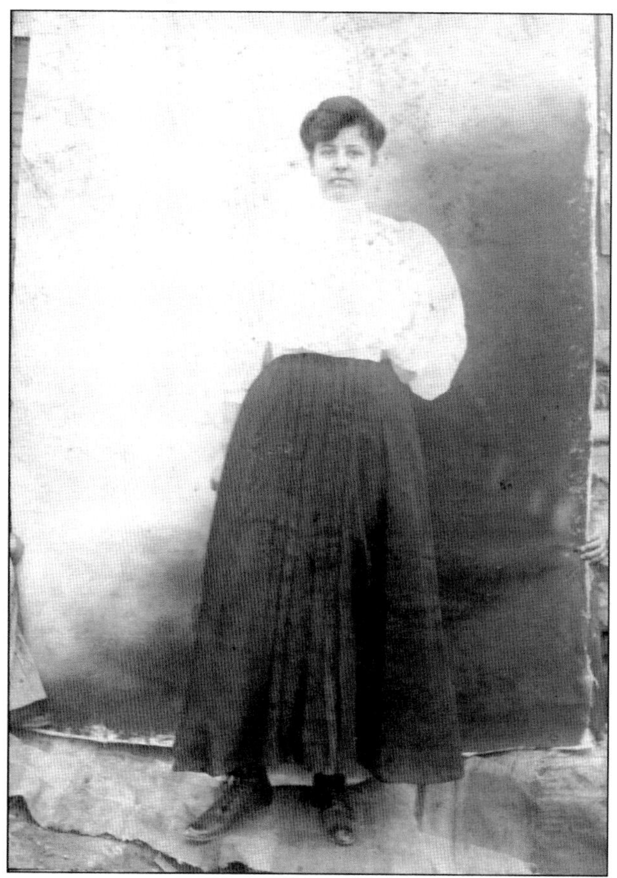

Belle Maddux Hickam married Charlie Hickam, and they had a son named Charles. Belle died when Charles was an infant. Charlie then married Ella Nye. Charles graduated from Hiltons High School and then went into active duty during World War II. (Courtesy of Elzoira Hickam.)

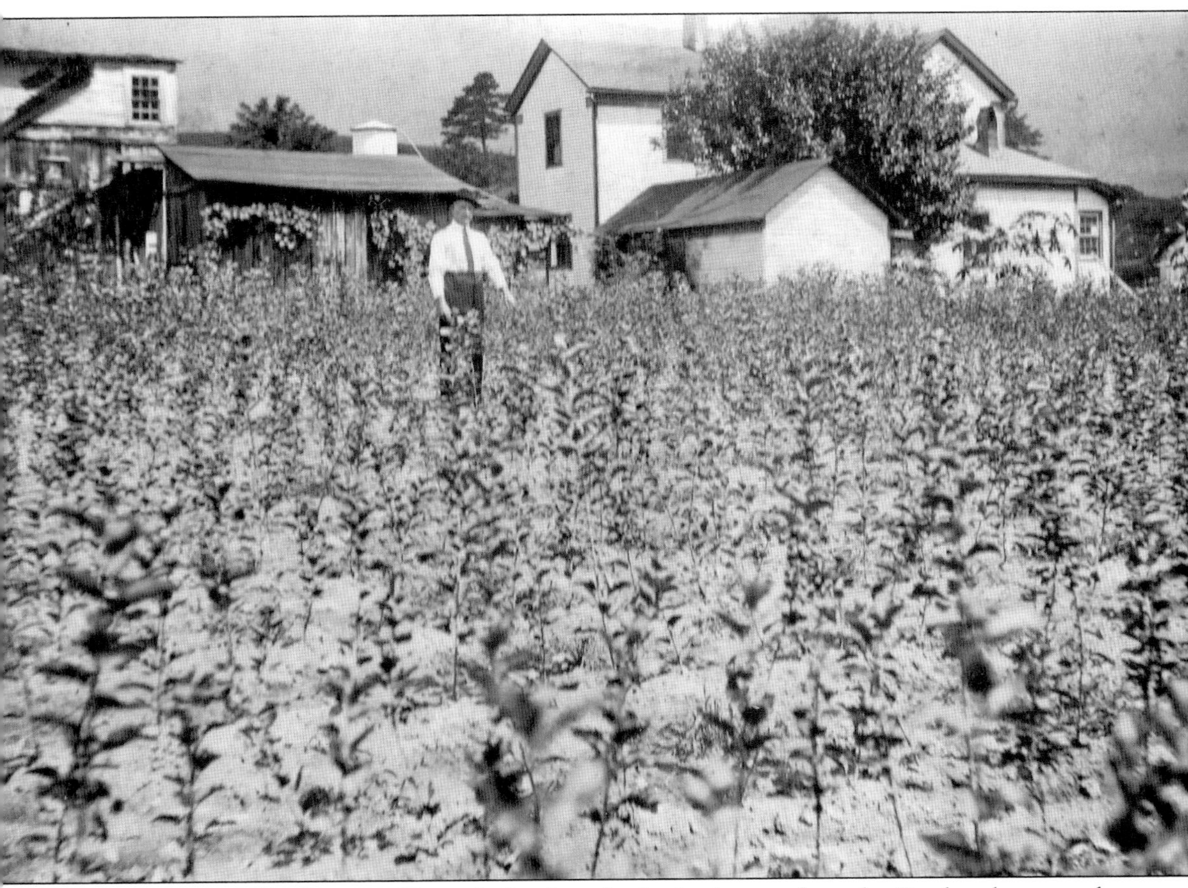

Standing in a field of crops is Henry J. Gardner. In the background are the Gardner house and store, where he served the community for many years. The store was located near the old train depot in Hiltons off the current A. P. Carter Highway. Gardner lived next door to the store with his family. (Courtesy of Mary Owens.)

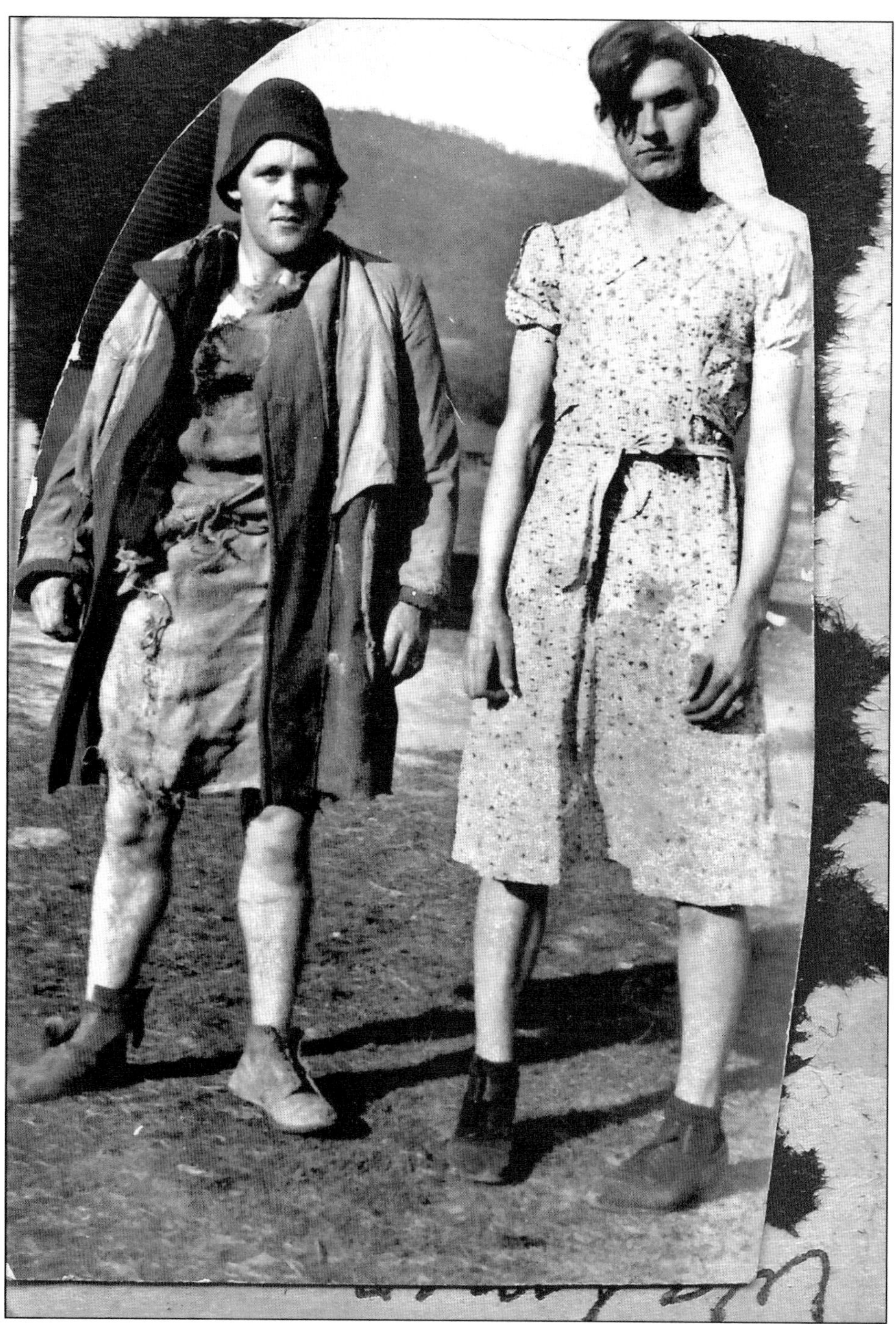

Pictured are Walmer Gardner (left) and John Carter. Carter is the son of the legendary "Big Tom" Carter and Clara Carrol. John's siblings are Ruth, Fred, Ward, Dale, and T. R. Carter Jr. Half brothers and sisters are Carlos, Cordia, Wertie, Robert T., Grace, Arnold, and Lawrence. The mother of these children was Leora Baker, who died before John married Clara Carrol. Walmer Gardner is one of several children of Andrew D. and Nannie Quillen Gardner and is a grandson to Hiram and Matilda Smith. (Courtesy of Elsie Gardner.)

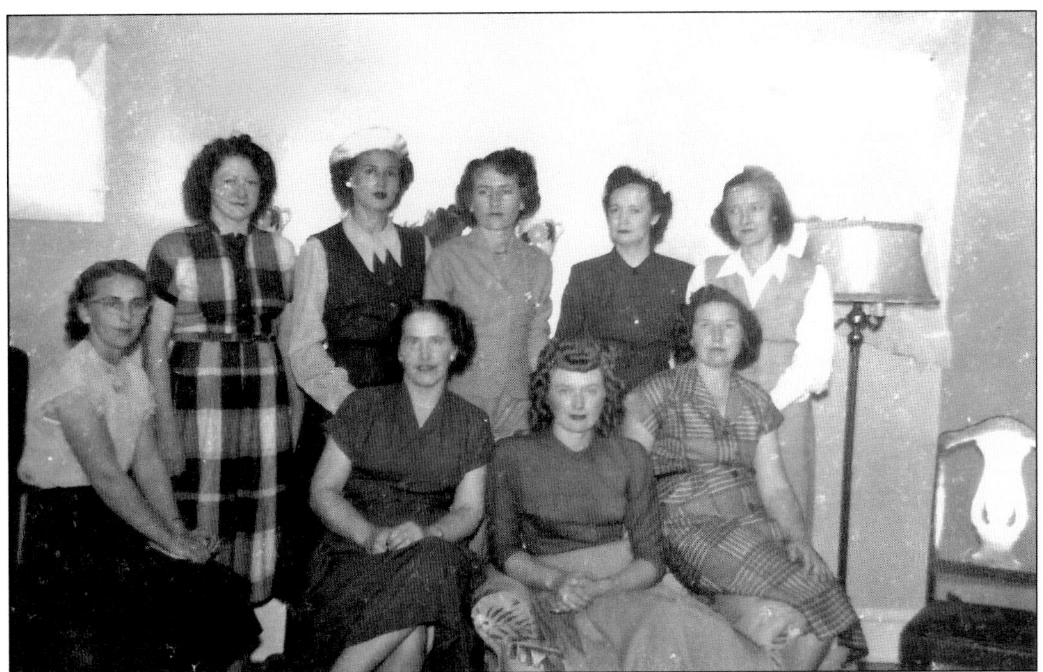

These members of the Hiltons Home Demonstration Club, pictured in the 1950s from left to right, are (first row) Minnie Johnson, Willierae Miller Gardner, and Evelyn Bralley; (second row) Trula Reedy, Betty Derting, June Wood, Mary Owens, Minnie Curtis, and Odis Maddux. (Courtesy of Marianna Gardner.)

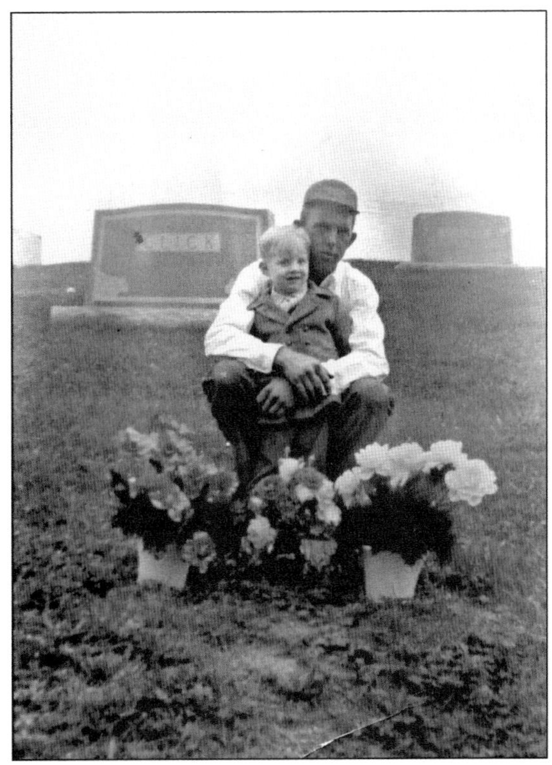

Pictured are Henry Lee Smith and his son Danny at Holston View Cemetery at the grave of Lee's father, William Lee Smith. Henry Lee died in 1975. He worked at the Kingsport Foundry. Danny worked there as well until it closed in December 2003. (Courtesy of Lois Grey.)

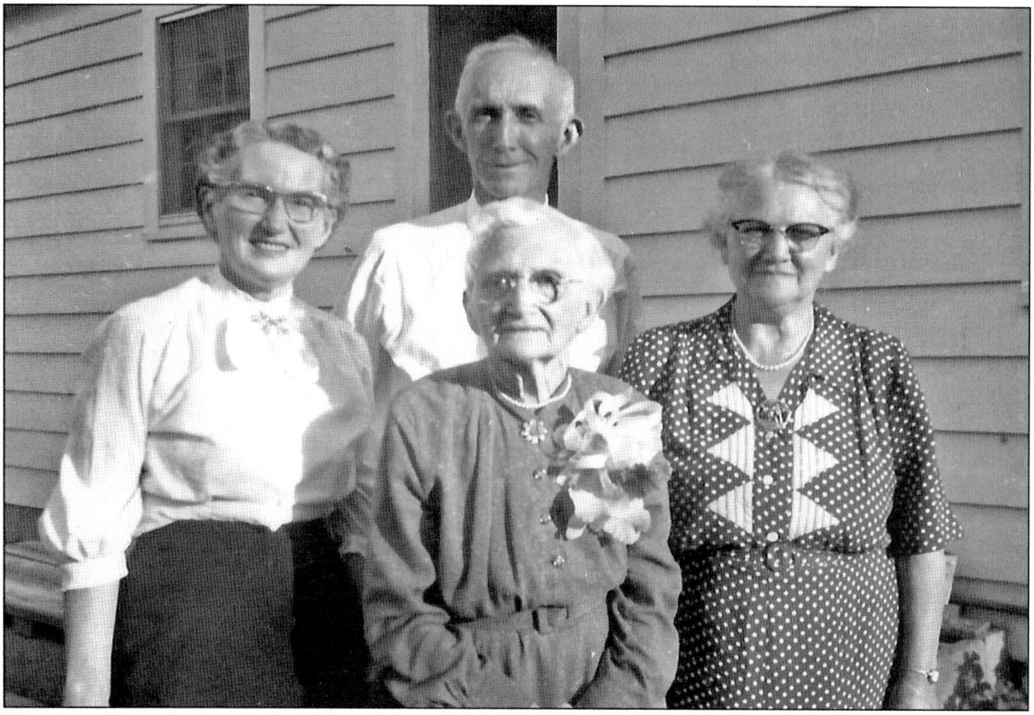

Claude Parker poses on October 14, 1956, with his sisters, from left to right, Florida Parker Baker, Salome Parker, and Nevada Parker Derting. Florida married Charles I. Baker on November 5, 1913. She later ran Park Street Antiques from her home in Gate City, Virginia. (Courtesy of Elsie Derting.)

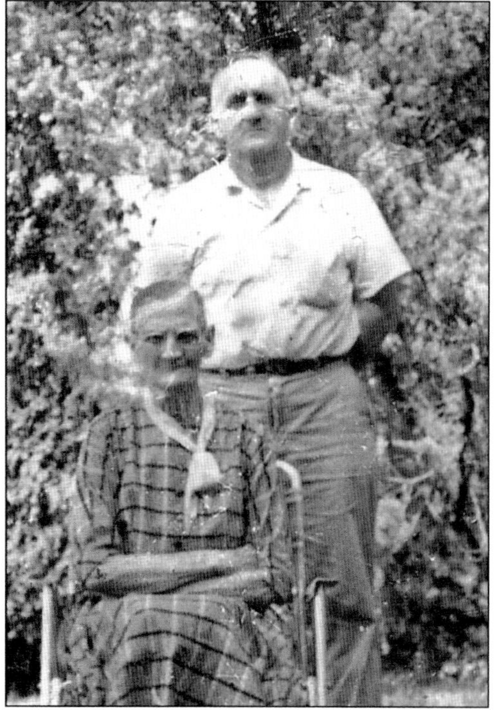

Susie Godsey (seated) and her son-in-law, Orin Bake, are pictured here. Susie was married to Isaac Godsey. The names of some of their children are Verge, Verdie, Oadie, and Gertrude. Orin Bake, who was raised in Ohio, married Verdie and worked many jobs, but for the most part, he ran a floral shop. (Courtesy of Opal McMurray.)

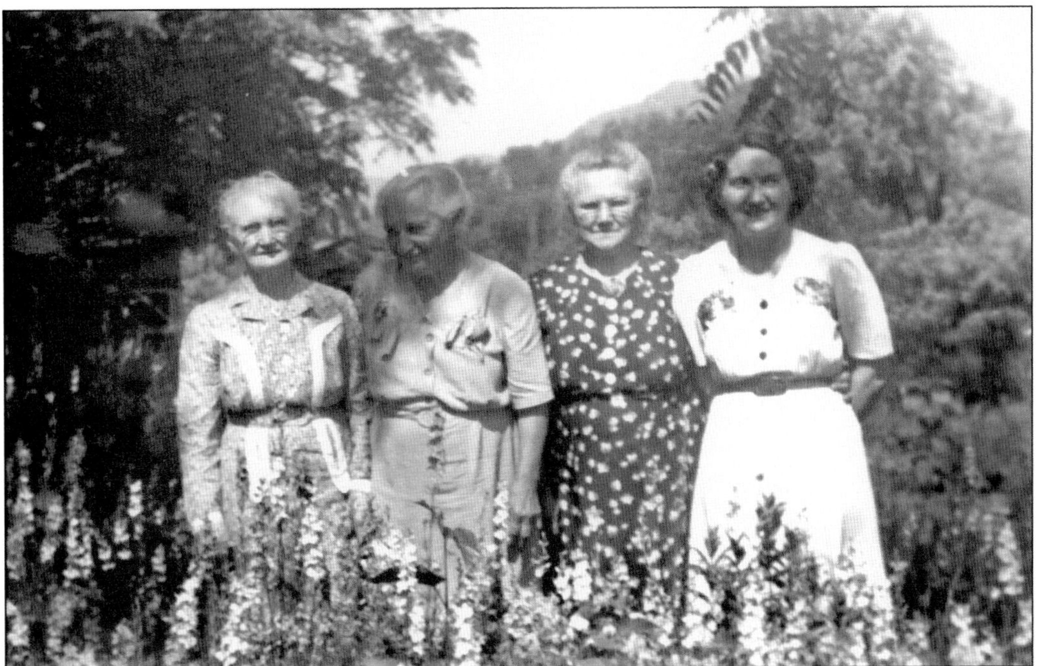

In this *c.* 1940 photograph are, from left to right, Salome Parker, Una Parker, Nevada Parker Derting, and Florida Parker Baker. All of these Parker sisters stayed near the Hiltons area except Una, who lived in Arizona and, at the time of this picture, was home visiting her family. (Courtesy of Elsie Derting.)

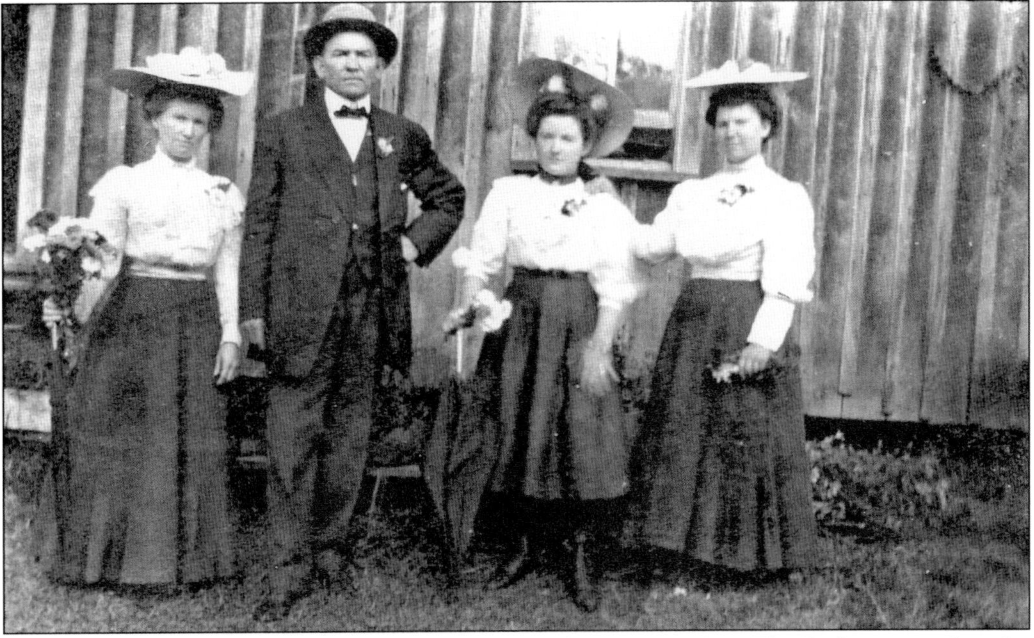

This picture shows the Parker sisters with their brother Price Parker. The Parkers moved to the Hiltons area in March 1867 and resided there most of their lives. "Auntie," as Salome Parker was known, helped care for her younger brothers and sisters in her youth and cared for her parents as they aged. In her advanced years, Auntie lived with her nephew. (Courtesy of Elsie Derting.)

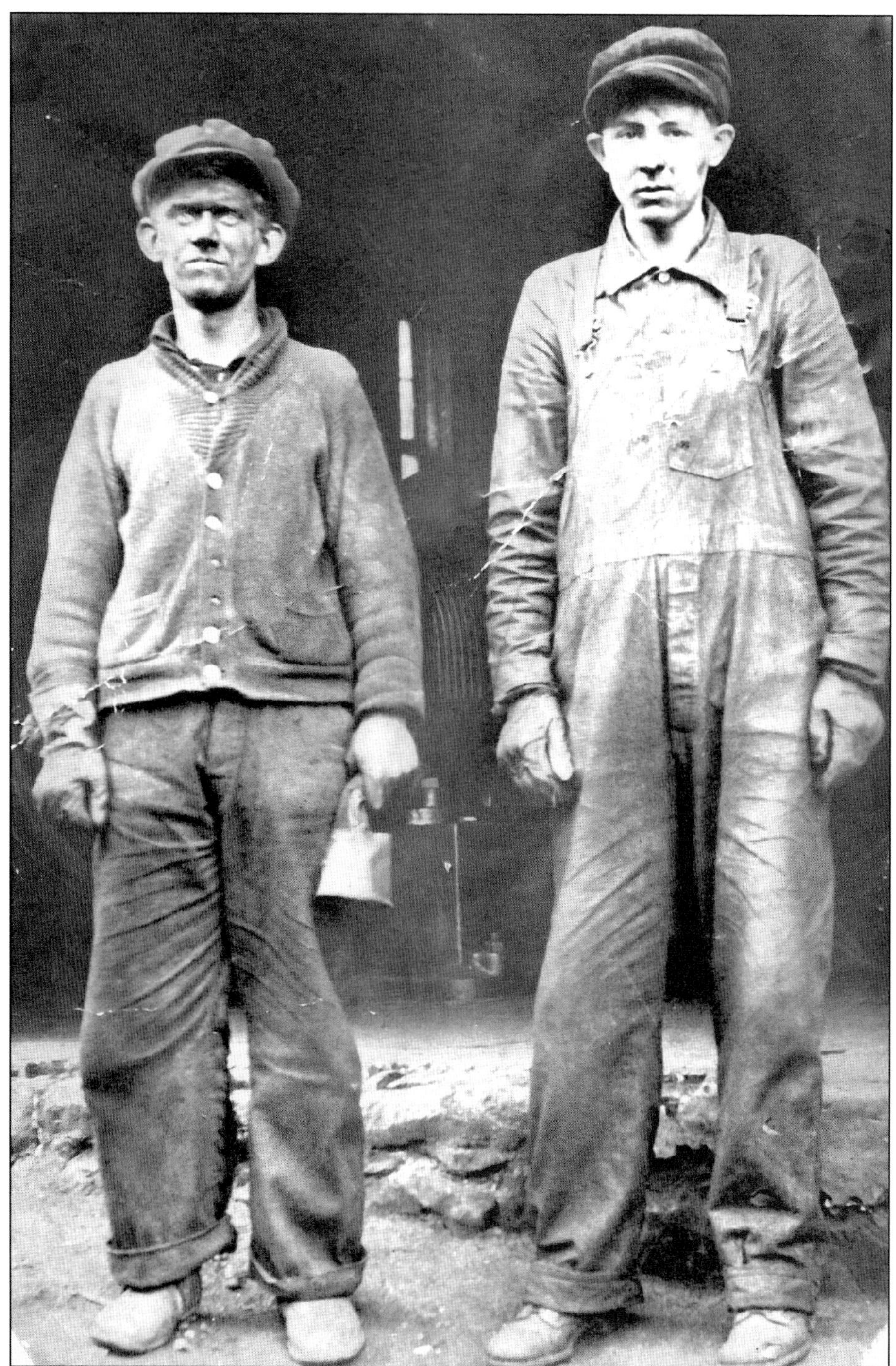

Oliver Burl Sanders and Claude Bulock are shown at work in Blackwood, Virginia, in 1918. Sanders was born in Ash County, North Carolina, on June 14, 1899. His parents were Thomas Cicero and Tansey Wyatt Sanders. He worked in the coal mine in Wise County, Virginia, in the early 1900s, and in the 1920s, he worked in Gas City, Indiana. He also worked at the cotton mill in Kingsport, Tennessee, for several years. (Courtesy of Elzoria Hickam.)

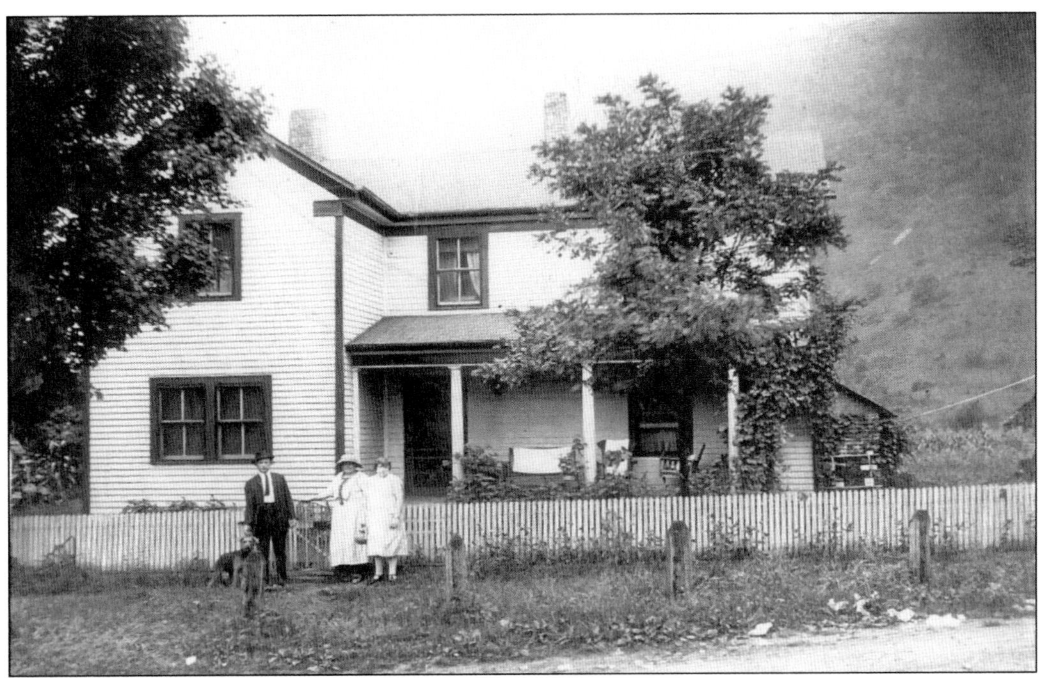

Pictured above are Henry J. Gardner, his wife, Mary Carmack Gardner (center), and Estelle Carmack in front of what is now known as the Hensley house. It is located near the old train depot off the current A. P. Carter Highway. They are again pictured below, but on the right the Gardner store that Henry ran for several years is visible. The Gardner store was on the lot where the old post office building now stands. Notice the street sign at the left of the picture. At the top of the sign appears to be a mile marker from Hiltons to Gate City and an advertisement for Polarine. (Courtesy of Mary Owens.)

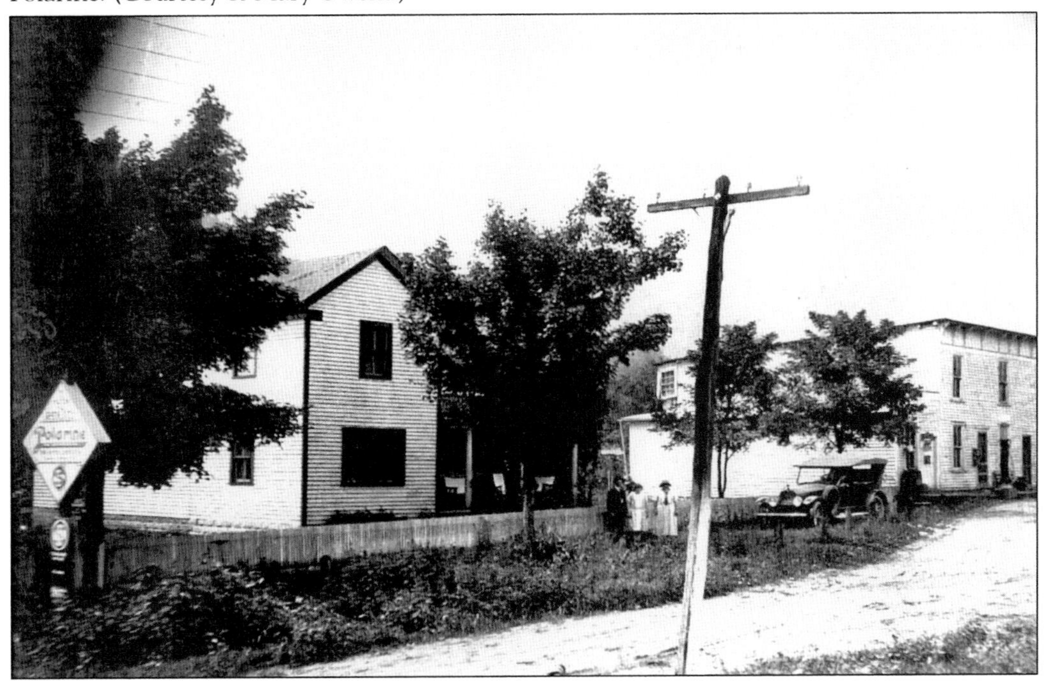

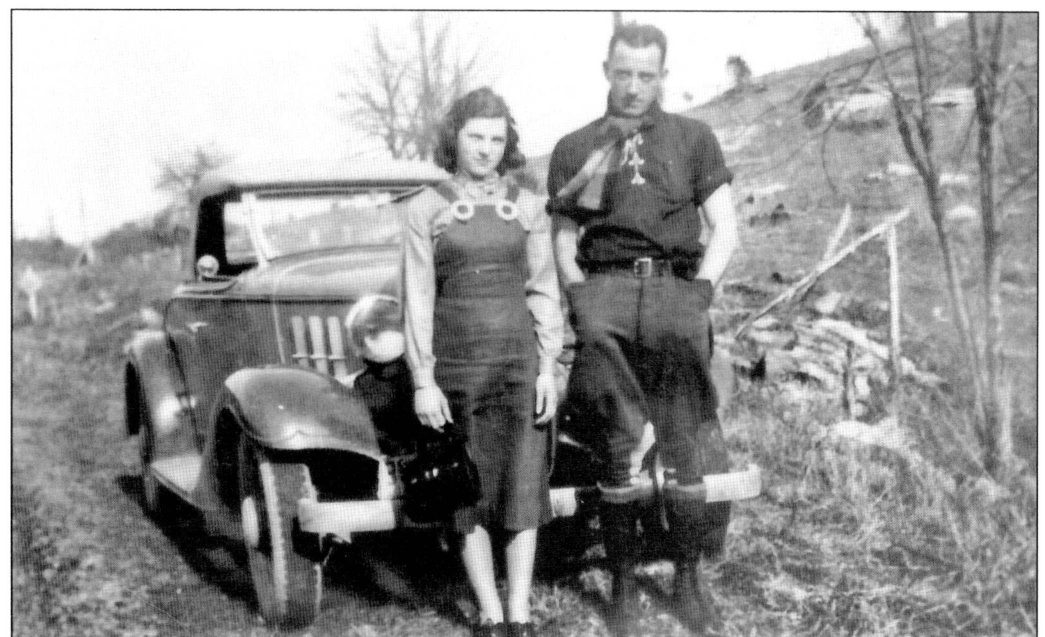

Chester and Estelle McMurray Hensley are pictured here in 1937 in front of an early 1930s Chevrolet. Their wedding was in 1943, and they stayed married for 53 years—until Estelle's death in 1996. Chester died in 2003. (Courtesy of Elsie Gardner.)

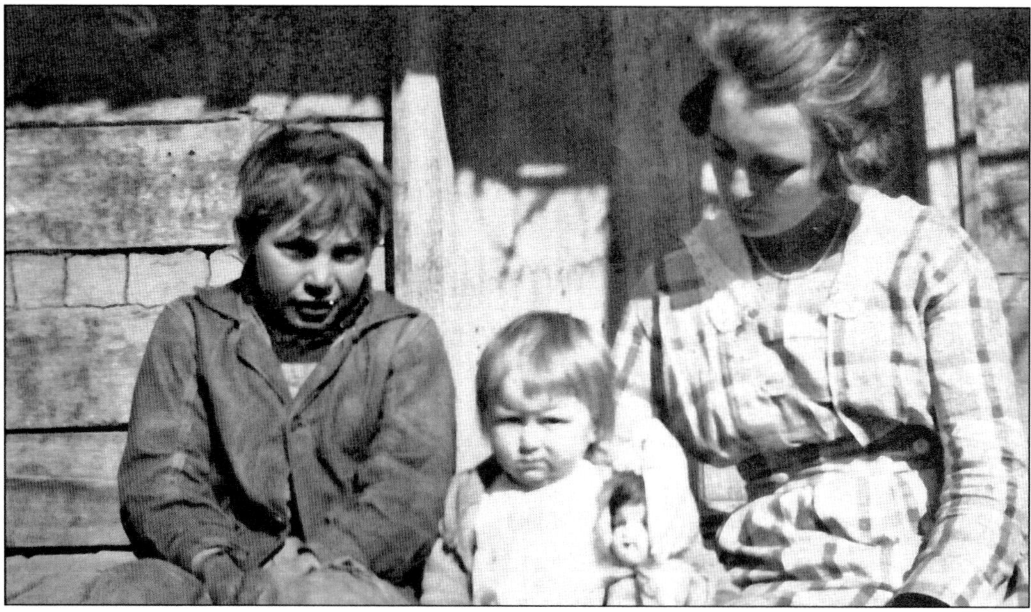

Pictured here are, from left to right, Joe Hensley, Ruth Pippin, and Mamie Daugherty. Hensley is the son of Bob and Ellen Gardner Hensley. He married Janie Crain, and they had two daughters, Dorothy and Mary. Ruth Pippin married Paul E. Pippin and is the daughter of Clyde Elbert and Phoebe McClain Jayne. The Pippins had seven children: Brenda, Sammy, Vickie, Nancy, David, Pamela, and Lesa. Ruth was a homemaker who loved to work in her garden. Mamie Daugherty was the daughter of William and Cora Gardner McClain. She married Claude Daugherty, and they had five children: Willie Kate, James, Beverly, Clifton, and Carol. (Courtesy of Elsie Gardner.)

Hiram Gardner Sr., born in 1858, was married to Matilda Smith Gardner, with whom he had 11 children: Rushen, Cora, William, Peggy, Andrew, Ellon, Miranda, Siby, Ward, Hiram Jr., and Dottie. The first Gardner in Scott County was William, who owned 160 acres on the North Fork of the Holston River. (Courtesy of Elsie Gardner.)

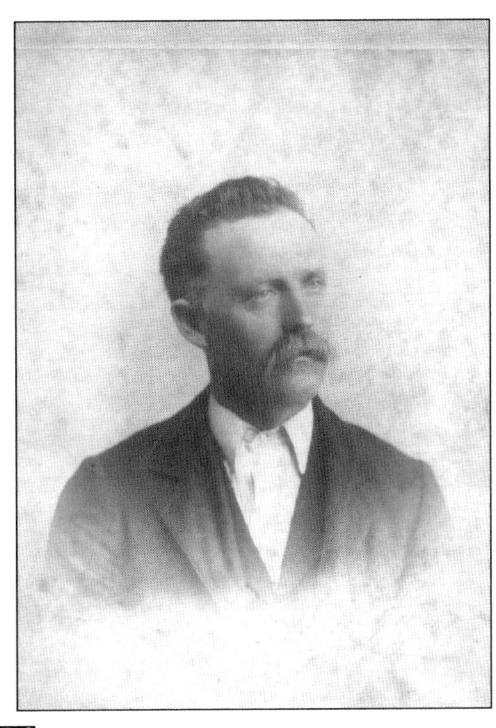

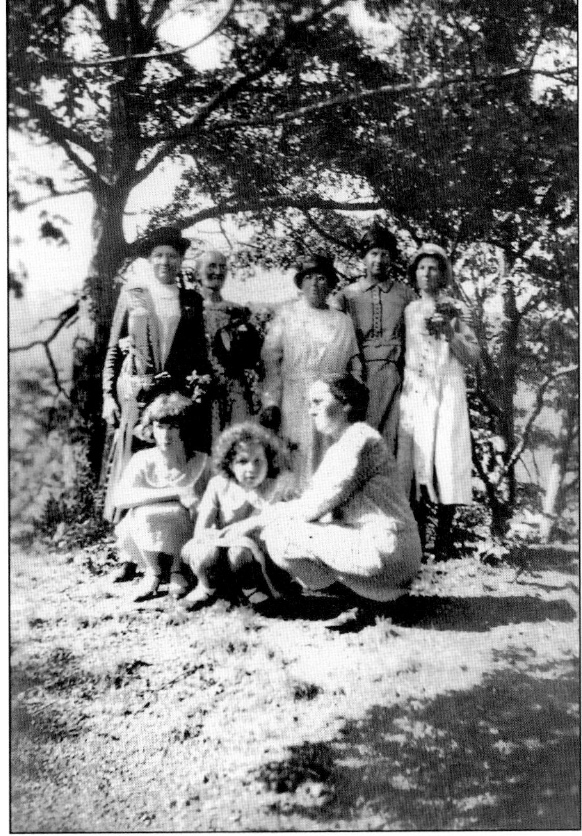

Pictured here from left to right are (first row) Hattie Curtis Myers, Evelyn Weatherly Bralley, and Nellie Reynolds Gibson; (second row) Liz Reynolds Quillen, unidentified, Mandy Reynolds Myers, unidentified, and Lotus Curtis Brooks. Lotus was the daughter of Thomas Parker and Mattie Emma Reynolds Curtis. She was the granddaughter of James Parker and Lucinda Meridith Curtis, and Jim and Harriet Smith Reynolds. (Courtesy of Marianna Gardner.)

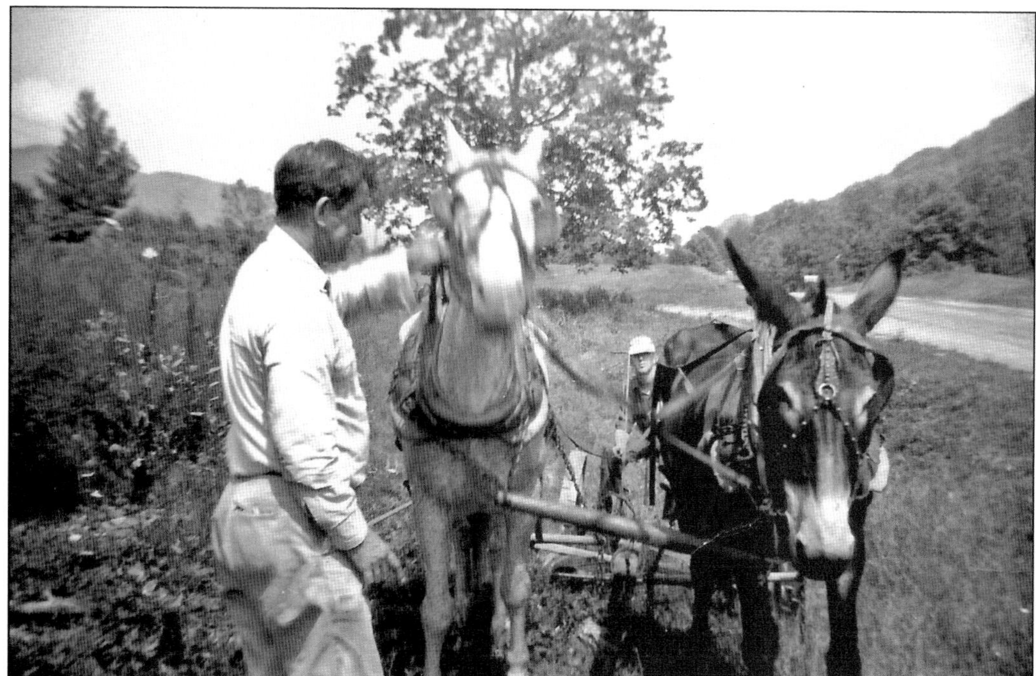

William Lee "Bill" Smith, was born on March 12, 1907, to A. B. and Susan Campbell Smith in Lee County, Virginia. He was married to Inez Gardner, and their children are Henry Lee, William Walton "Cotton," Nora, and Willie Lorain "Jean." Bill worked at Borden Mill until shortly before his death in 1954. (Courtesy of Lois Grey.)

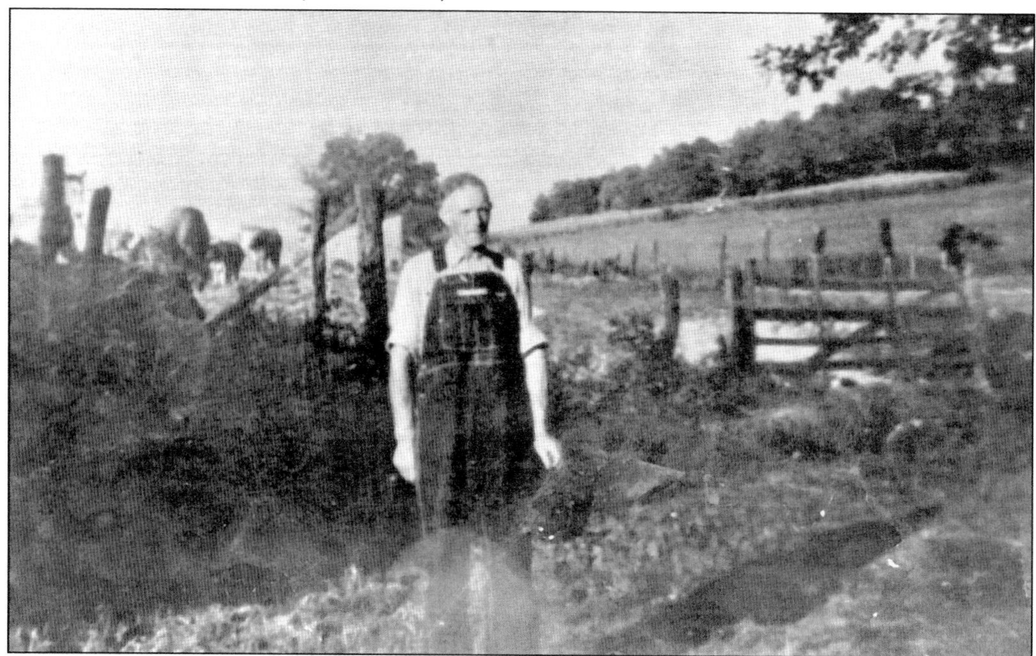

Noah McMurray was married to Della Ramey McMurray Johnson. He was the father of William Harley, Willard, Leland, Mabel, Florance, Genevieve, and Nelsie. They lived in the Spice Wood Hollow area, where he was a farmer. Noah died around 1941. (Courtesy of Opal McMurray.)

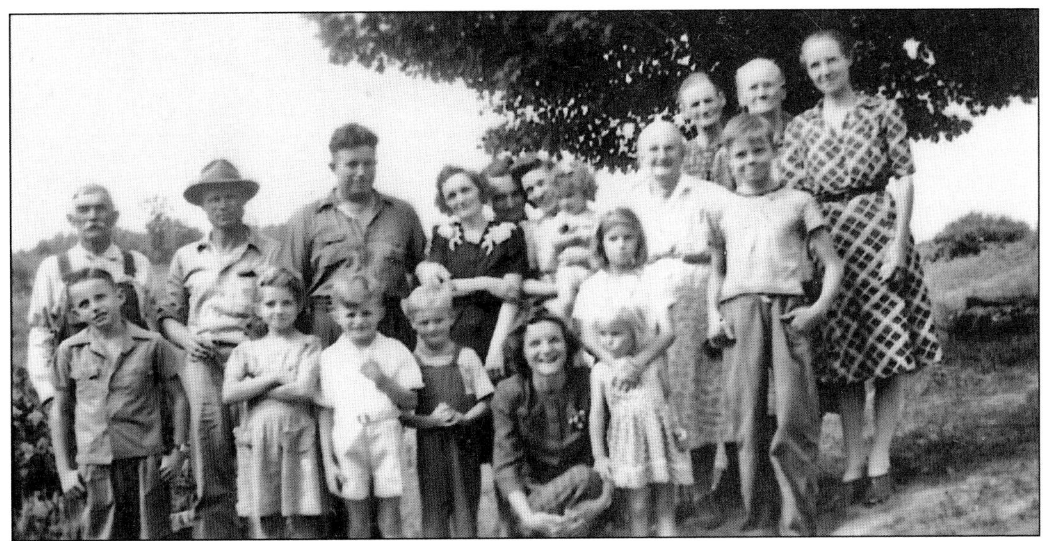

Pictured here on Isaac Godsey's farm, from left to right, are (first row) Bobby Hensley, Helen Hensley, George Hensley, Russell McMurray, Odie McMurray, Betty McMurray, Muriel McMurray, and Douglas McMurray; (second row) Isaac Godsey, Harley McMurray, J. Kay Hensley, Verda Godsey Hensley, Dee Ketron, Darsy Ketron, Peggy McMurray, Bordie Hensley, Susie Godsey, Opie Bright, and Virgie Bright. (Courtesy of Opal McMurray.)

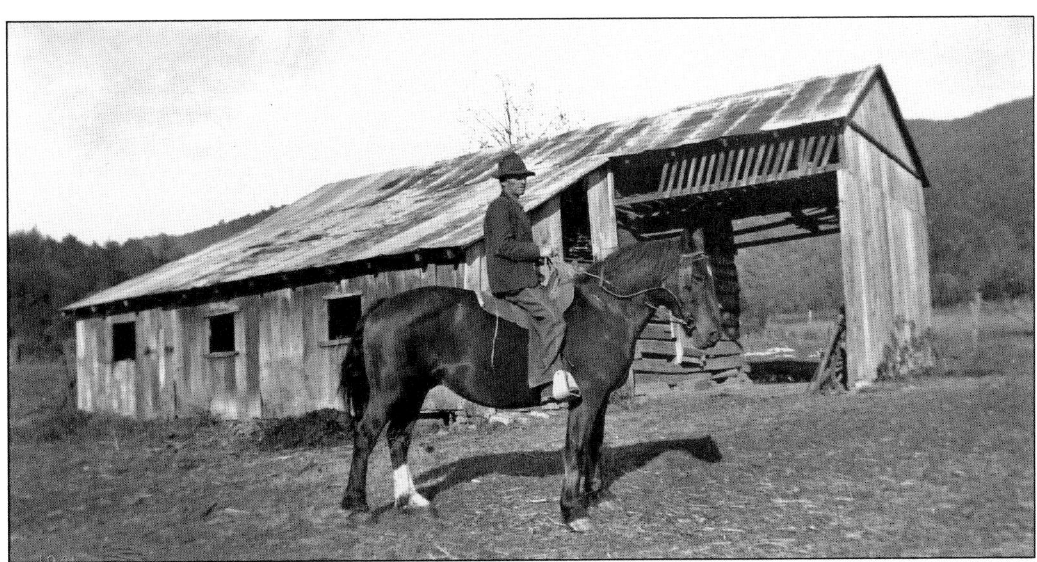

Martin Luther Derting is shown on his horse in front of his barn. Derting used his horses to plow his ground and also to pull his wagon. He would hitch his wagon and take his children to school on cold winter mornings. The barn sat where Mountain View Apartments are now standing. Martin divided his huge farm between his six sons. (Courtesy of Elsie Derting.)

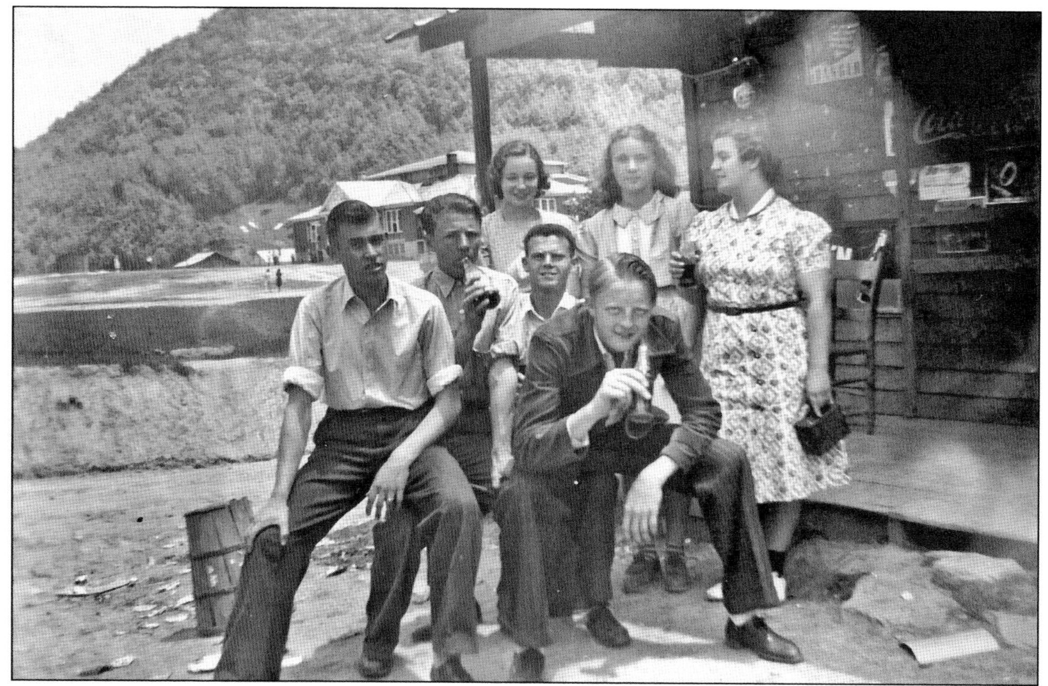

Local teens enjoyCoca-Colas on the porch at Mel Hensley's store. This was a favorite meeting place for teens after school because it was across the street from Hiltons High School. Pictured from left to right are the following: (first row) Warren Baker, Ralph Gardner, Joe Derting, Ted Harris; (second row) Elsie Maddux, Lucille Fugate, and Sara Gardner. (Courtesy of Elsie Derting.)

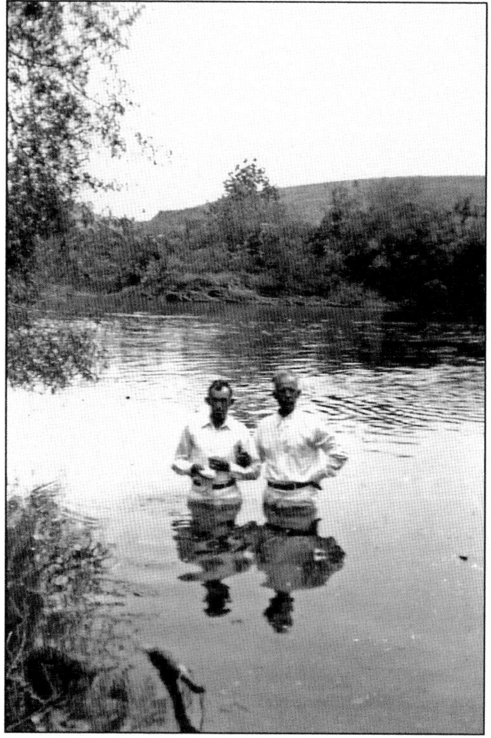

Here the Reverend J. R. Cochran is baptizing his son, Charles, in the Holston River. This was a common scene in the days before church baptisms. Many times, people were baptized in the river, even during the winter months, because that was the only place they had. Charles is pictured in the military chapter in front of the Missionary Baptist Church. (Courtesy of Elsie Derting.)

From left to right are (first row) Flanders Maddux, Harry H. B. McNutt; (second row) Lilburn Blalock, and two unidentified members of the Curtis family. (Courtesy of Elzoria Hickam.)

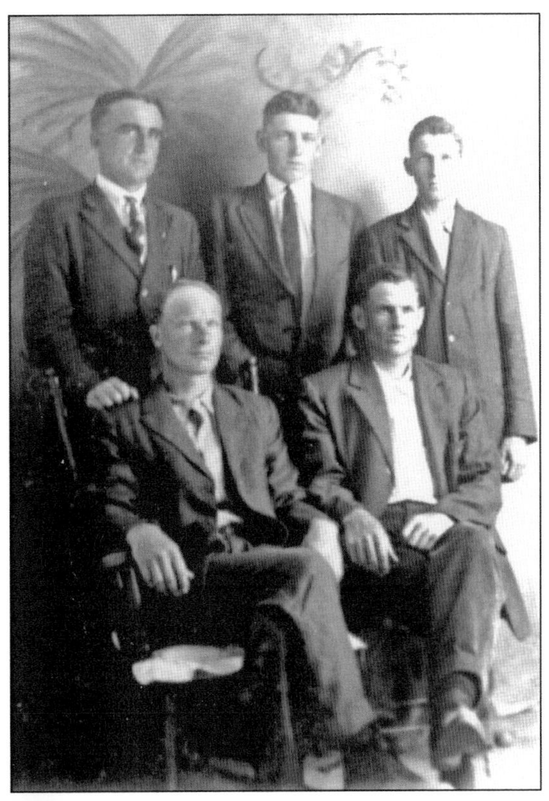

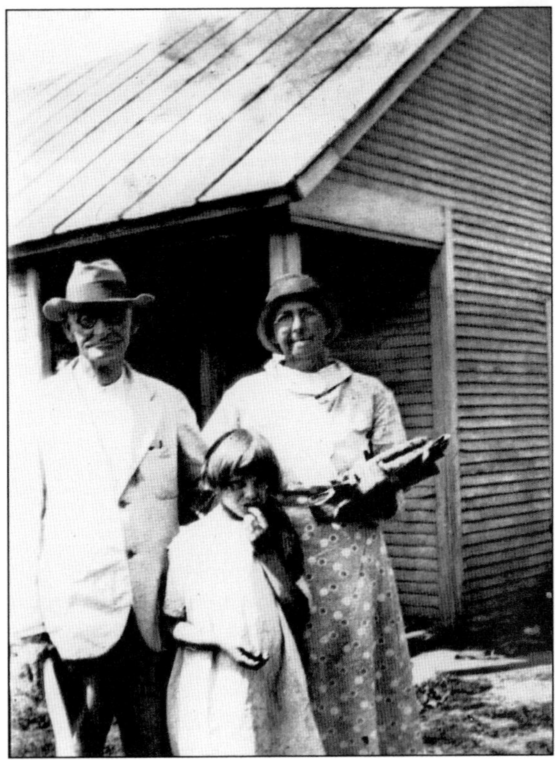

Pictured are the Reverend C. L. Poulston (left), Margaret Poulston, and Opal Vivian Metcalf (in front). Reverend Poulston was the first pastor of Hiltons United Methodist Church. He was a circuit rider for a time and would often preach at the Old Chestnut Flats Church. Reverend Poulston would ride his horse from church to church. (Courtesy of Mary Owens.)

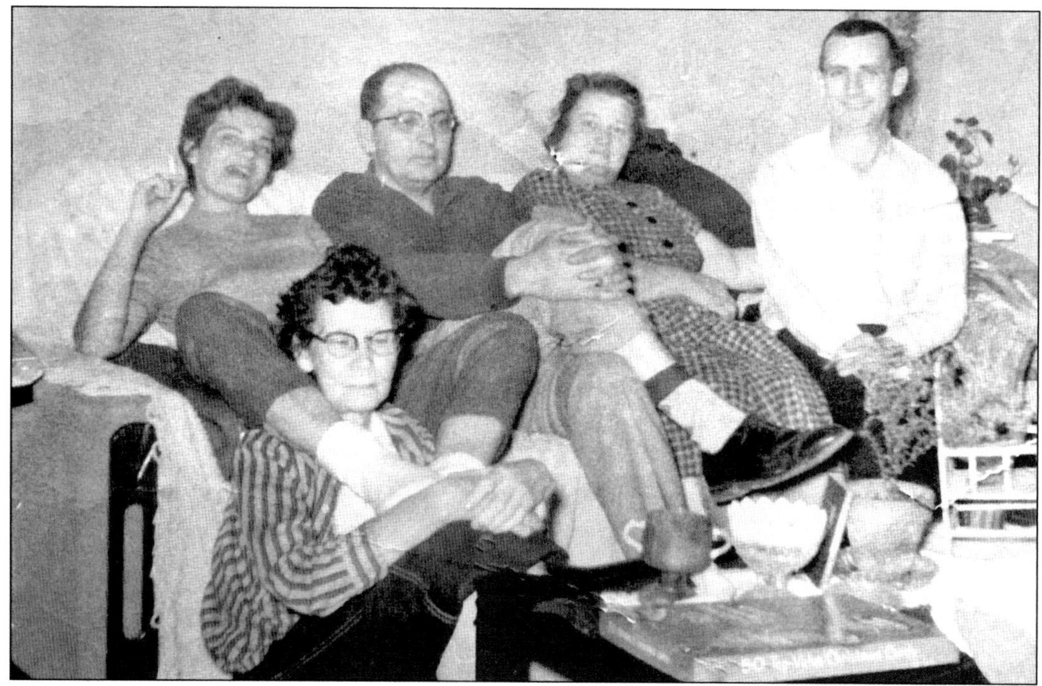

Shown here are, from left to right, Pauline Blaylock, Lucian Blaylock, Elsie Gardner, and Sam Hobbs. Nannie Smallwood is sitting on the floor. Lucian Blaylock was one of the charter members of the Hiltons Ruritan Club, which began in April 1957. The Hiltons club was the 834th in the nation. (Courtesy of Elsie Gardner.)

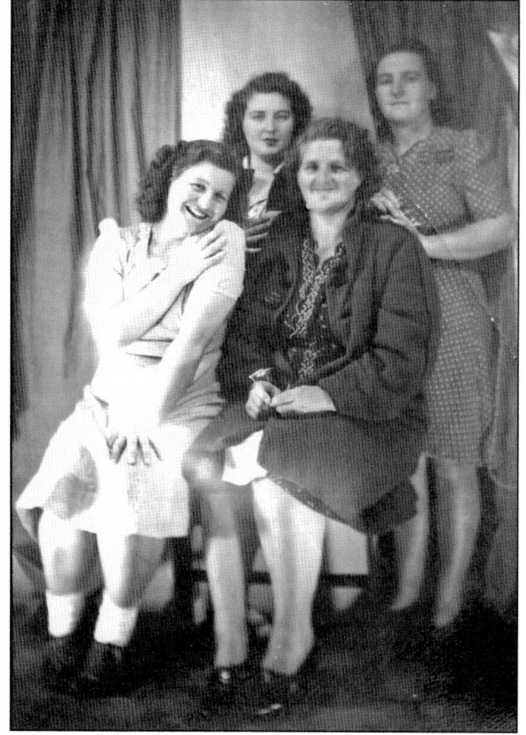

Pictured here from left to right and front to back are Ruby Gardner, Alice Gardner, Delma Gardner, and Sarah Gardner, who are sisters to Elsie Gardner. Her brothers are Walmer, Ward, Harrie, and Ed. Their grandfather walked to the Gold Rush in California. (Courtesy of Elsie Gardner.)

Elsie and Clyde Gardner were married on April 1, 1939, in Blountville, Tennessee. After living in California, they moved back to the Hiltons area in December 1945. They had 10 children: Mary Kathleen, Judith Marie, Daniel Keith, Carol Lanore, Paul Rex, Max, Owilda Jean, Deloris Gay, Marvin Kent, and Terry Lee. Clyde attended Maces Springs and Hiltons School, and Elsie attended Stony Point School. (Courtesy of Marianna Gardner.)

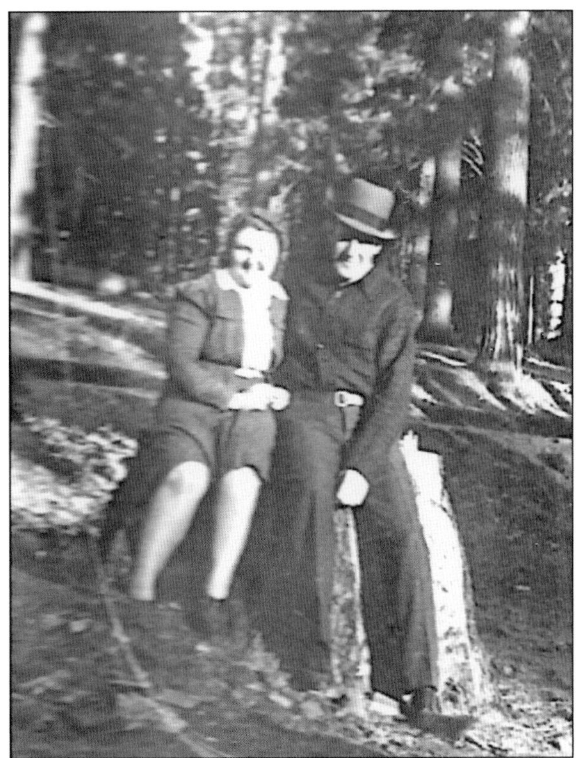

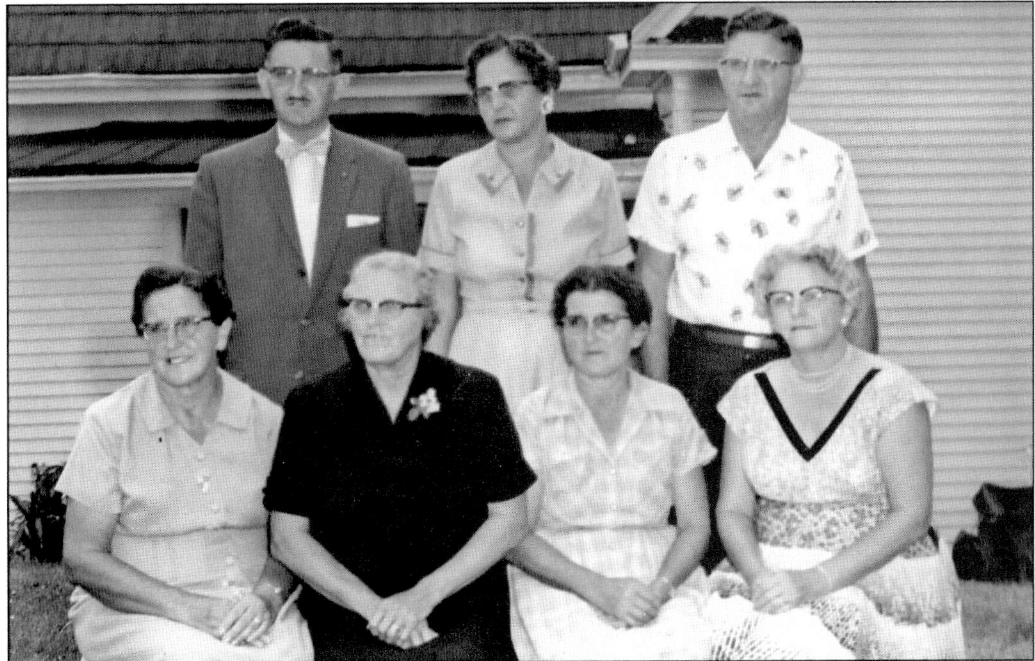

Pictured from left to right are (first row) Earlie Hunsucker Good, Charmie Hunsucker Dickson, Edith Bright, and Ethel Rutherford; (second row) J. D. Hunsucker, Bonnie Bright, and Dewey Hunsucker. Earlie married James C. Good, and they had four children: Charles Thomas, Carmen, Elmer, and Dan. (Courtesy of Carmen Good.)

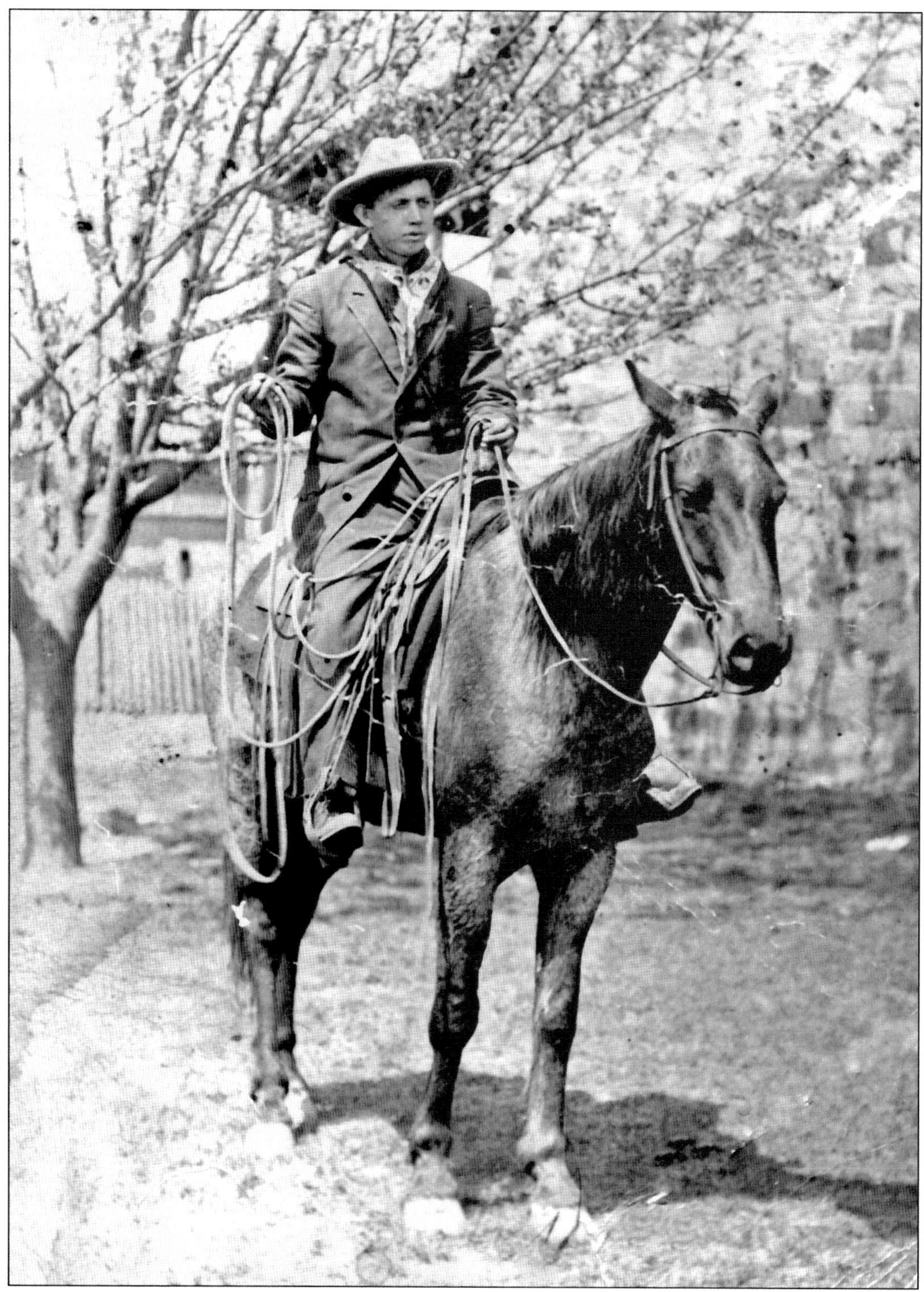

This is a picture of Pete Smith, Bill Smith's brother. They were sons of Augin Smith. Their mother died at a young age, and their father later remarried. Bill married Inez Gardner, and they had four children: Dalton, Loraine Jean, Nora, and Lee. (Courtesy of Opal McMurray.)

Pictured is John Hooker, who married and had four daughters: Lilly, Nannie, Jenny, and Susie. Hooker came to the Hiltons area from the Sandy Ridge area of Coeburn, Virginia. Although it is not known which side he fought for, John Hooker was a Civil War veteran. (Courtesy of Opal McMurray.)

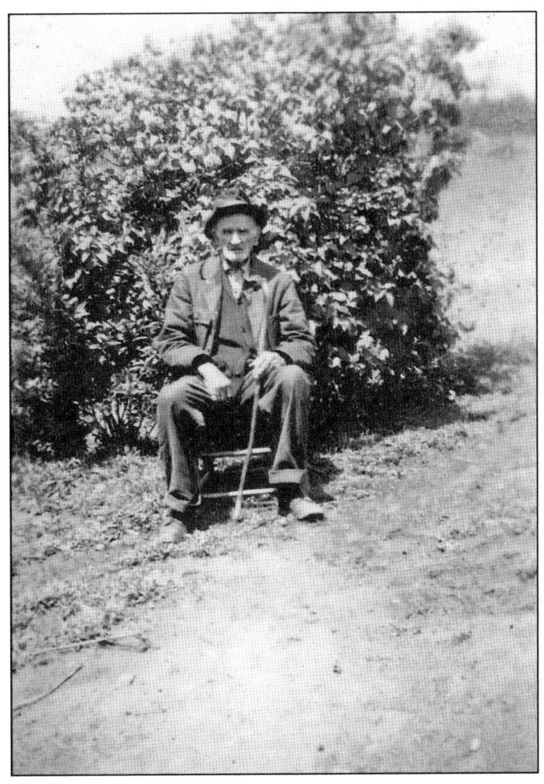

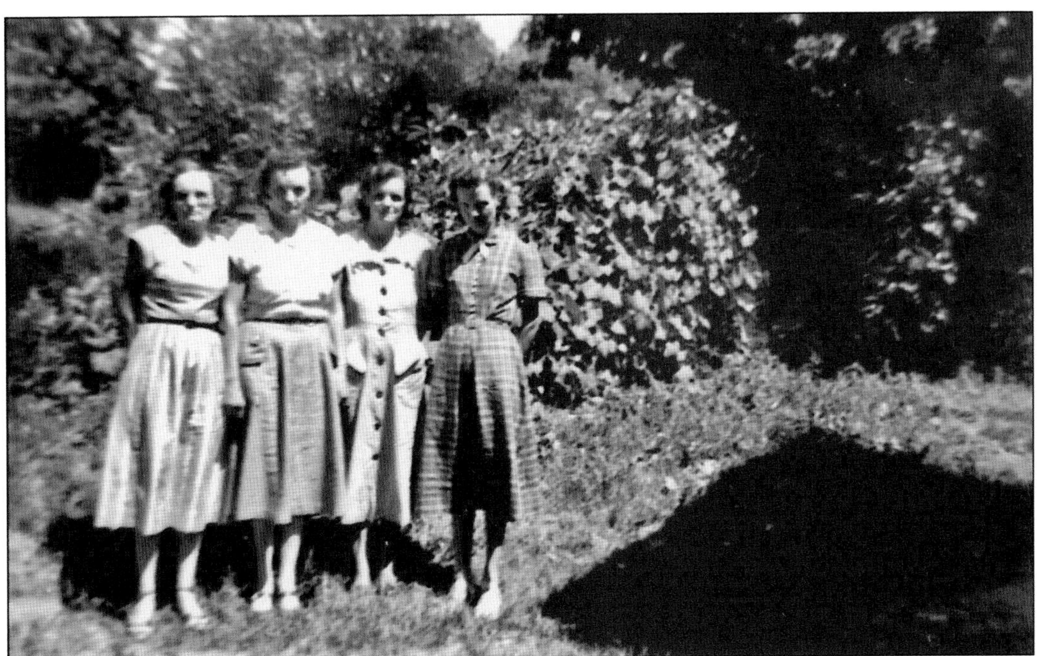

Pictured are sisters Verdie Hensley (left), Verge Bright (center), and Odie McMurray. Also pictured is Esther McMurray, their first cousin as well as the mother of Gary and Eugene McMurray. Sanford McMurray was Gary and Eugene's grandfather. (Courtesy of Opal McMurray.)

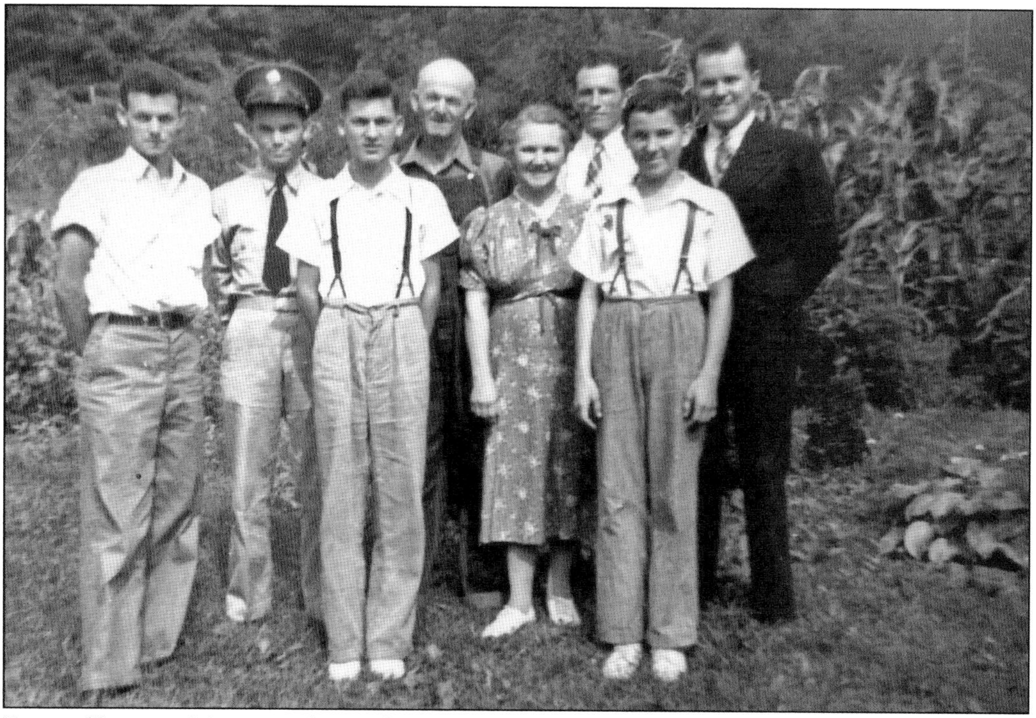

Pictured here are Martin Luther and Nevada Parker Derting with their six sons (in no particular order): Earl, Carl, Homer, Joe, Ralph, and Roy. Although Martin primarily did farm labor, he also worked at Borden Mill in Kingsport for a while, worked part time with the Scott County Road System, and worked part time with the Virginia Forestry Division. He loved to ride his horse and would often go to the top of Clinch Mountain. (Courtesy of Elsie Derting.)

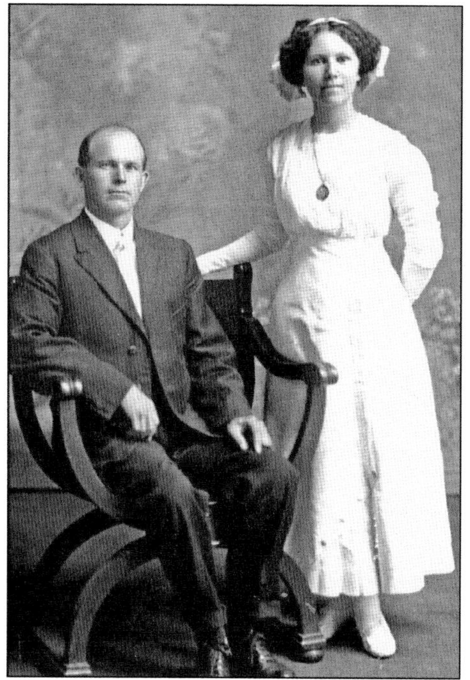

This is the wedding photograph of Martin Luther and Nevada Parker Derting. They were married on June 25, 1913. Nevada was born in September 1890, the ninth of 11 children. She loved school and enjoyed community activities. She often walked several miles to join in on such things as spelling bees. (Courtesy of Elsie Derting.)

William and Rachel Owen Parker were married in the late 1800s. They had 11 children, one of whom was Claude Parker. Claude helped his father work on the farm in his childhood and soon was working his way through Indiana. In Sioux City, Iowa, he began his career as a bridge contractor in 1913. In the 1920s, he worked on present-day Highway 126 from Kingsport to Bristol. (Courtesy of Elsie Derting.)

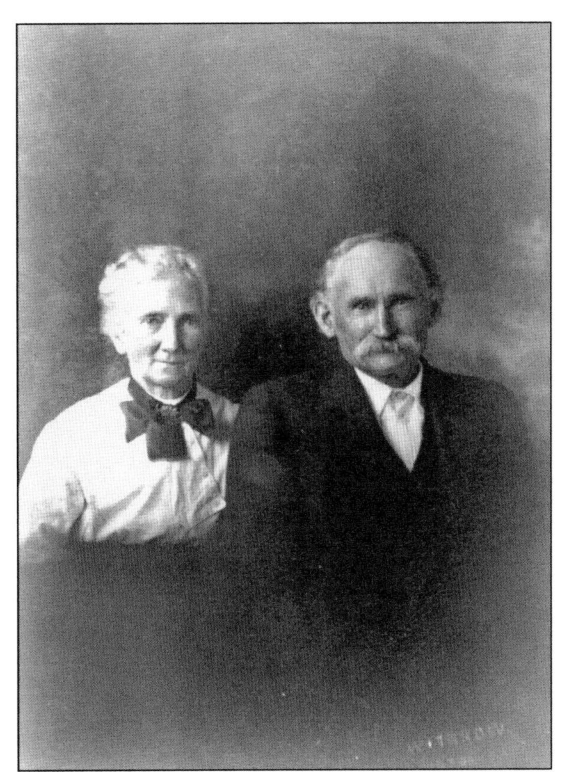

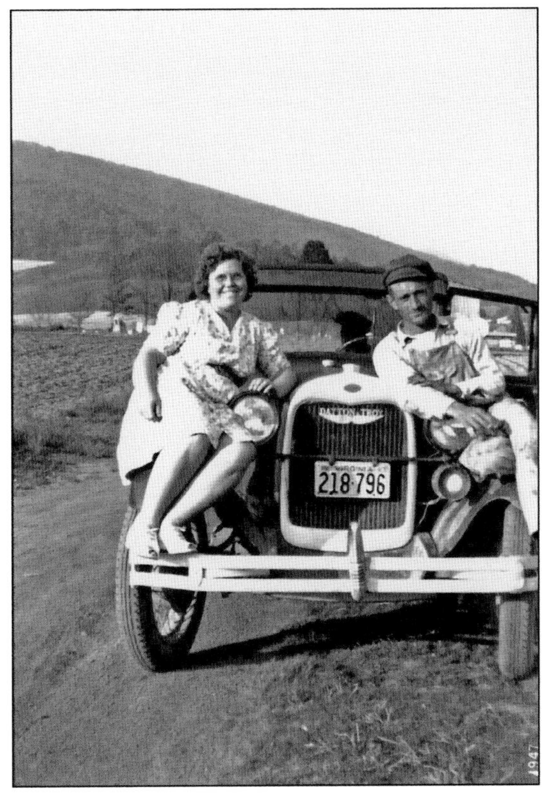

Elsie Sanders Sorah and Junior Sorah lived in the Bright Hollow area of Hiltons. Junior had a brother, Cotton Sorah. Elsie was Elzoria Sanders Hickam's sister. (Courtesy of Elzoria Hickam.)

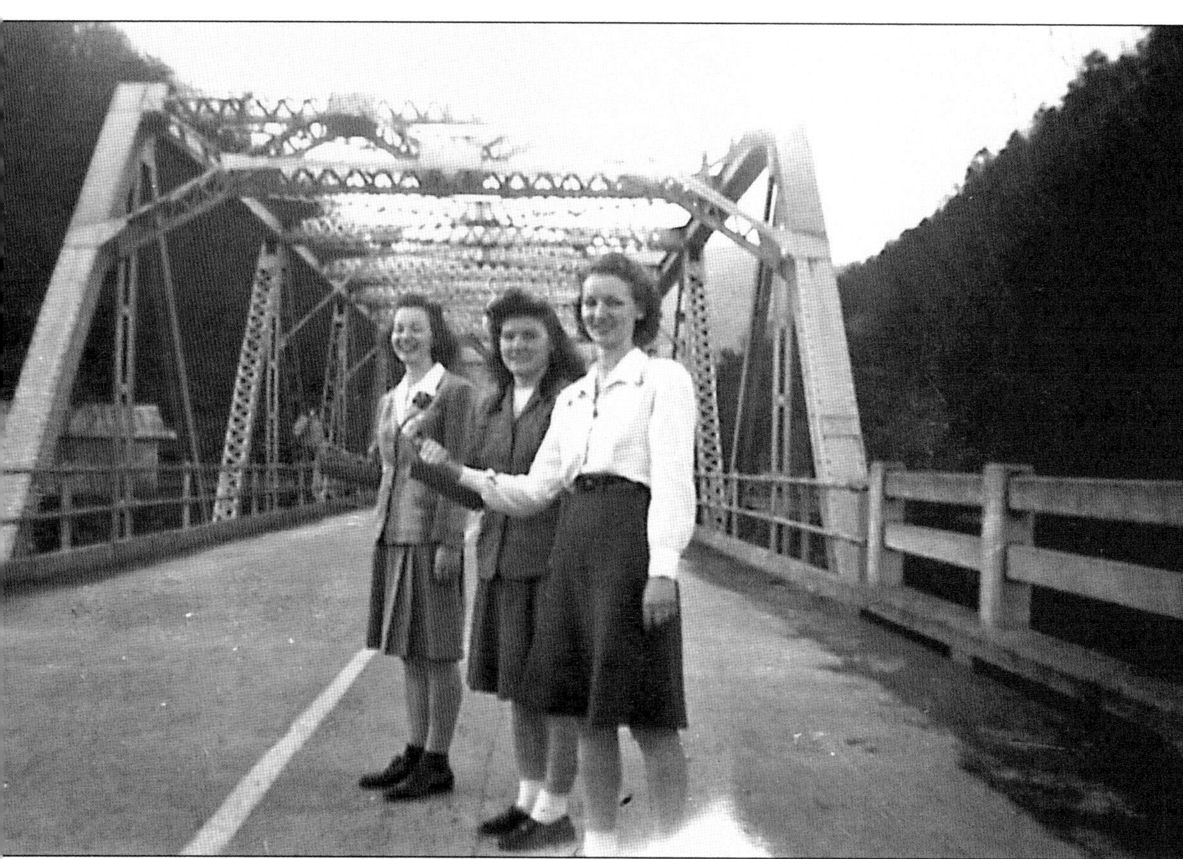

Elsie (left), Mary (center), and Juanita Maddux are shown at the Hiltons River bridge on Highway 58. The opening of the bridge was important to those who lived in Hiltons, and many of the families have photographs made on or in front of the bridge. (Courtesy of Elsie Derting.)

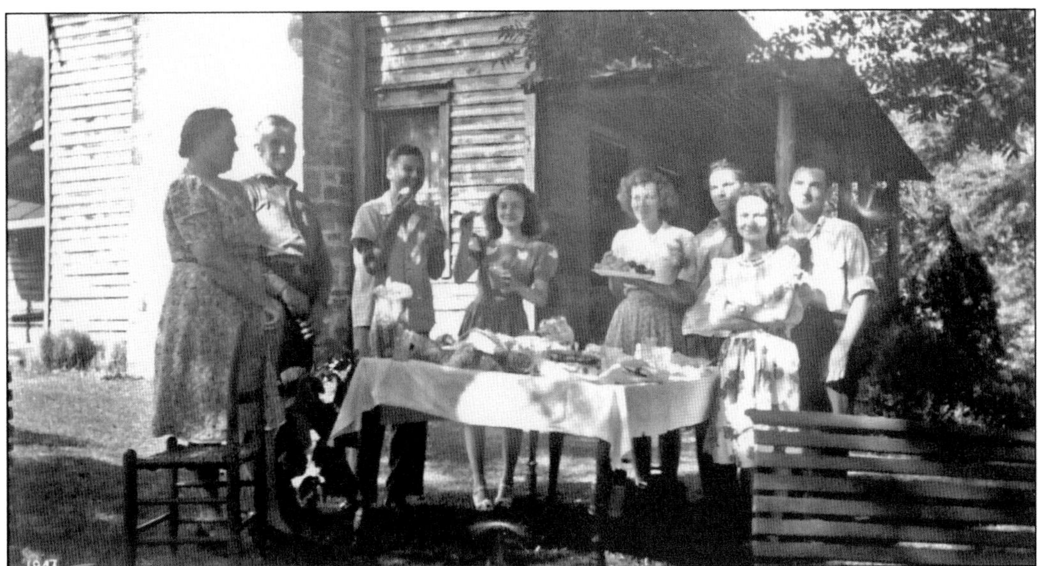

This moment was captured at a Fourth of July picnic at Ezra Addington's home in 1947. Pictured from left to right are Jessie Addington, Ezra Addington, Ralph Derting, Claudia Addington, Elsie Derting, Roy Derting, Betty Gardner, and unidentified. The photographer was Homer Derting. Elsie said that she had never before seen so much homemade candy and that it was the best she had ever put in her mouth. (Courtesy of Elsie Derting.)

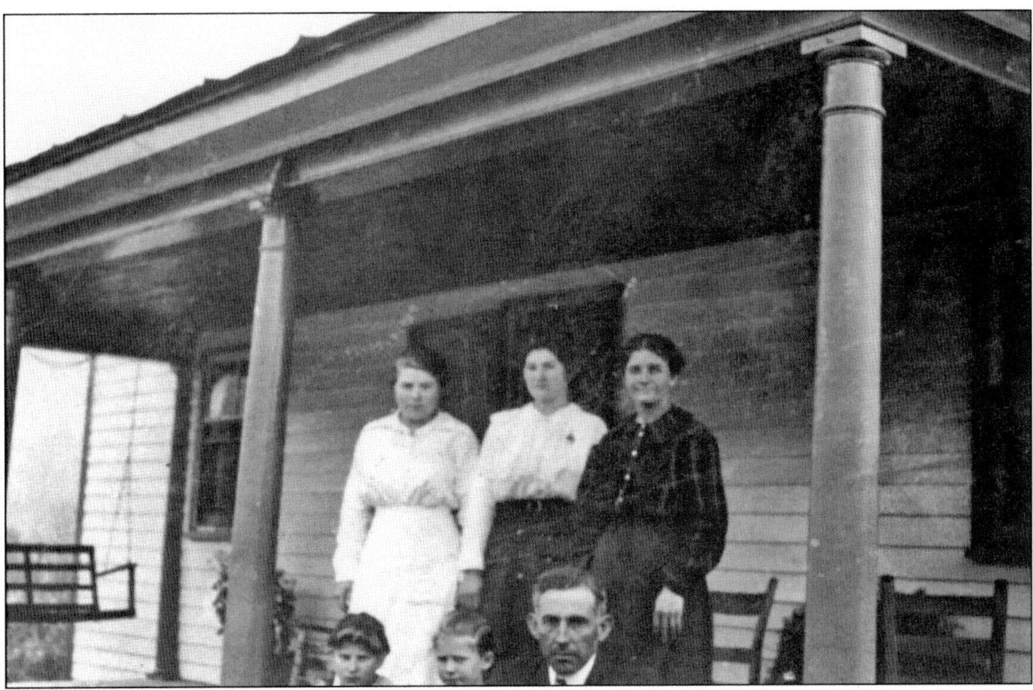

Shown here are (standing, from left to right) Ida Hickam Gardner, Marinda Hickam Nichols, and Myrtle Whetsel; (seated) Dr. Sylvester Gardner. This is the Luther Hickam house that burned on Mendota Road near Hiltons. The children are Thelma (left) and Nina Hickam. (Courtesy of Elzoria Hickam.)

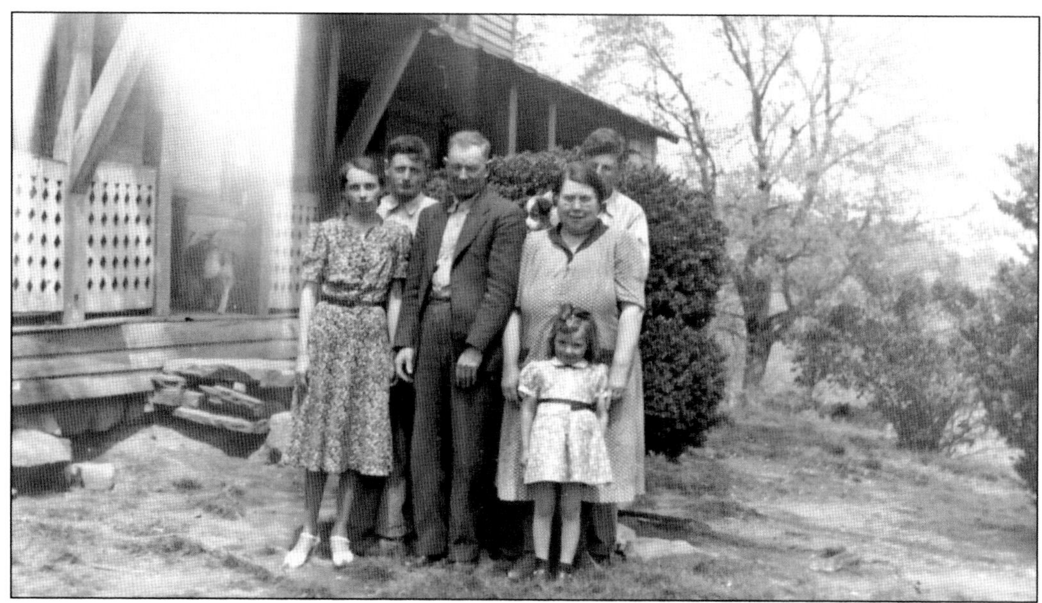

Pictured from left to right are (first row) Madge Hickam Parson, C. H. "Charlie" Hickam, and Loraine Parson in front of Sarah Hickam; (second row) Charles Hickam and Glenn J. Hickam, sons of C. H. Hickam, half brother to Madge Parson. (Courtesy of Elzoria Hickam.)

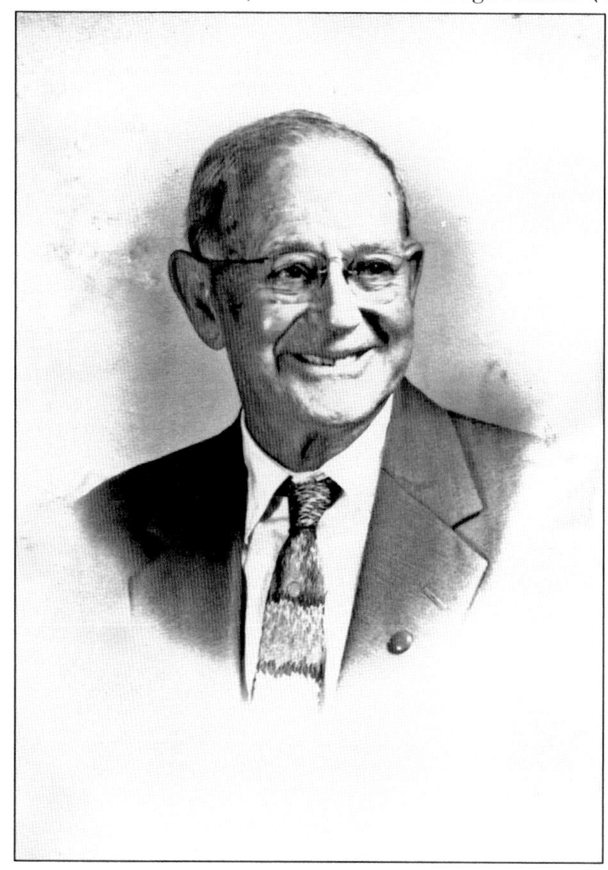

Charles Hickam Sr., the grandson of Emanuel Hickam of the Civil War era, was married to Belle Maddux Hickam, and they had three children. He was the grandfather of Stanley Hickam. (Courtesy of Stanley and Lennea Hickam.)

Pictured here are Nathan Ezra and Jessie Mae Hilton Addington and their son, James. Jessie is the great-granddaughter of John Hilton, who originally owned the most land in Hiltons. Nathan Ezra Addington taught at Hiltons School for 32 years and for a total of 52 years at several different schools. This picture was made in the 1920s. Both Ezra and Jessie were well educated, and Jessie attended Radford College in the early 1900s to be a teacher. (Courtesy of Stanley and Lennea Hickam.)

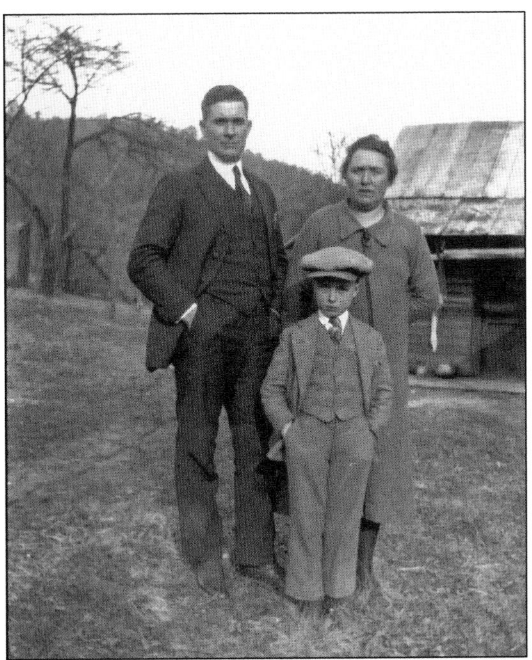

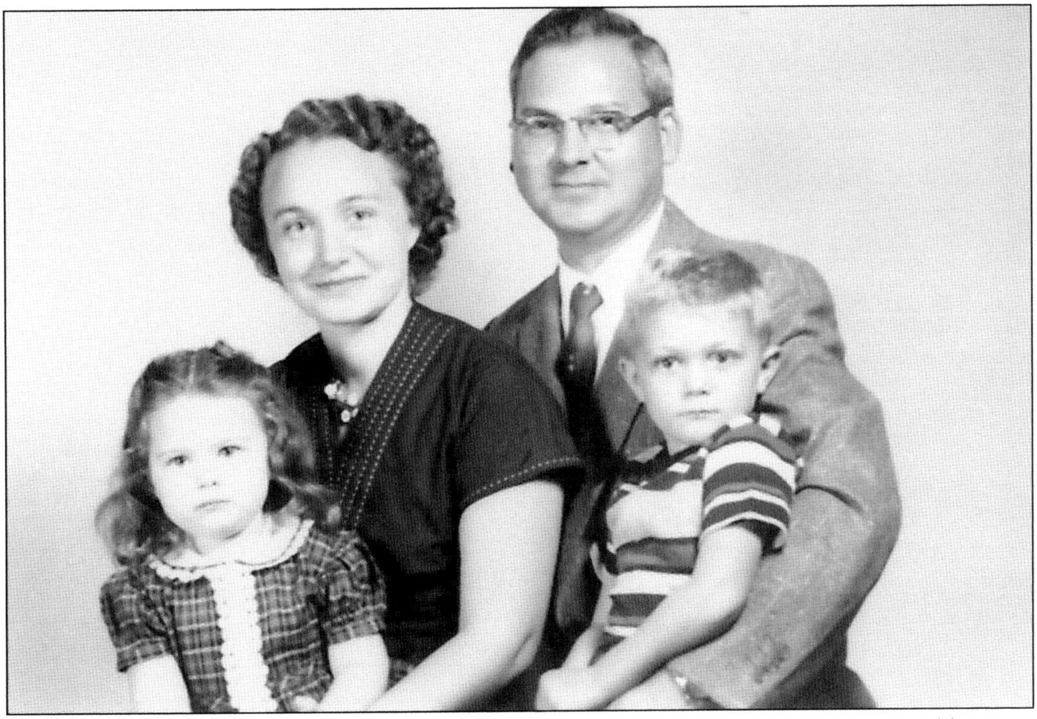

Shown here around 1956 are Claudia Addington, the daughter of Ezra and Jessie Addington, and Ralph Derting. Claudia taught music from 1946 to 2005 in the community at her home or at Hiltons Elementary School. Also pictured are their children, Lennea and Keith. Ralph Derting served as a social worker in Scott County for 30 years. Keith works for the University of South Carolina, and Lennea works in the Kingsport Public Library. (Courtesy of Stanley and Lennea Hickam.)

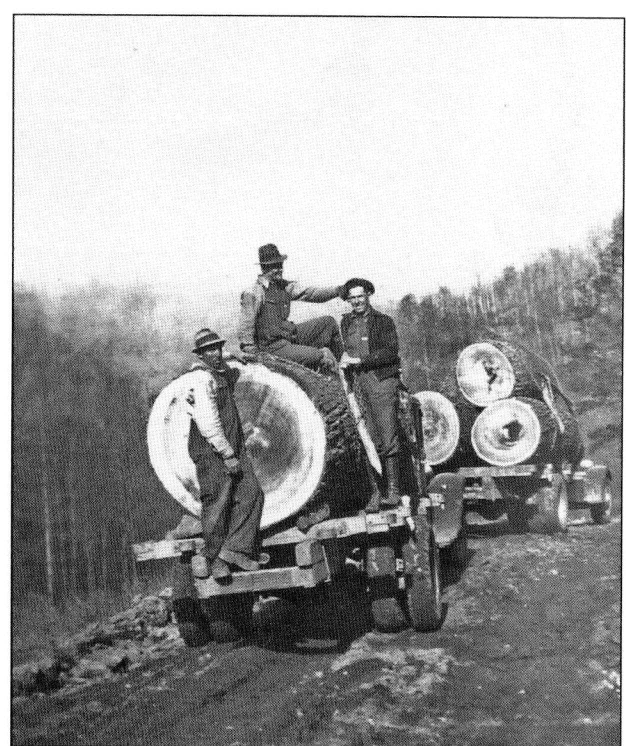

Pictured here are, from left to right, Joe Hensley, Andrew Gardner, and Jim Taylor logging on Brumley Mountain. Notice the large log on the truck the men are standing on. Gardner married Nannie Quillen, and they had several children. Nannie died young, and the children went to live with their grandparents. (Courtesy of Elsie Gardner.)

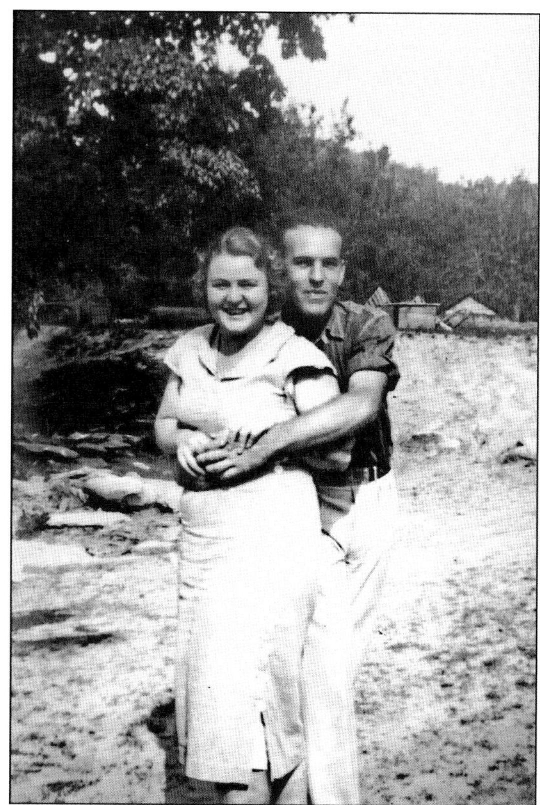

Pictured here are Elsie Gardner and Claude McMurray. McMurray eventually became principal of the Rye Cove School in Scott County, Virginia. (Courtesy of Elsie Gardner.)

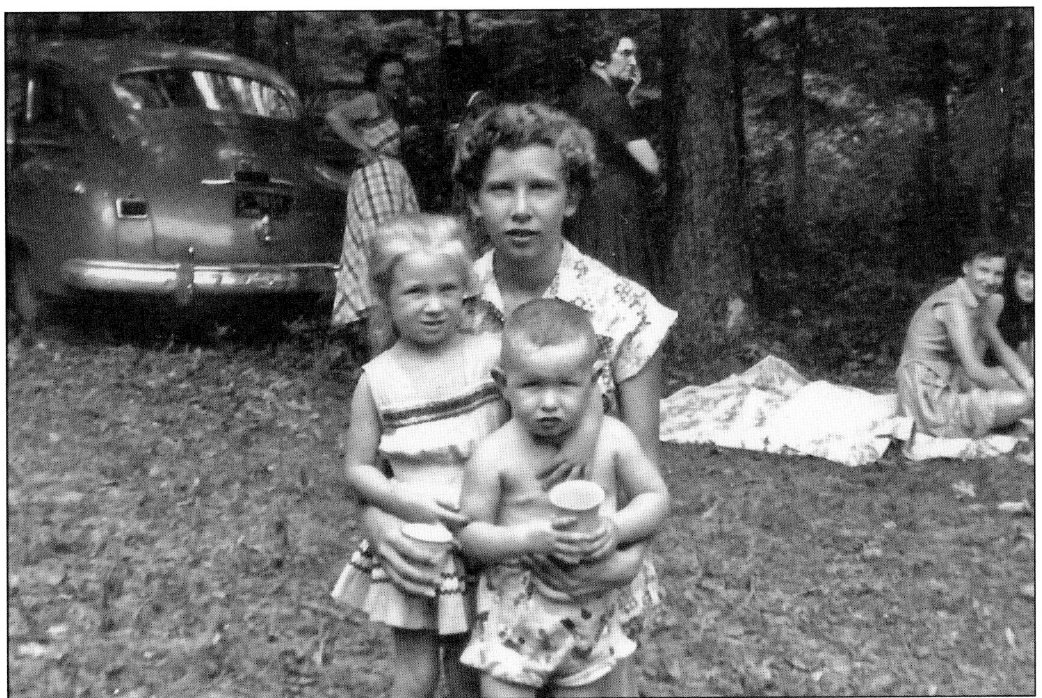

Pictured here are Sandy Bralley Miller (in the back), Marianna Brooks Gardner, and Steve Rose. Marianna is the daughter of Thomas Arthur "Jiggs" and Lotus Curtis Brooks. She married Marvin Gardner, and they have one child, Amanda Kay. Marianna and Marvin live on the North Fork of the Holston River, and Marvin farms the home place in his spare time from his regular job. In the back in the dark dress is Mamie Blockard Curtis, and to the right on the blanket is Helen Derting Weatherly, whose parents owned the store behind the cemetery. (Courtesy of Marianna Gardner.)

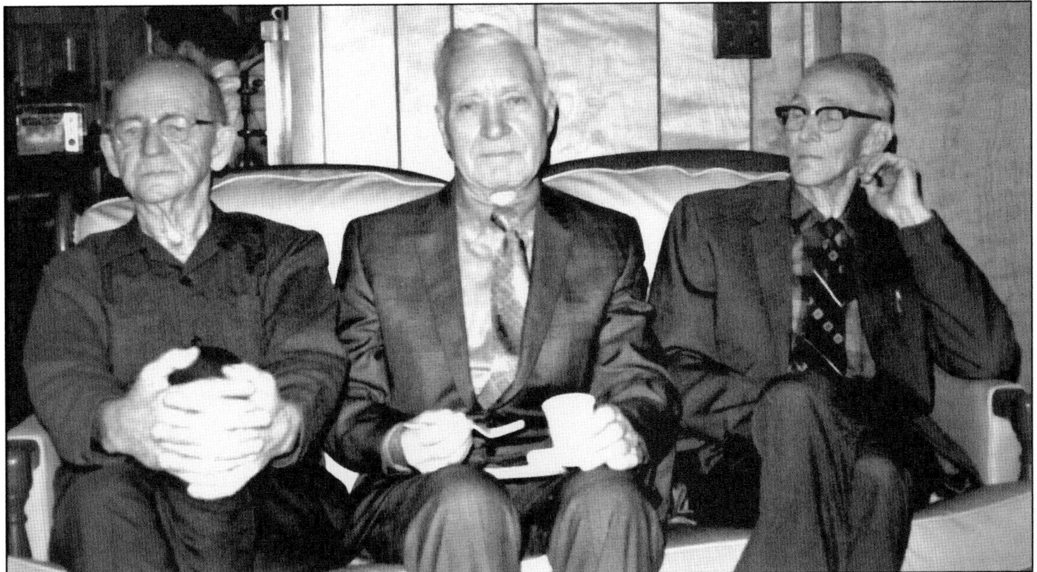

From left to right are James C. Good, Brian Hilton, and Guy Cross. Hilton is the retired postmaster of the Hiltons Post Office. (Courtesy of Marianna Gardner.)

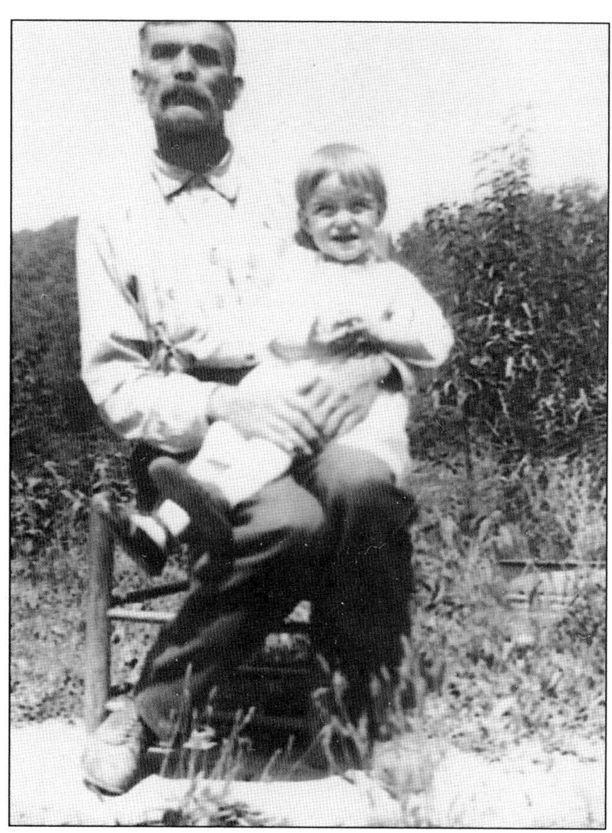

Isaac Godsey and his daughter, Ida Mae, were photographed around 1910. Ida Mae was one of two daughters who died within months of each other of typhoid fever in 1911. The other daughter was Allafare. (Courtesy of Opal McMurray.)

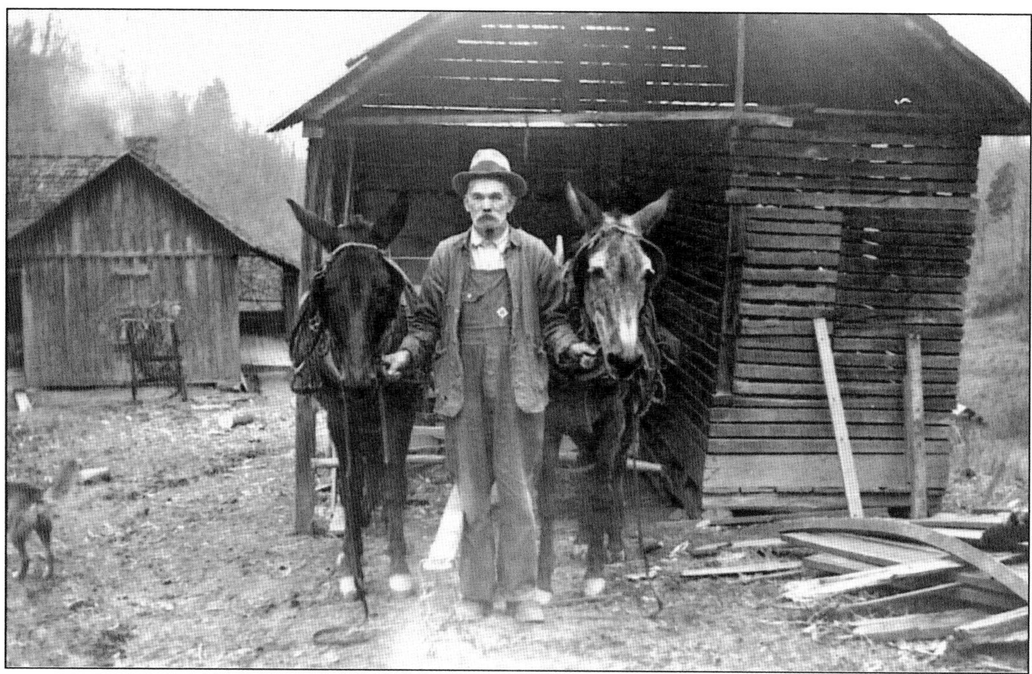

Isaac Godsey poses with his two mules, Bill and John, on Godsey's farm, where he used the team of mules to work the land. Isaac's wife's name was Susie. (Courtesy of Opal McMurray.)

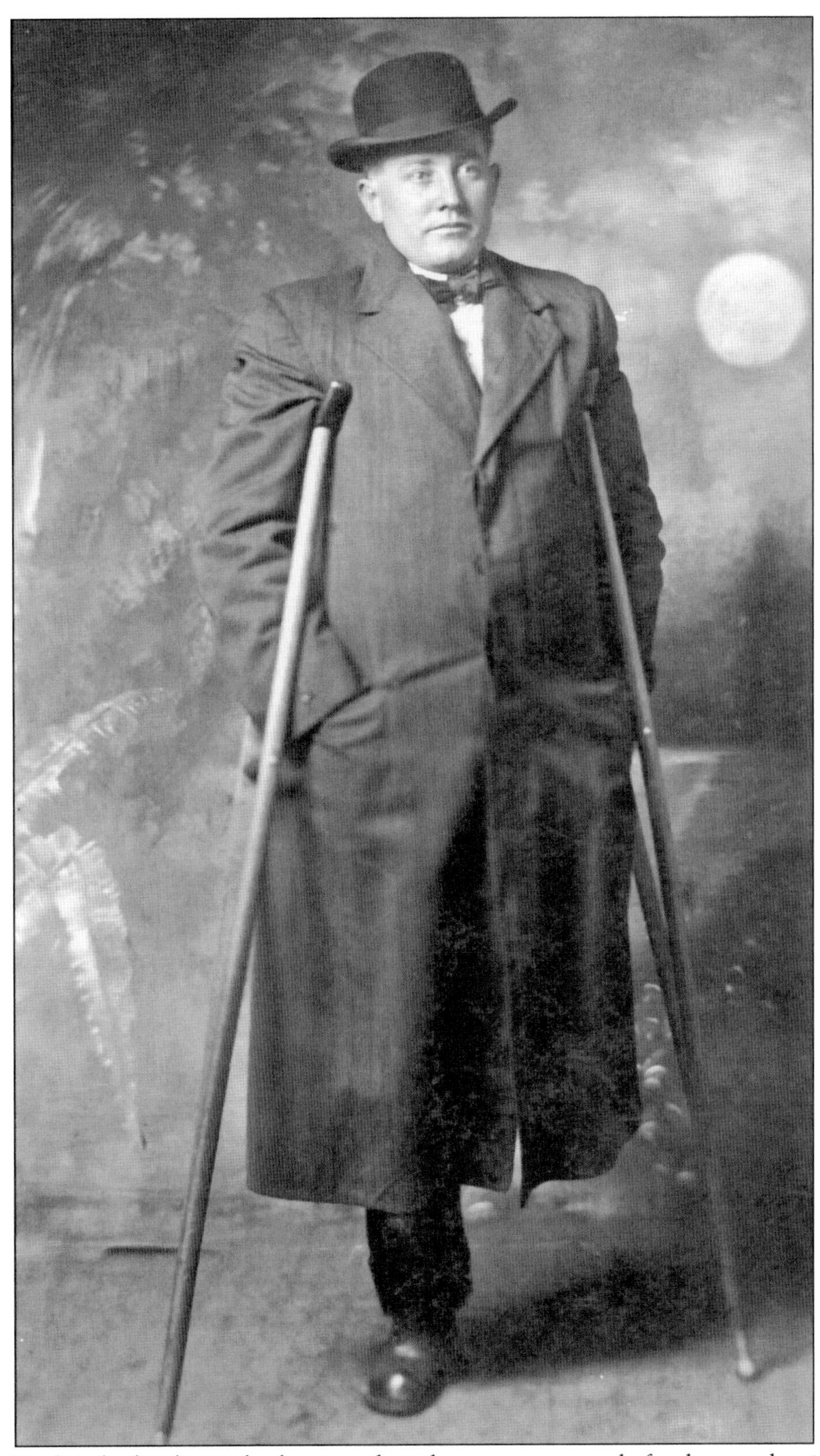

Chester Gardner had only one leg because the other was amputated after he was shot in the leg when caught destroying hobby horses with a knife. (Courtesy of Elsie Gardner.)

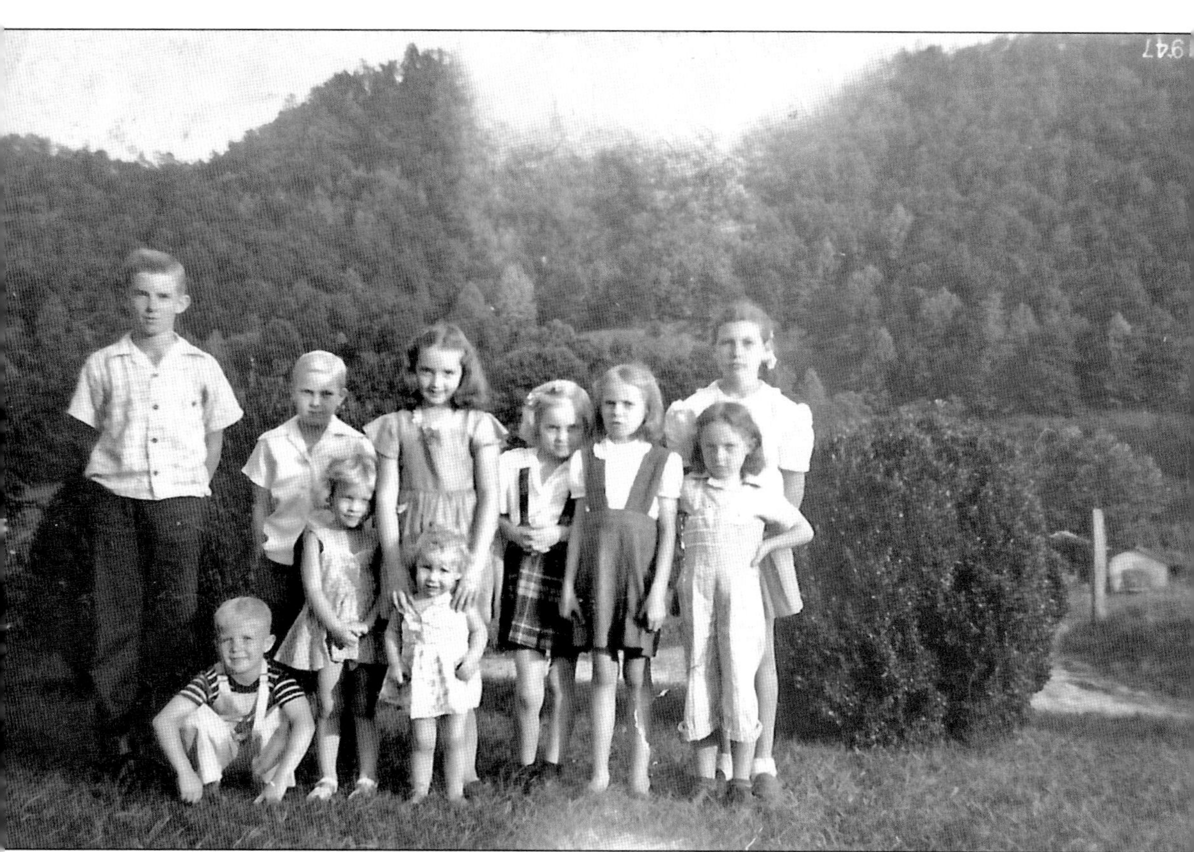

In the back row of this photograph, from left to right, are Doug Mann, Jack Smith, Connie Curtis, Rose Smith, Eleanora Curtis, Judy Curtis, and unidentifed (standing in front of Judy). Donnie Mann is crouched in front. The two smaller girls standing next to Donnie are unidentified. Connie Curtis married Darrell Gardner. They had two sons, Robin Darrell and Andrew Curtis. Connie is the daughter of Conley and Minnie Curtis. (Courtesy of Marianna Gardner.)

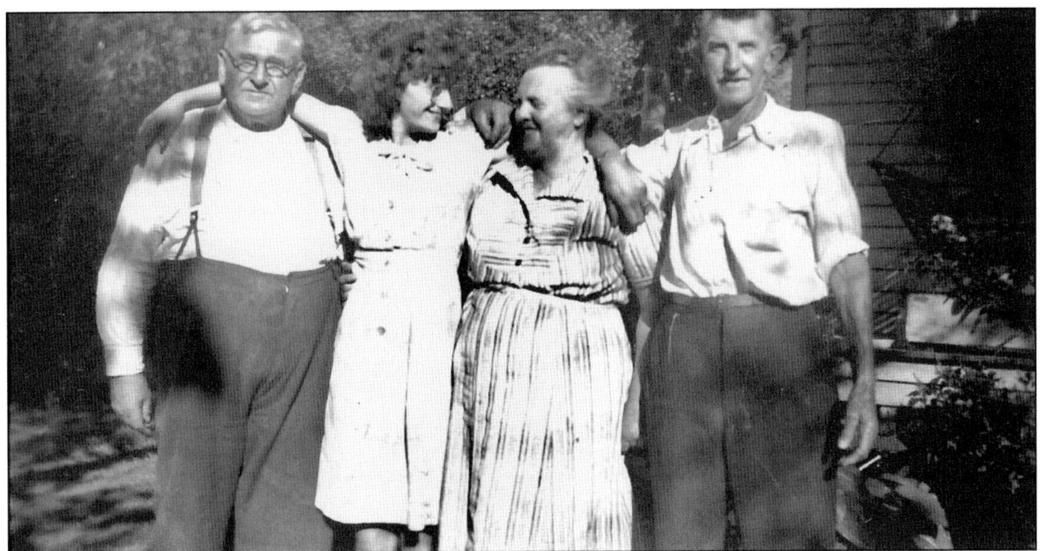

From left to right are Charlie Shaffer, Edith Hunsucker, Meg Shaffer, and Bruce Hunsucker. (Courtesy of Carmen Good.)

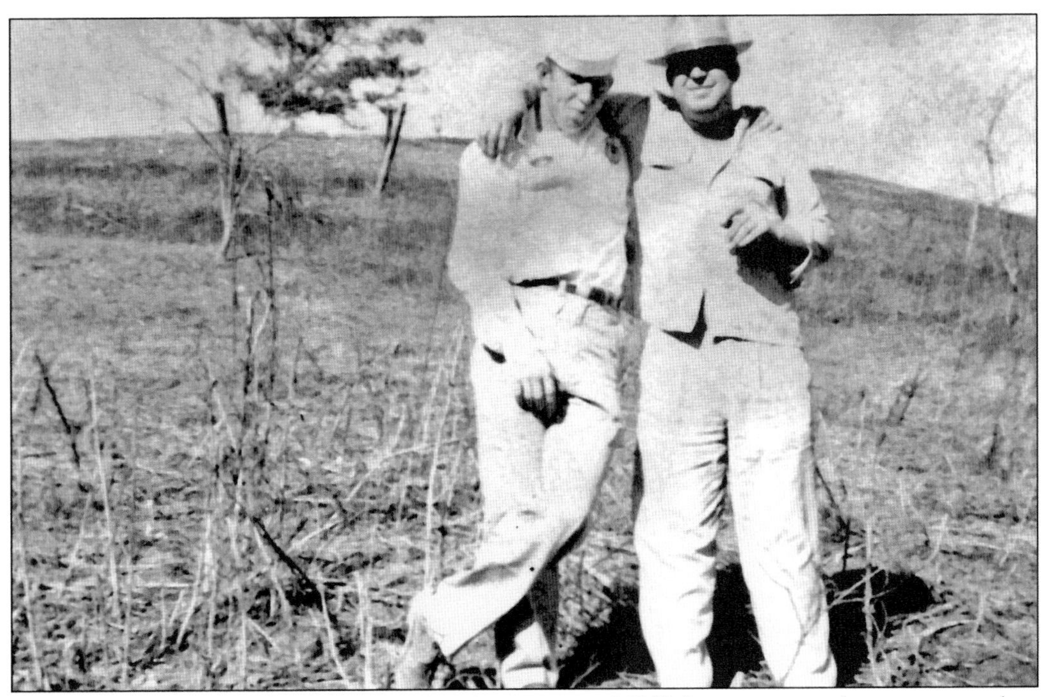

Lee Smith (left) and William "Cotton" Smith pose around 1951. Lee went on to become a preacher. He was a good mechanic and a farmer. Cotton joined the U.S. Navy and later moved to Anna Cortez, Washington. Their sister, Nora, now lives in Florida. (Courtesy of Lois Grey.)

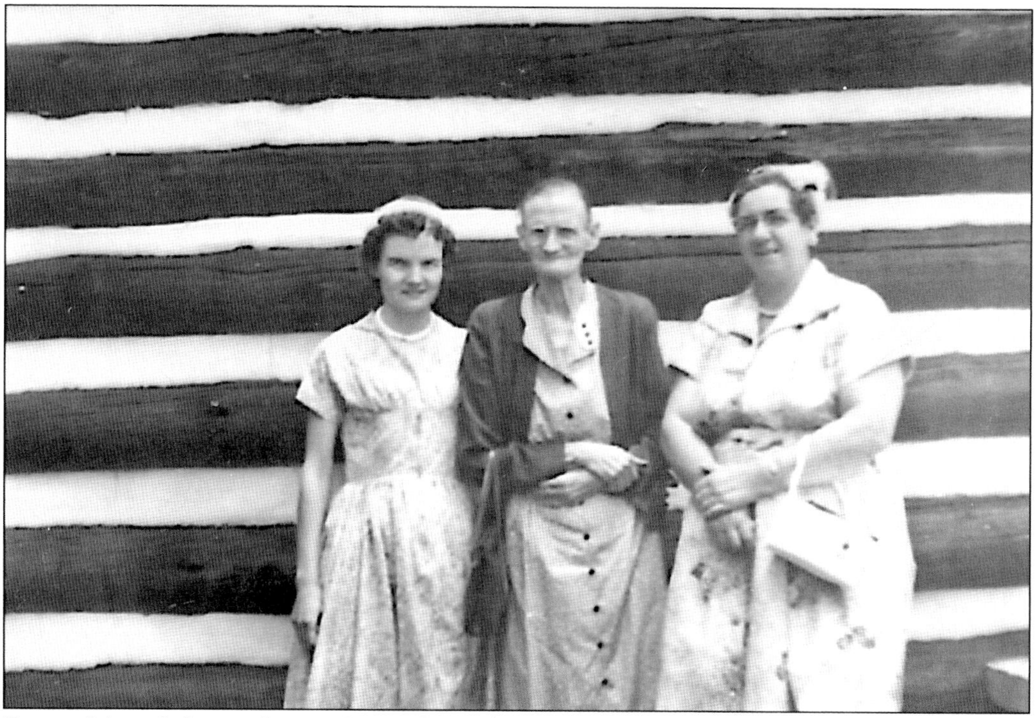

Pictured from left to right are Gertrude Godsey, Susie Godsey, and Towns Godsey. Gertrude Godsey married Ross Bright. Towns Harkleroad Godsey married Charlie Godsey, who was a first cousin to Susie and Gertrude. After Charlie's death, she married Joe Hickman. She had two sisters, Hazel and Lolan, and three brothers, Jack, Gate, and Roy. (Courtesy of Opal McMurray.)

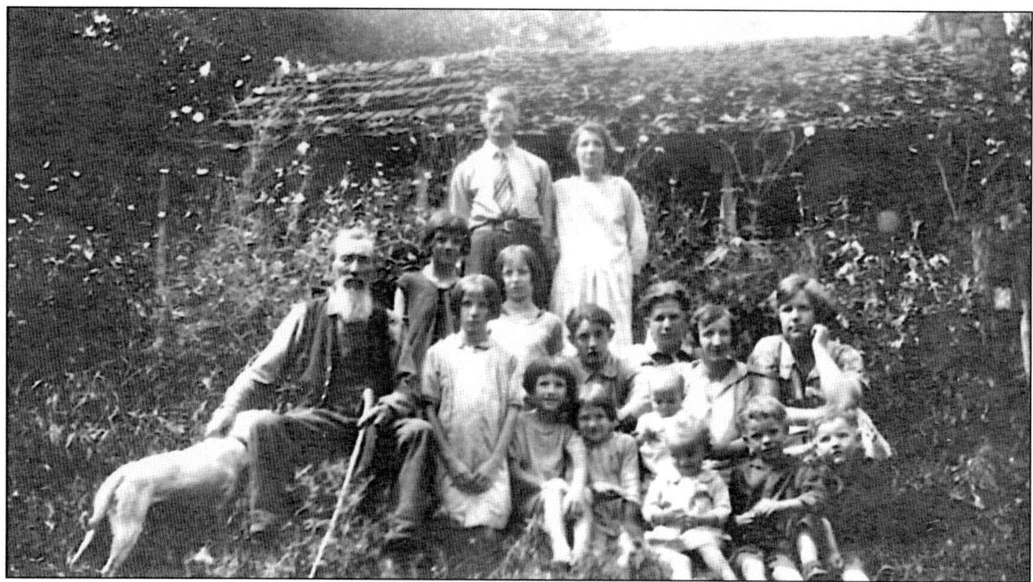

This is a picture of Martin Godsey, Bill Hooker, and Mattie Hooker. The children in the picture are unidentified but probably belonged to Bill and Mattie. The Hookers were married around 1904 and had five children: Lessie, Evie, Pearl, Davie, and Dorsey. (Courtesy of Opal McMurray.)

Coolidge Derting taught school for many years and lived in the Beech Grove community. Now retired, he lives in the Johnson City, Tennessee, area. (Courtesy of Elsie Gardner.)

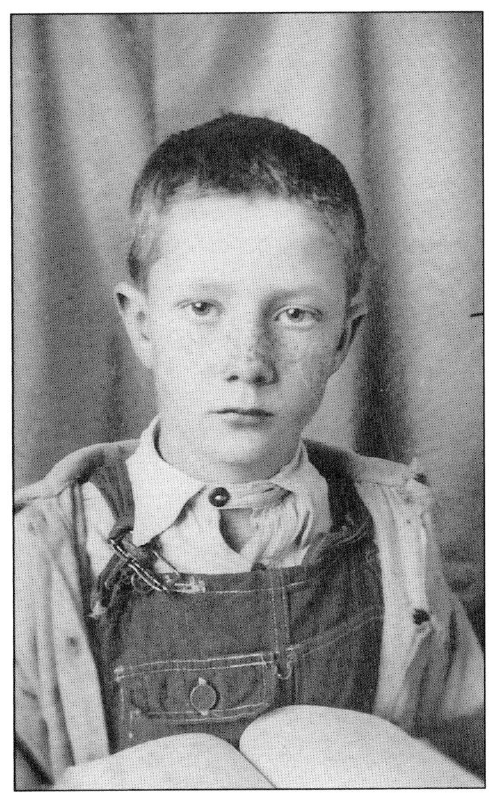

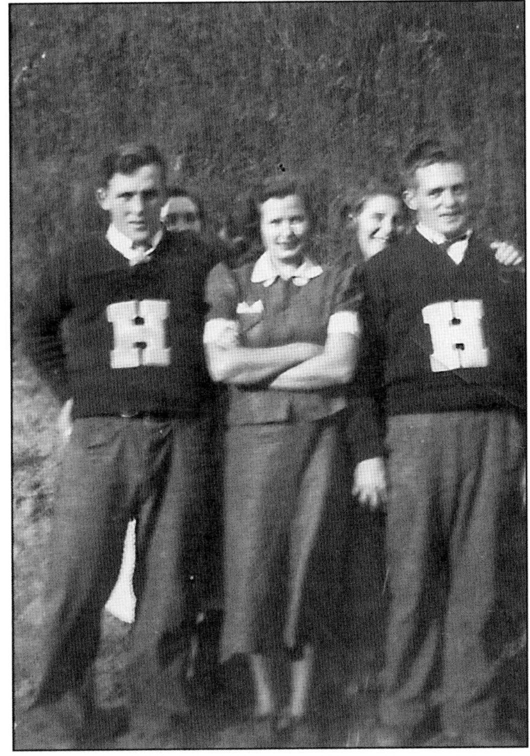

Pictured from left to right are Walmer Gardner, unidentifed (obscured), Ruby Gilly (center), Sara Gardner, and Ward Gardner. Shepler at Hiltons High School. Walmer and Ward Gardner are two of the sons of Andrew D. and Nannie Quillen Gardner. Their grandparents were Hiram and Matilda Smith. (Courtesy of Elsie Gardner.)

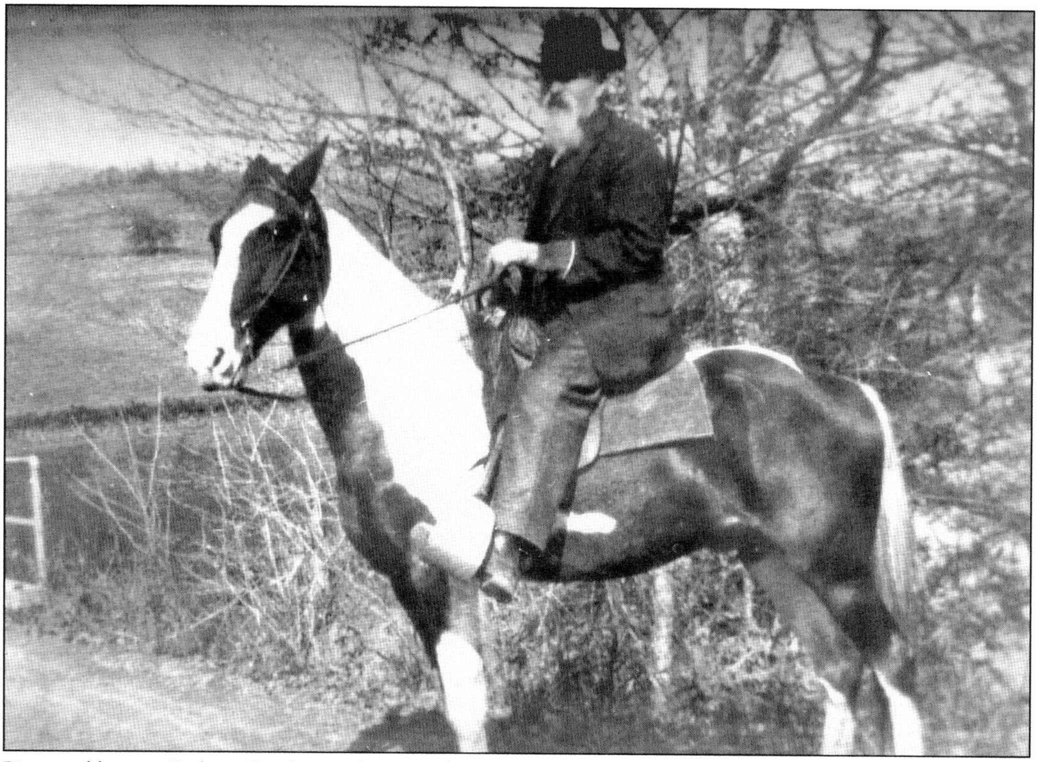

Pictured here is Ruben Gardner, who was the son of Ewell and Margaret Barnhart Gardner. Ruben was born in 1841 and died in 1931. He married Sibbie Derting and served in the Civil War. This picture was taken near the new bridge in Hiltons. (Courtesy of Elsie Gardner.)

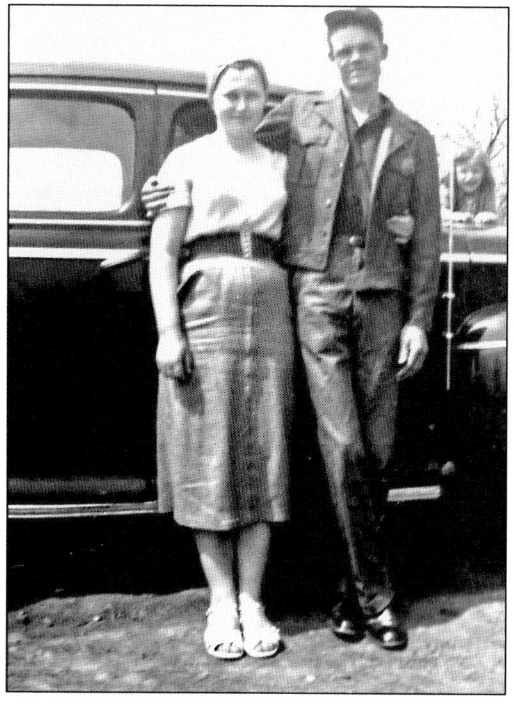

Pictured are Margaret Ketron and Doug McMurray. Margaret had a brother named Jay and a sister named Evie. Her father was Lloyd Ketron. Margaret lives in the Lynn Garden community of Kingsport, Tennessee. (Courtesy of Lois Grey.)

Harley McMurray (left), pictured with his brother Willard McMurray, married Odie Laura Godsey and had seven children: Douglas, Betty, William Harley Jr. "Junior", Russell, Reba Muriel, Peggy, and Donnie. Reba Muriel married William Lloyd Matthews, and they had four children: Ricky, Ronnie, Rhonda, and Billy. (Courtesy of Opal McMurray.)

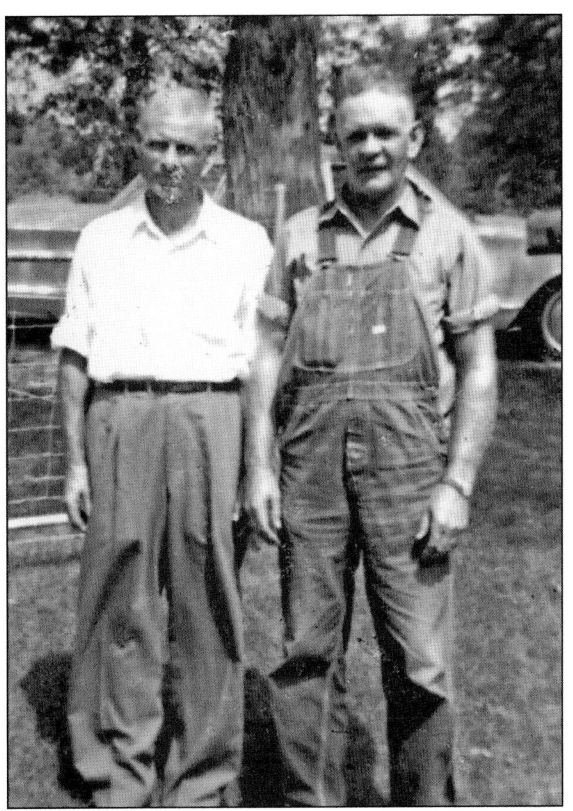

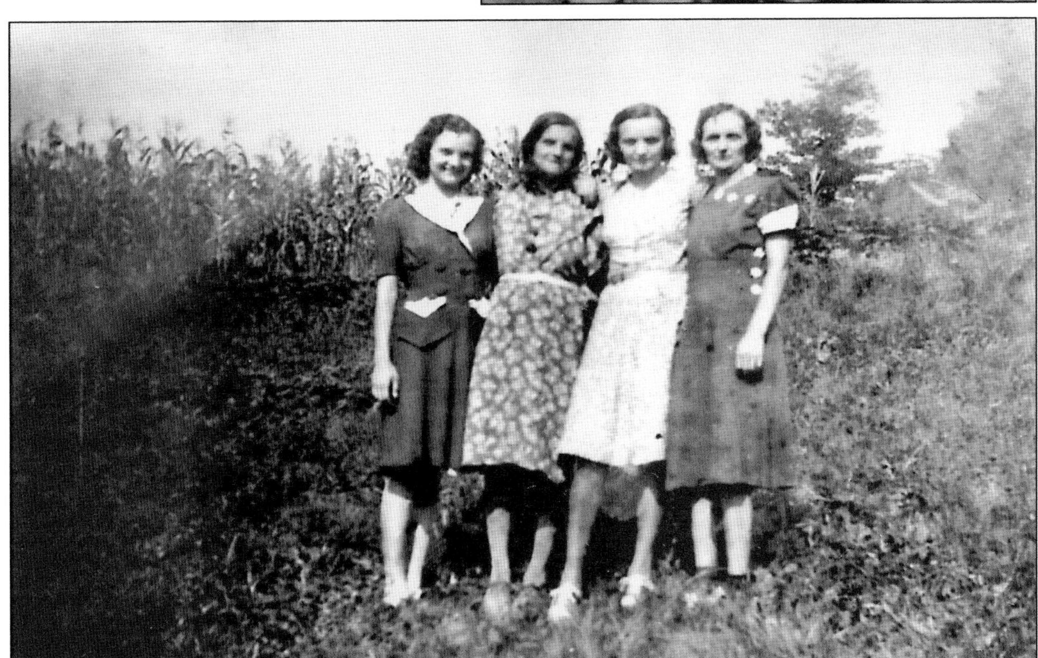

Shown here are four of Isaac Godsey's daughters. They are, from left to right, Gertrude, Odie, Verge, and Verdie. Verge married Opie Bright, and they had three children: Ross, Florance, and Pauline. Verdie married Orin Bates, and Gertrude married Ross Bright. (Courtesy of Opal McMurray.)

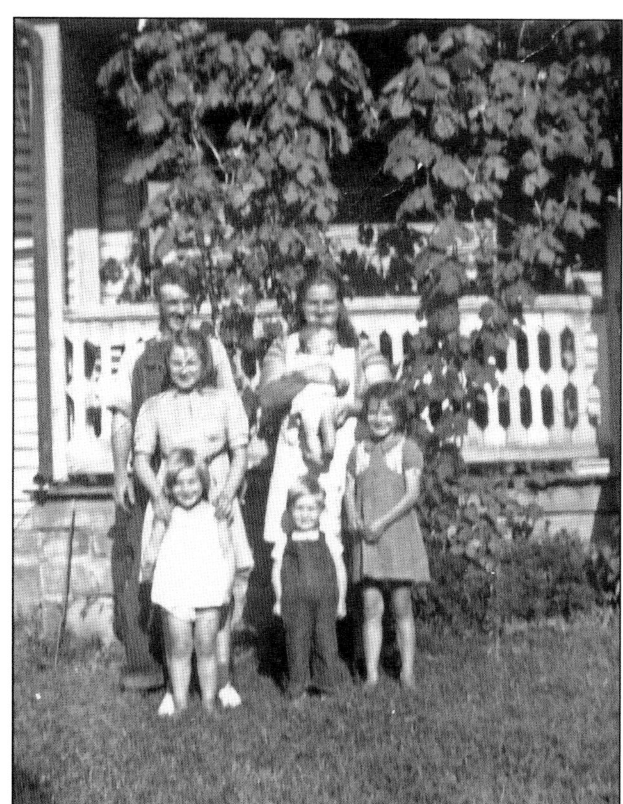

Roy and Ruby Gardner Bright pose with their children. From left to right are (first row) Sue, Joe "Buddy," and Patsy; (second row) Margaret and Tressie; (third row) Roy and Ruby. (Courtesy of Elsie Gardner.)

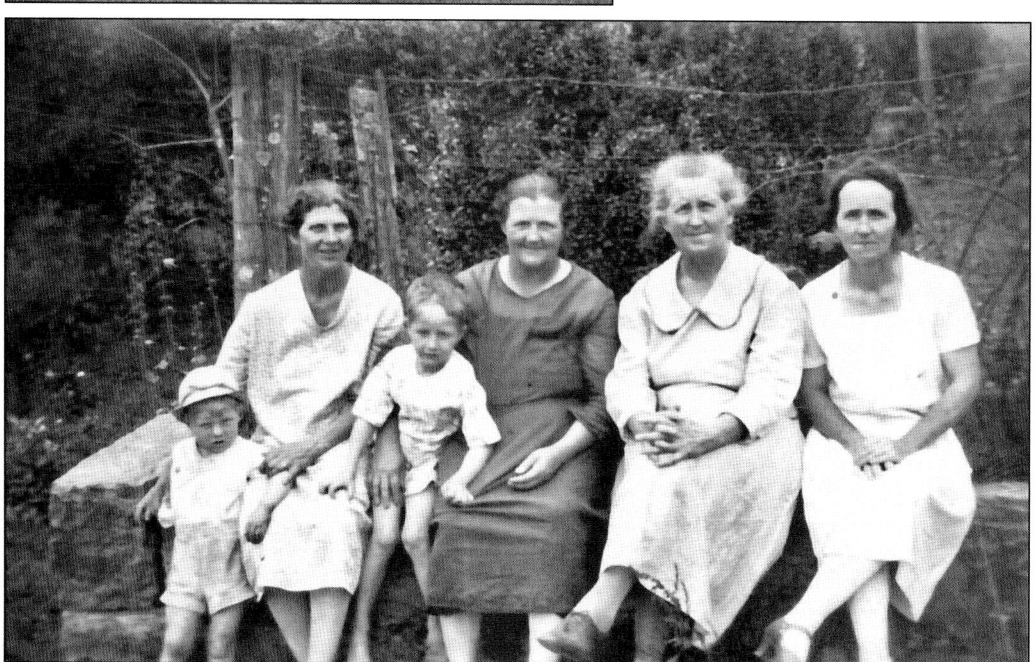

From left to right are Demsy Wilson and her mother, Sibbie Wilson; Calvin Derting and his mother, Peggy Derting; Cora McClain; and Renda Lunsford, whose family owned the Lunsford Mill. (Courtesy of Elsie Gardner.)

This is the original T. P. Curtis home place. Pictured are Mack, Dee, Poppy, Mommie, Conley, and Minnie Curtis. Through the years, Conley and Minnie have restored and preserved the home place, and the family still lives there today. (Courtesy of Marianna Gardner.)

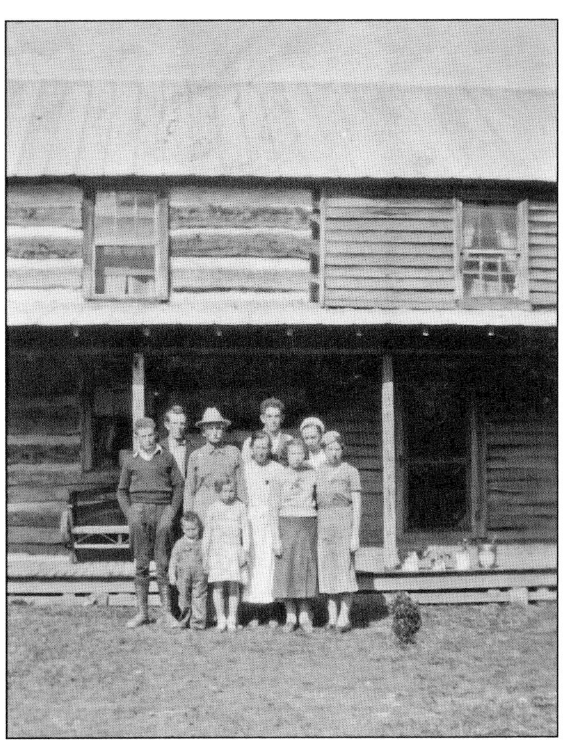

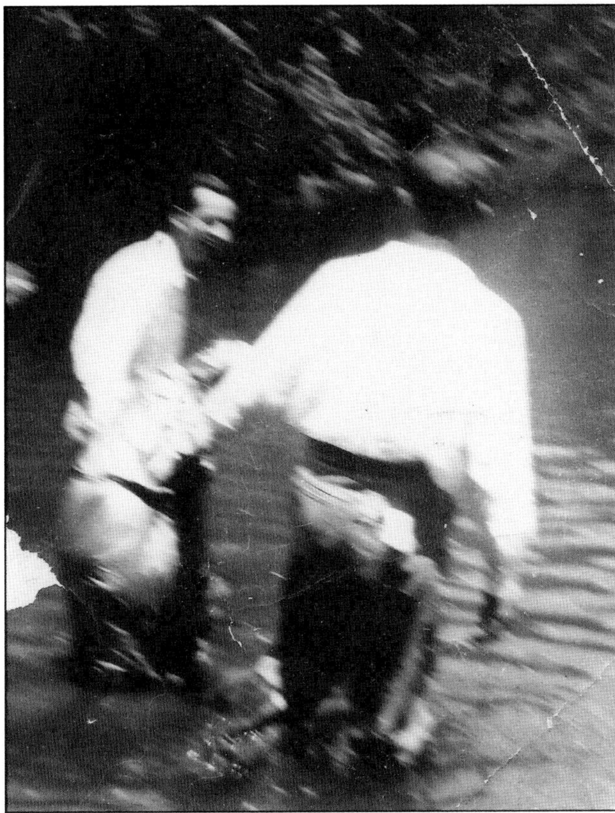

This is a picture of Betty McMurray during her baptismal. The man baptizing her is George Willis, and the other man is unidentified. Before the days of church baptismal, this was a common scene by the river. During the winter, the congregation members would actually break the ice to have a baptism. (Courtesy of Lois Grey.)

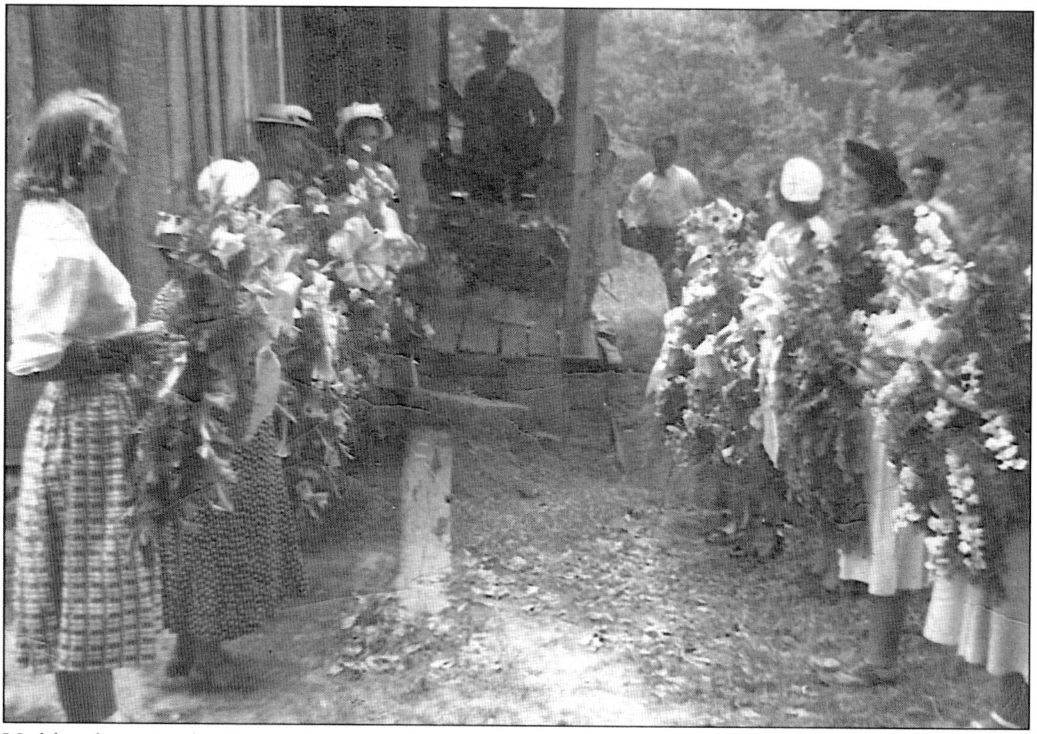

Unlike those in the funeral homes of today, memorial services were once held in the home of the deceased. This picture was taken at Isaac Godsey's memorial service and includes Georgie Hensley, Evie Hooker Fleenor, and Cordy Godsey. Cordy was one of seven children. Her siblings were Charlie, Abe, Steve, Milburn, Dicey, and Julie. (Courtesy of Opal McMurray.)

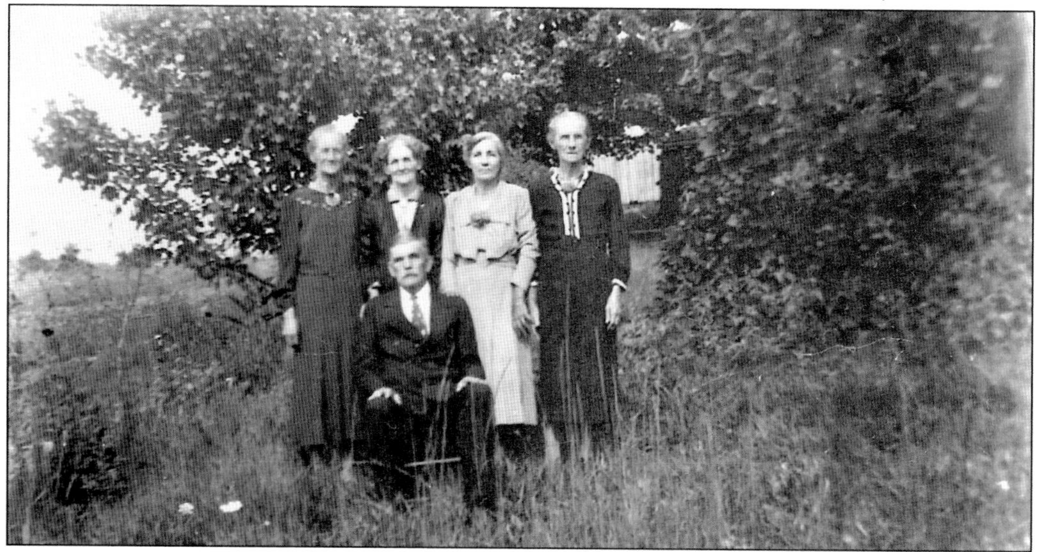

Pictured from left to right are Berthie Godsey Eaton, Jenny Godsey Upchurch, Mattie Godsey Hooker, and Willie Godsey. Isaac Godsey is seated in front. Berthie Godsey was Isaac Godsey's sister, and she married Jim Eaton. They had seven children: Rossie, Walter, Jim, Joe, Earnest, Nell, and Garvey. Jenny was one of Isaac's sisters. She moved to Knoxville, Tennessee, and lived there most of her adult life. (Courtesy of Opal McMurray.)

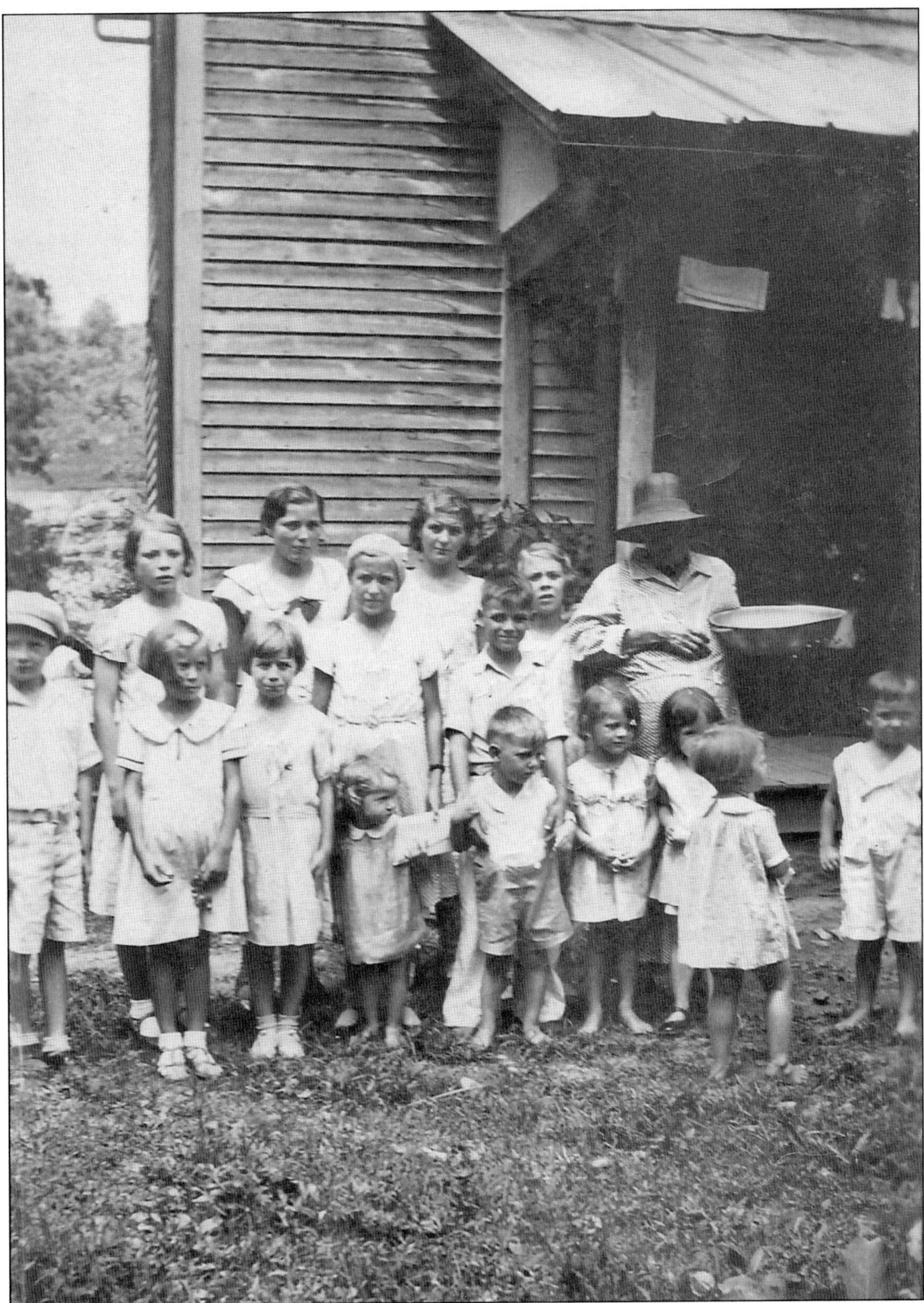

Matilda Gardner stands with her children and great-grandchildren. Matilda married Hiram Gardner Sr., and they helped raise several generations of Gardners on the North Fork of the Holston River. (Courtesy of Elsie Gardner.)

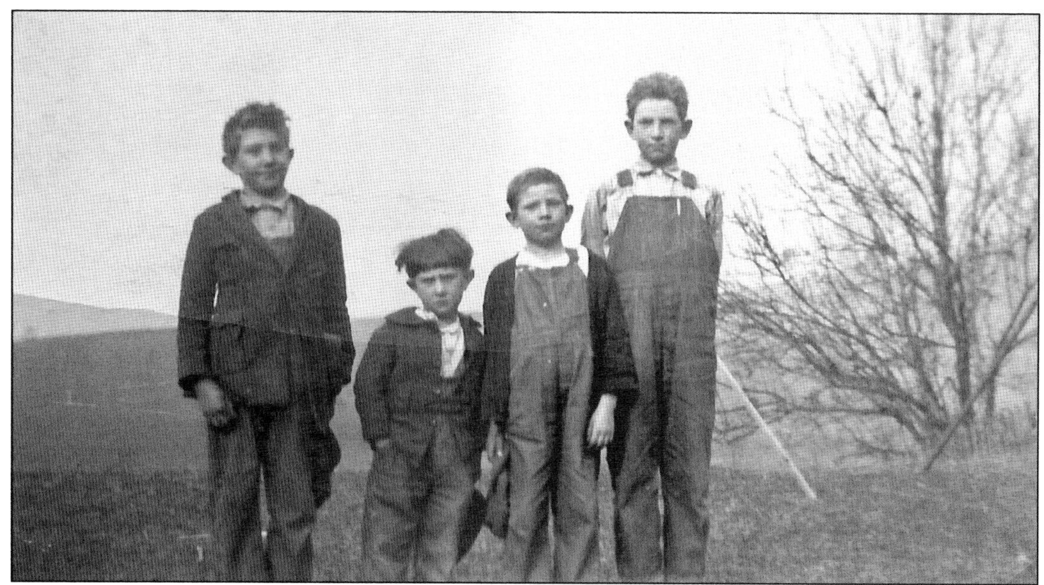

From left to right are Sylvester Blackard, Bill Blackard, Mack Curtis, and Conley Curtis. (Courtesy of Marianna Gardner.)

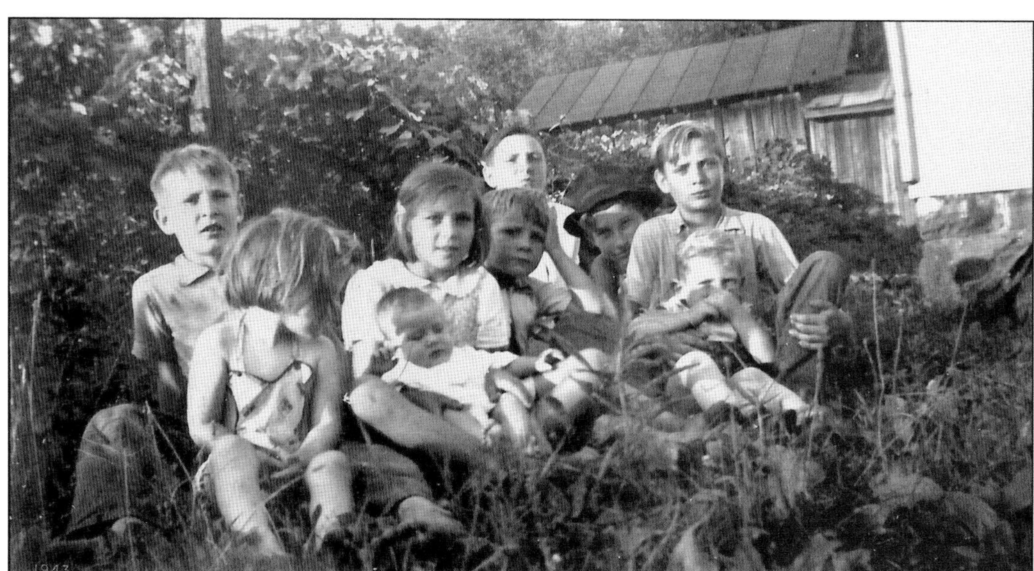

In this 1943 photograph are two of Clyde and Elsie Gardner's children, Carol and Danny. Also pictured, in no particular order, are Harrie and Mary Gardner's children: Peggy, Lois, Jim, Jack, Dan, and Gail. (Courtesy of Elsie Gardner.)

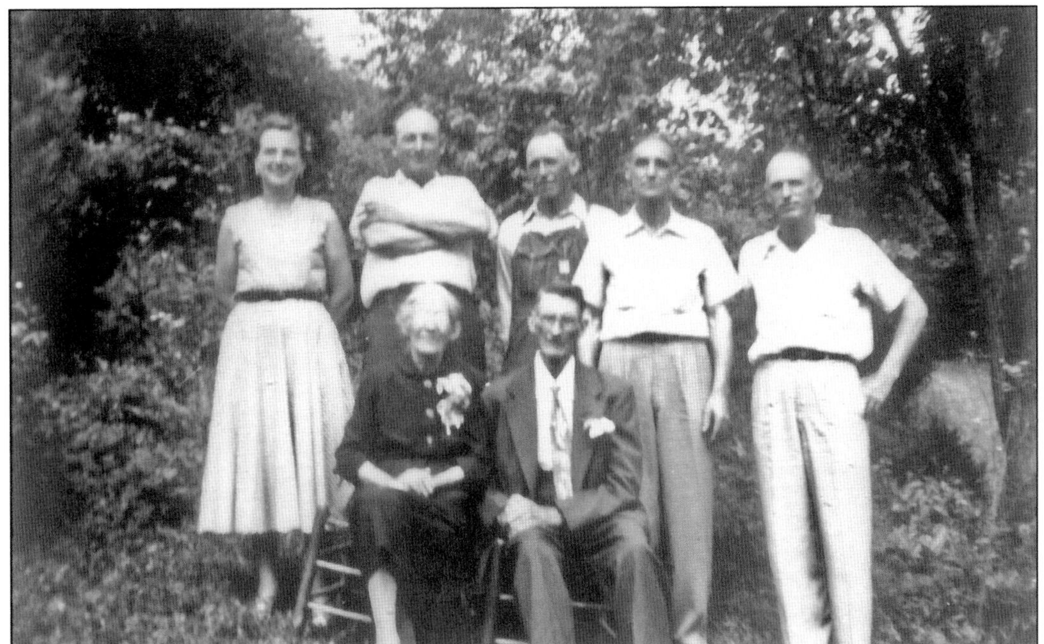

Included in this picture are Charley Hensley, who pastored a church near Blountville, Tennessee, for many years; Edith Hooker (standing, far left); Johnnie Hooker; Dee Ketron; Pleasant McMurray; and Bill Hooker and Mattie Hooker (seated). This picture was taken around 1954 at Bill and Mattie's 50th wedding anniversary party. (Courtesy of Opal McMurray.)

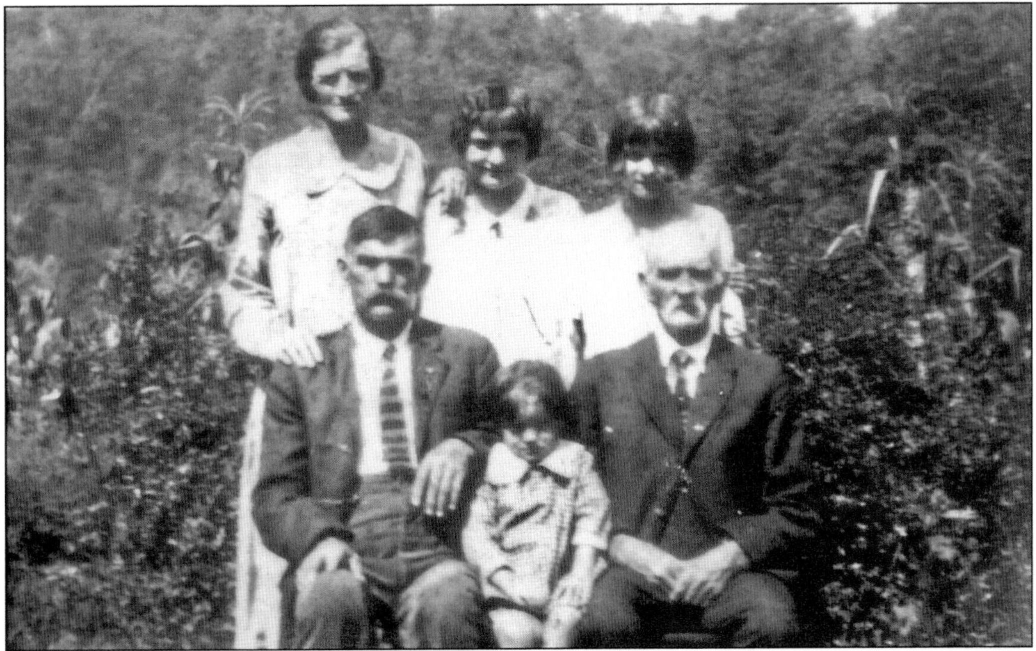

Pictured from left to right are (seated) Isaac Godsey, unidentified, and John Hooker; (standing) Susie Godsey, unidentified, and Odie Godsey McMurray. John Hooker's wife's name is unknown, but she attended school at Tom's Creek near Coeburn, Virginia, when she was a girl. (Courtesy of Opal McMurray.)

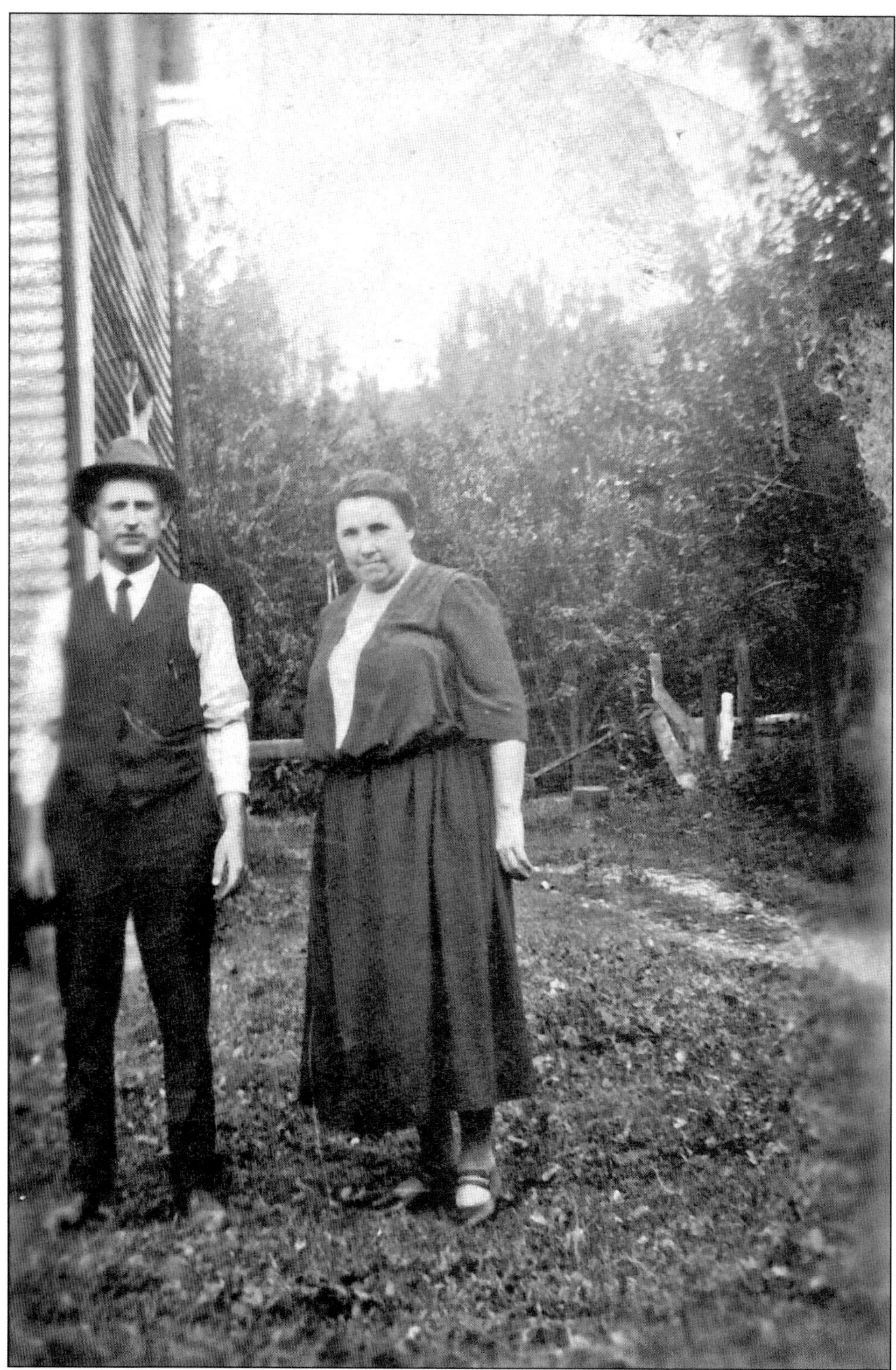

Pictured here are Henry Gardner and his wife, Mary Carmack Gardner. Henry was a brother to Hiram Gardner Sr. Henry's grandson, Raymond Gardner, served in the military for several years. (Courtesy of Elsie Gardner.)

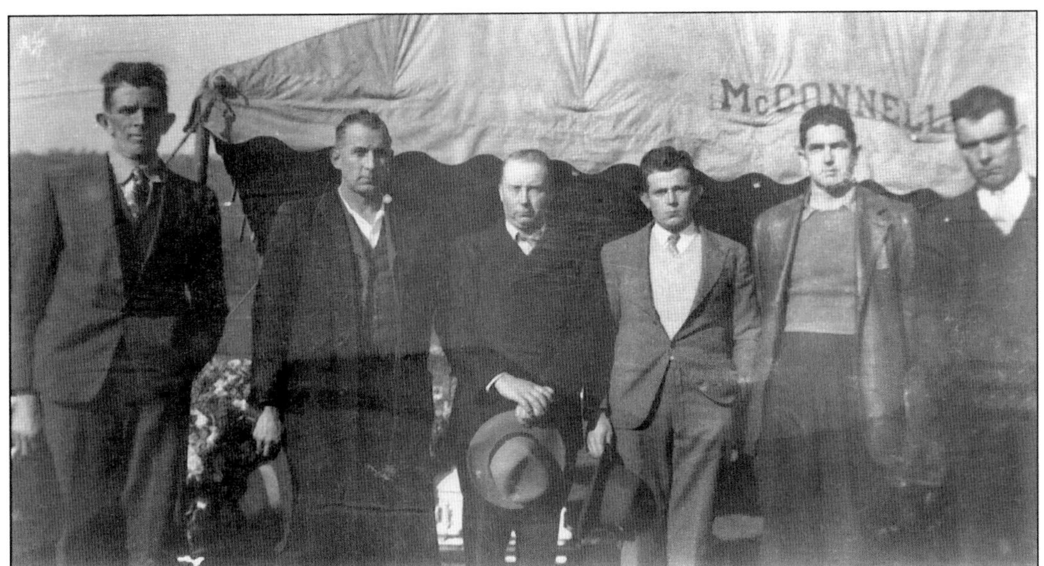

Gathered at a funeral, from left to right, are Dee Curtis, James Curtis, Johnnie Mann, Mack Curtis, Conley Curtis, and Towns Curtis. Mack and Conley Curtis are brothers, and the others are cousins to them. (Courtesy of Marianna Gardner.)

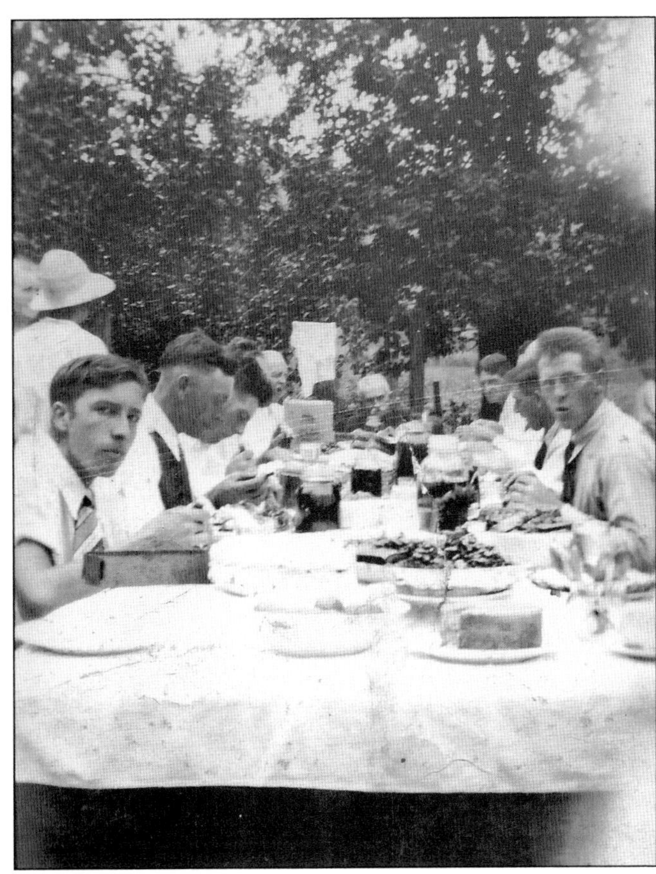

At the Gardner family reunion, everyone sits around the picnic table eating the good food and visiting with family and friends. (Courtesy of Elise Gardner.)

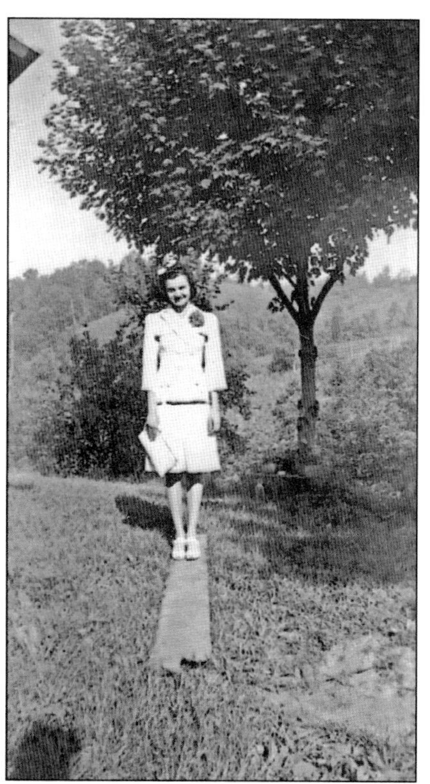

Gertrude Godsey Bright married Ross Bright, who was the only son of Opie and Verge Bright. Ross had two sisters, Florence and Pauline. Verge Godsey Bright was a daughter of Isaac and Susie Godsey, who are pictured below. (Courtesy of Opal McMurray.)

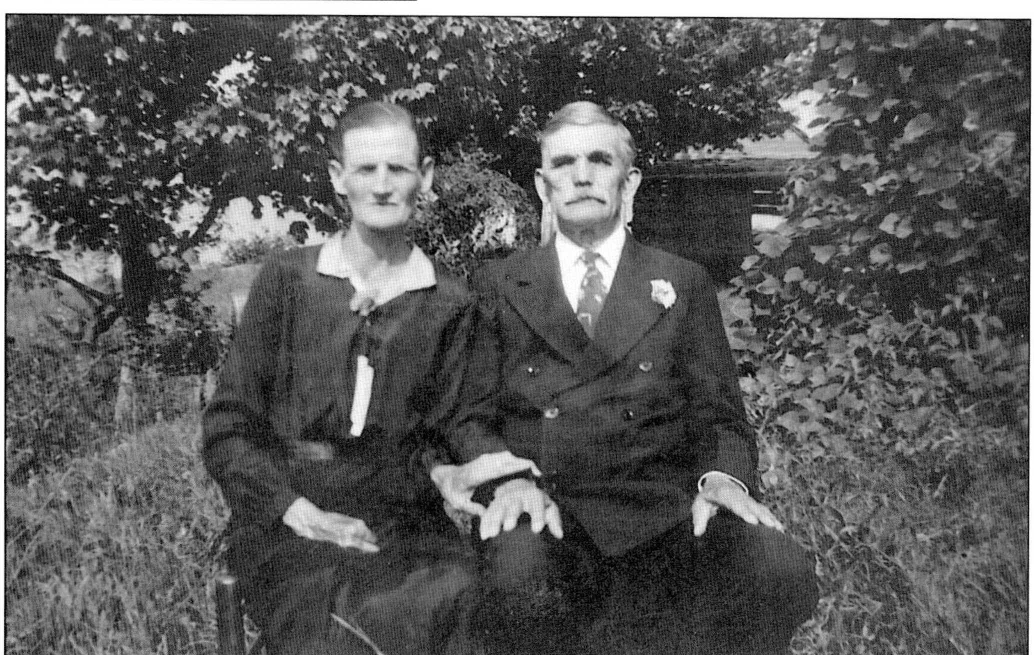

Susie and Isaac Godsey had seven daughters: Gertrude, Odie, Verdie, Verge, Ida Mae, Allafare, and Bessie. Bessie married Sanford McMurray, and they had two daughters. Jeanette married Bates Hensley, and Ester married Glen McMurray. One of Ester's sons, Gary, now works for the Carter-Trent Funeral Home in Kingsport, Tennessee. (Courtesy of Opal McMurray.)

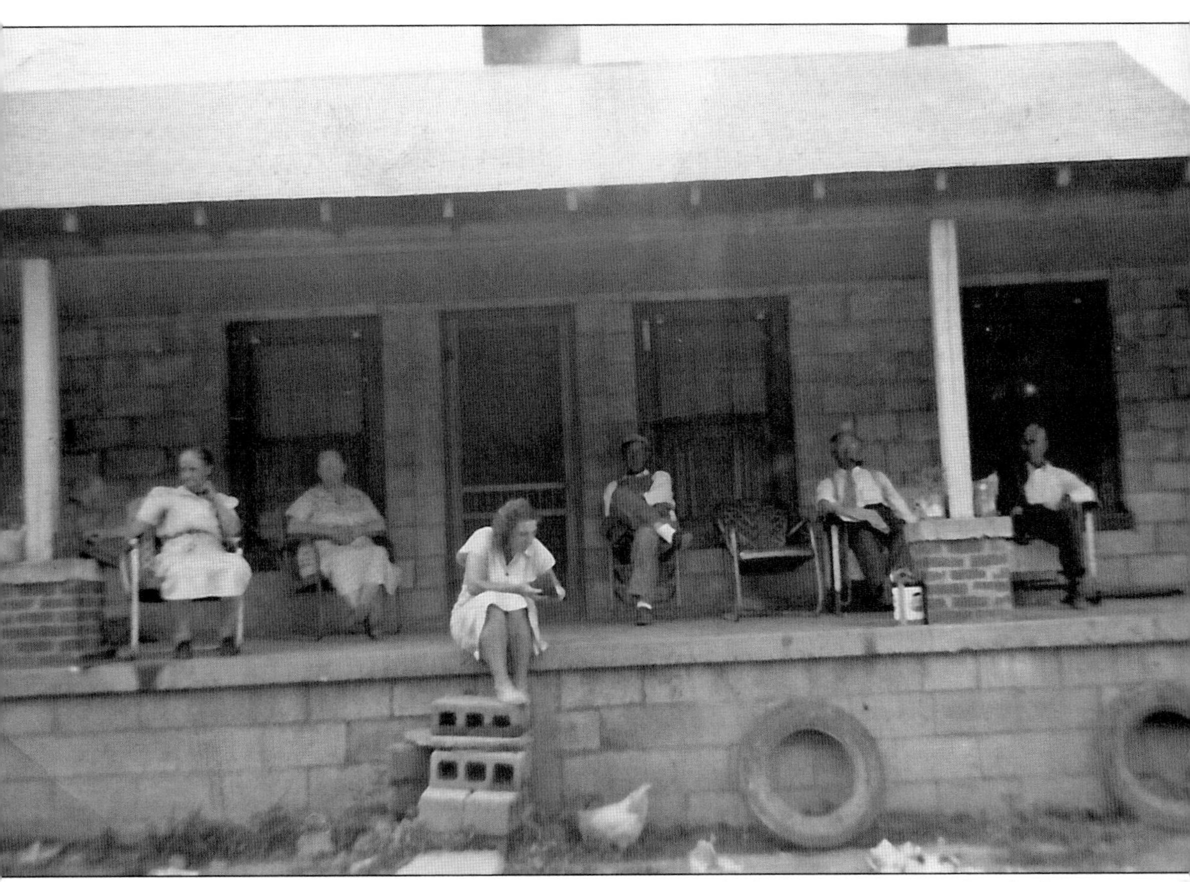

Pictured here, from left to right, are Easter Smith, unidentified, Betty McMurray Smith, James Hensley, Philmore Gardner, and Frank Smith. When this picture was taken, Betty, who is sitting on the porch with her feet on the steps, was nine months pregnant with her son Danny. (Courtesy of Lois Grey.)

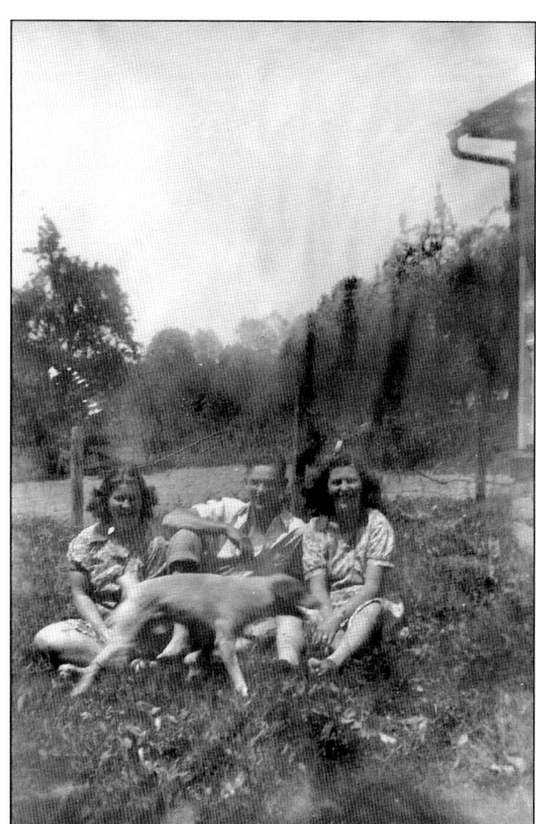

Pictured from left to right are Ettnie McMurray, Erwin McMurray, and Sarah Gardner. They are playing with Jailer, the dog. (Courtesy of Elsie Gardner.)

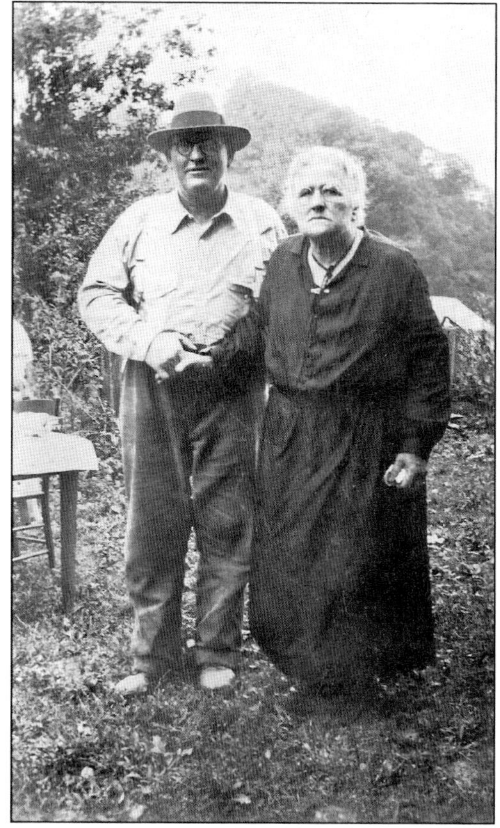

Pictured here are Will Gardner and Darla Hart. Margaret "Darla" Gardner Hart was a sister to Hiram Gardner Sr. and Ruben Gardner. She married Elijah Hart. (Courtesy of Elsie Gardner.)

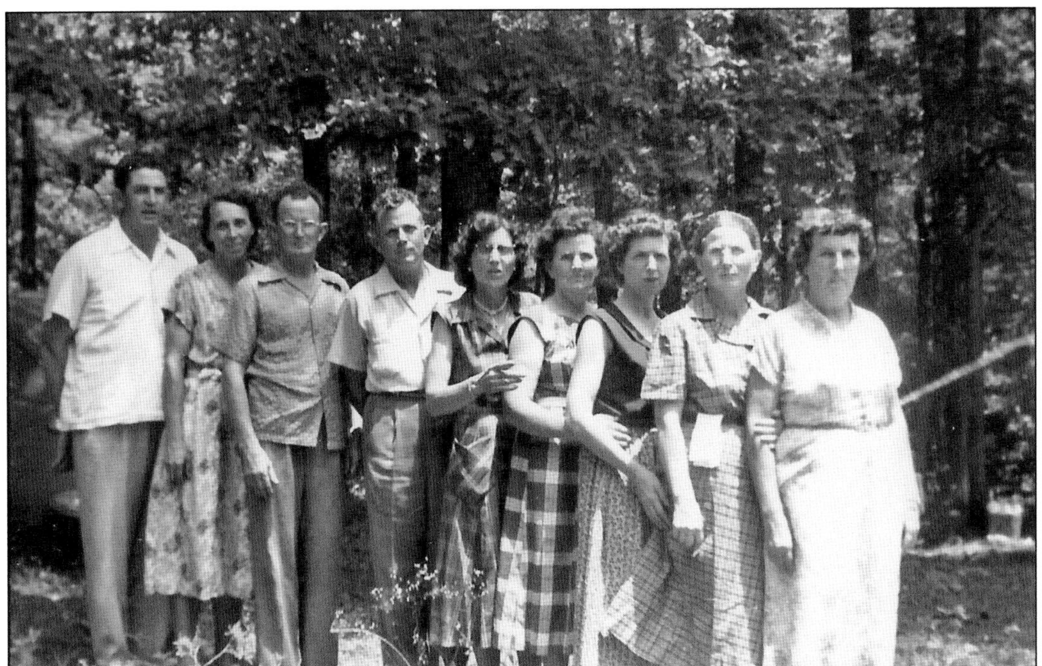

In this photograph is the Curtis family. Pictured from left to right are Conley; Bertha, who was the wife of the late Dee Curtis; Ben; Mack; Carrie; Florence; Lotus; Hattie; and Ethel Curtis. The parents of these siblings are Thomas Parker and Mattie Emma Reynolds Curtis. The grandparents are James Parker and Lucinda Meridith Curtis, and Jim and Harriet Smith Reynolds. (Courtesy of Marianna Gardner.)

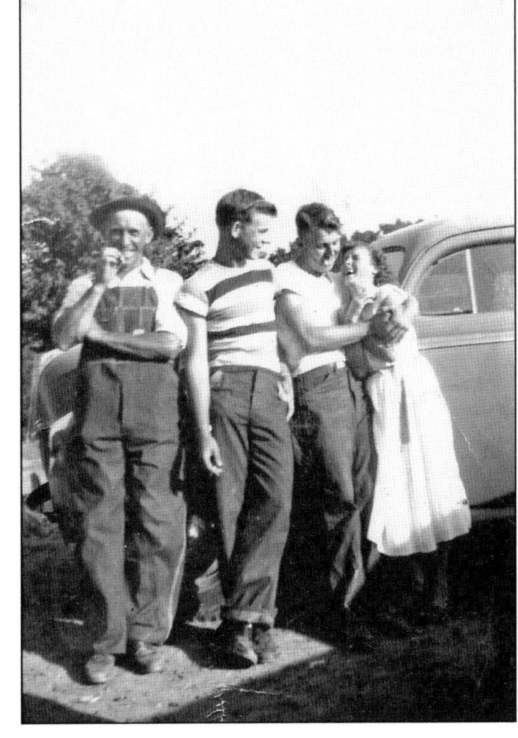

Leaning against the car, from left to right, are Charlie Hensley, Bobby Blaylock, Lee Smith, and Betty McMurray. Betty and Bobby had been dating for a while. That day, Lee charmed Betty away from Bobby, and they later married. Lee and Betty had several children and lived together until Lee's death. (Courtesy of Lois Grey.)

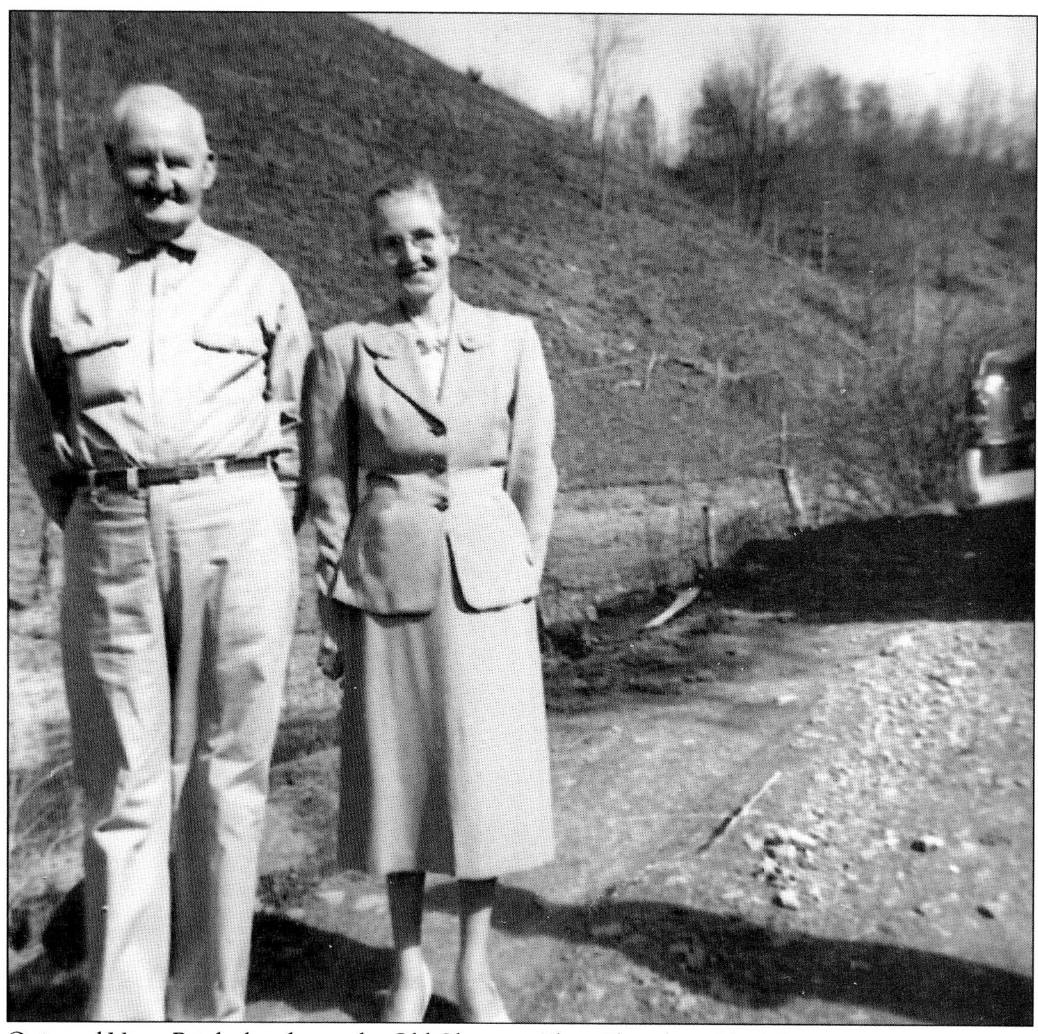
Opie and Verge Bright lived near the Old Chestnut Flats Church and had three children: Florence, Ross, and Pauline. (Courtesy of Opal McMurray.)

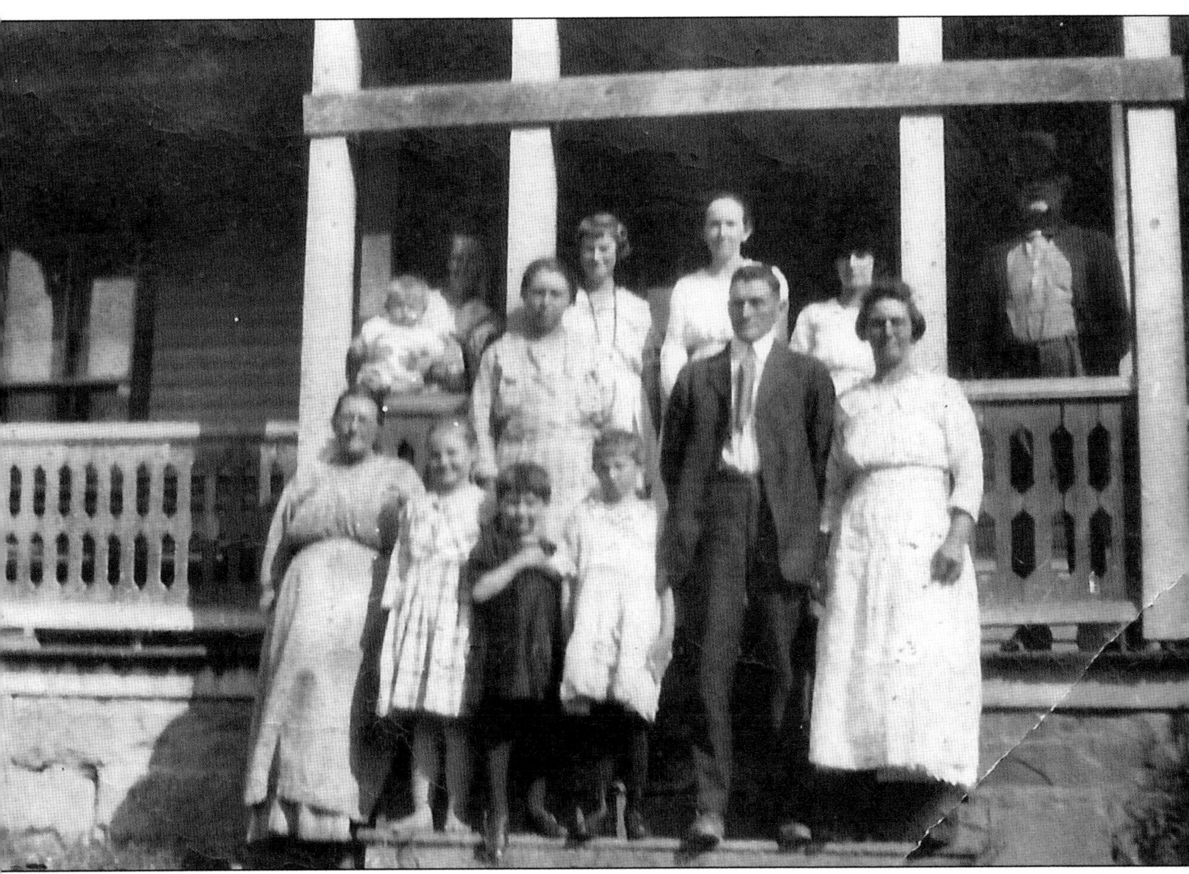

Included here are Matilda Gardner, Elsie Gardner, John Salley, ? Salley, Hiram Gardner, and Clara Gardner. (Courtesy of Elsie Gardner.)

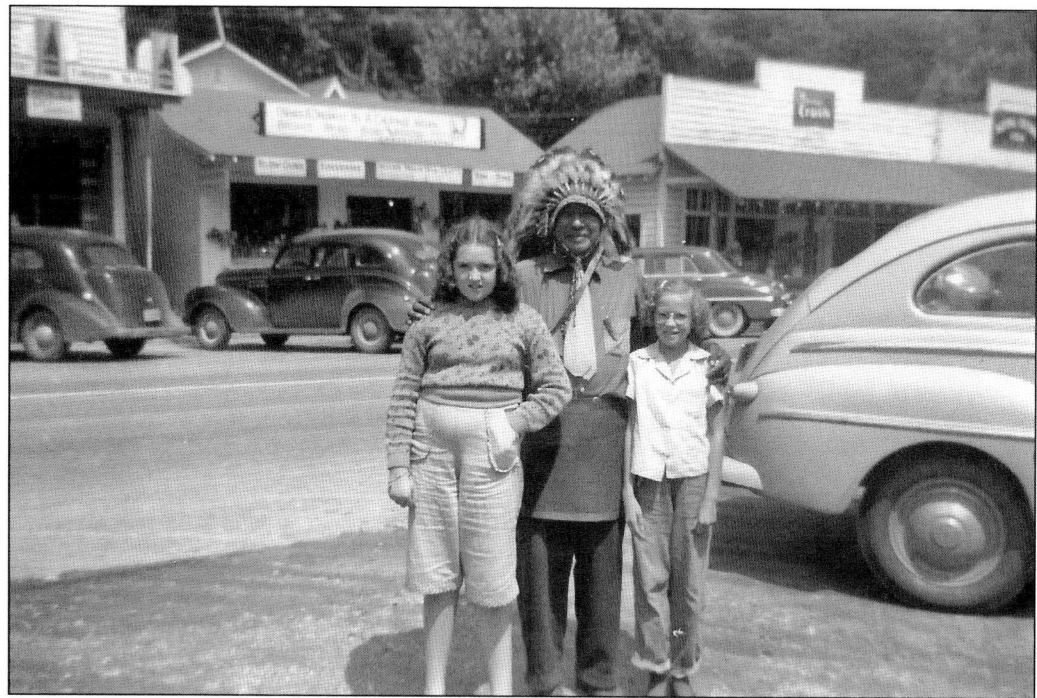

One of the pastimes of the residents of the Hiltons area was to travel to Cherokee, North Carolina. Connie Curtis and Eleanor Curtis pose with one of the Native Americans in the Great Smoky Mountains. (Courtesy of Marianna Gardner.)

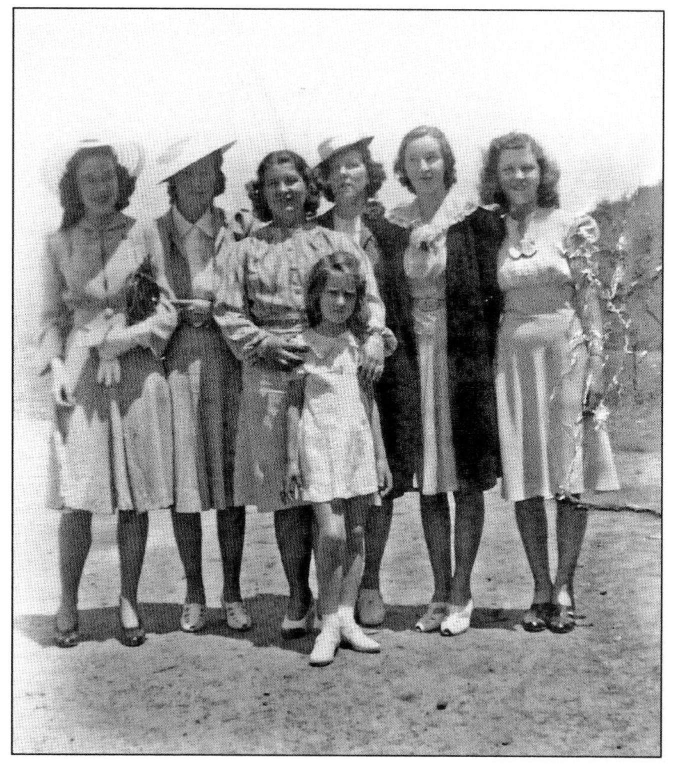

Pictured here from left to right are Carmen Stellard, Nell Wood, Sara Gardner, Elsie Maddux, Ettnie McMurray, and unidentified. In front is Beth Grove, who was the daughter of G. D. Grove, the principal of Hiltons High School. (Courtesy of Elsie Derting.)

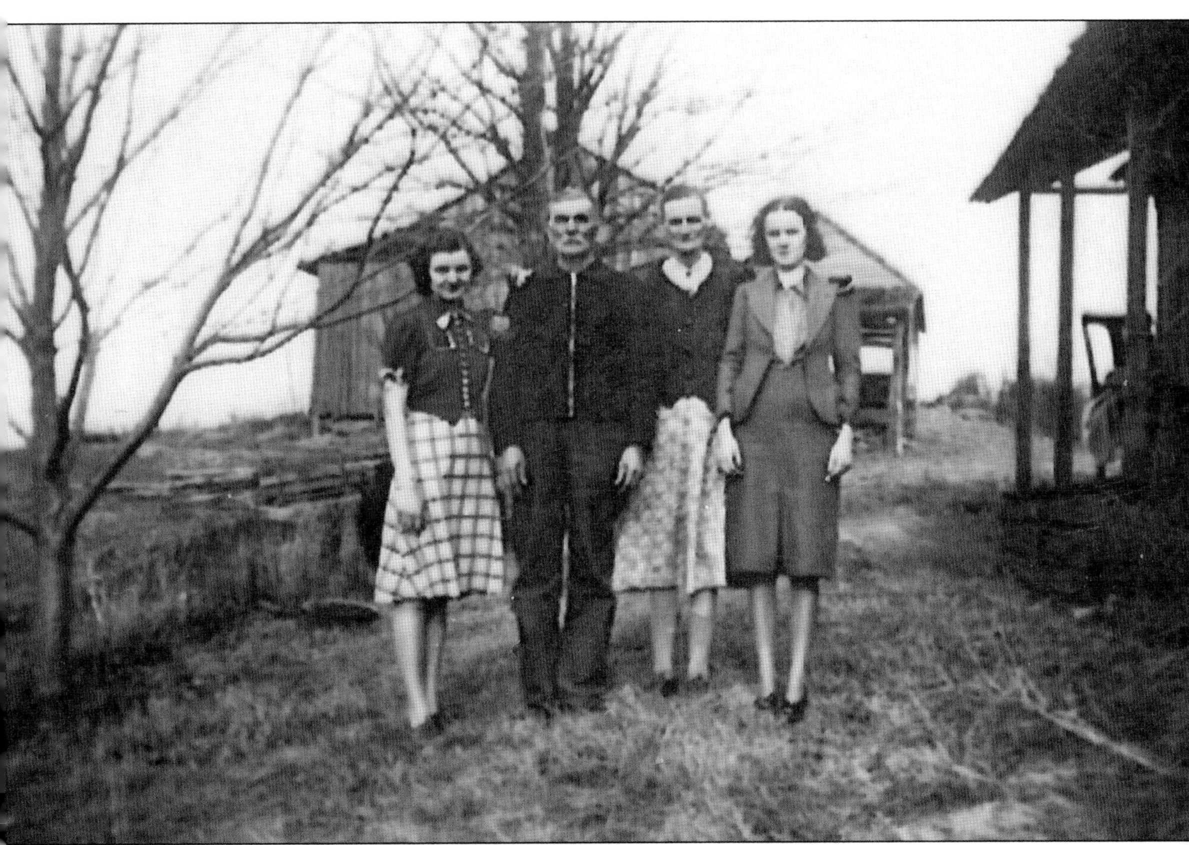

From left to right are Gertrude Godsey, Isaac Godsey, Susie Godsey, and Esther McMurray. Esther is the mother of Gary and Eugene McMurray. Gary has worked for several local funeral houses and also drove the school bus for several years. (Courtesy of Opal McMurray.)

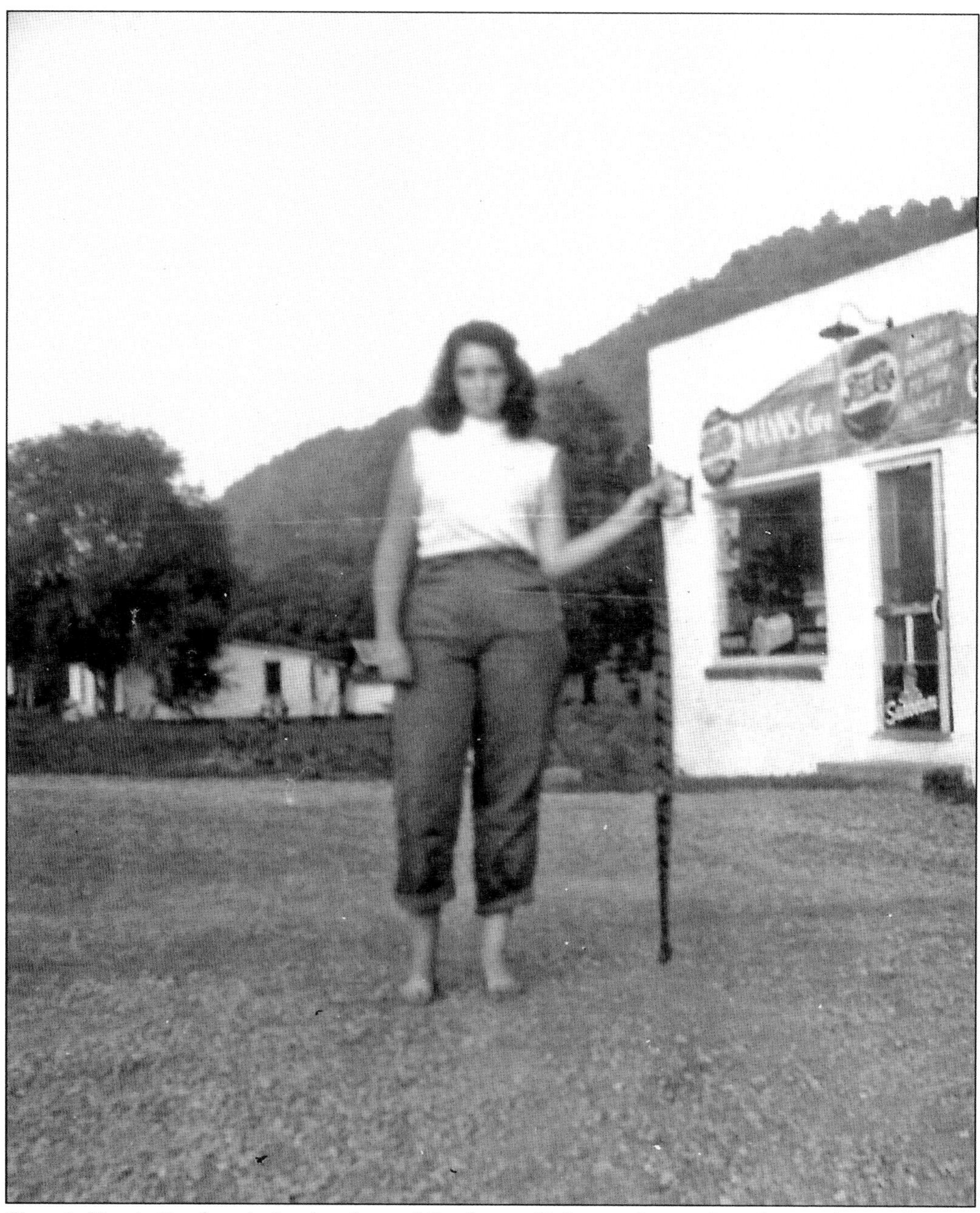

Connie Curtis Gardner is the daughter of Conley and Minnie Curtis. Standing in front of a store owned by her uncle and aunt, Johnnie and Carrie Mann, she is holding a dead Clinch Mountain rattle snake. The store was later known as Field's Grocery. (Courtesy of Marianna Gardner.)

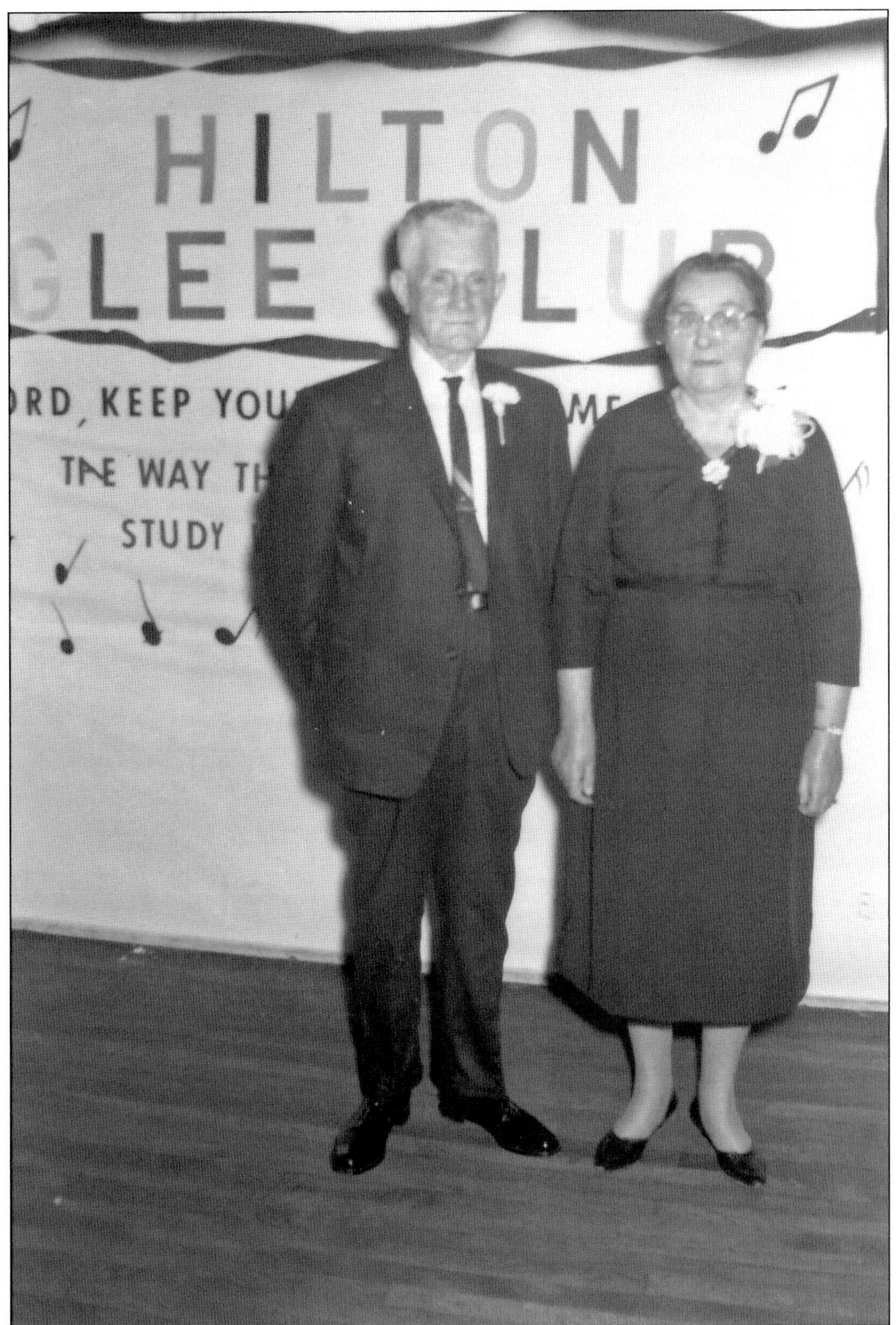

Each year, the Hilton Glee Club honors members of the community for their service. In the late 1960s, Ezra and Jessie Addington were honored for all the service and the loyalty they had shown to the Hiltons community. (Courtesy of Elsie Derting.)

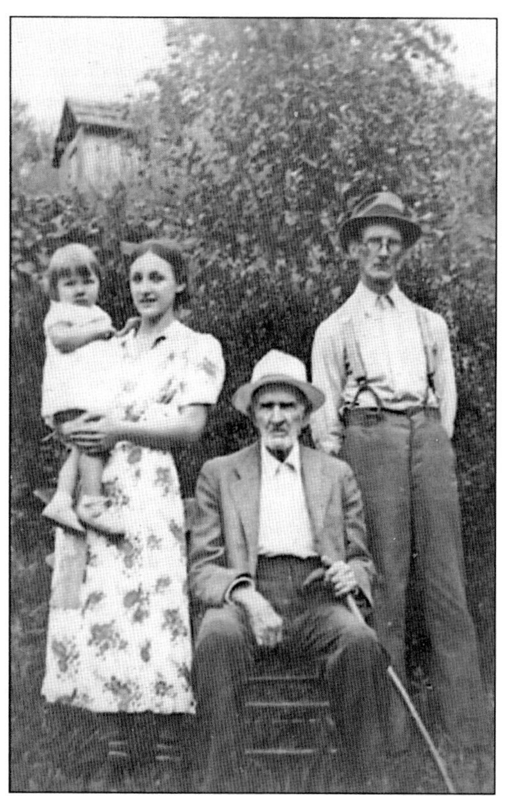

Pictured from left to right are Charlecie Hensley, holding her daughter, Edna; John Hooker; and Bill Hooker. Charlecie Hooker Hensley married Charley Hensley. The three Hookers are the children of Bill and Mattie Hooker. (Courtesy of Opal McMurray.)

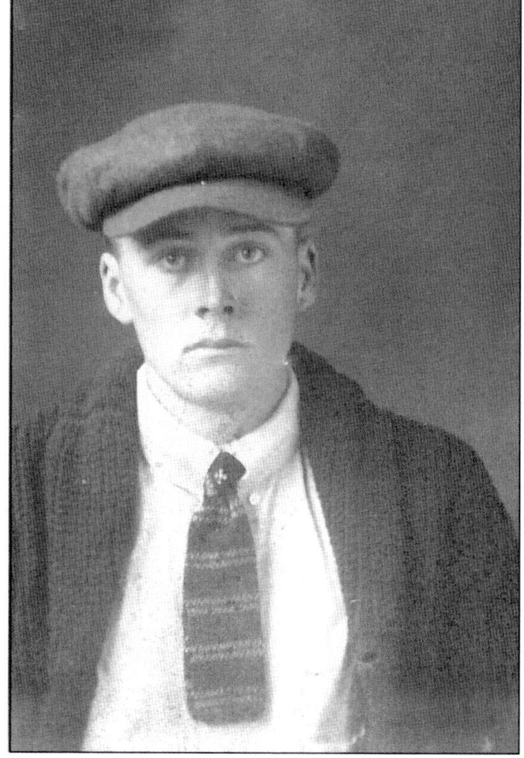

Jasper Gardner had two sisters, Berdie Gardner McMurray and Lizzy Gardner Baker. Their parents were Henry and Salley Addington Gardner. Jasper left Scott County, Virginia, in the 1930s to live out his life in California. He never married but enjoyed spending time with friends and family. (Courtesy of Elsie Gardner.)

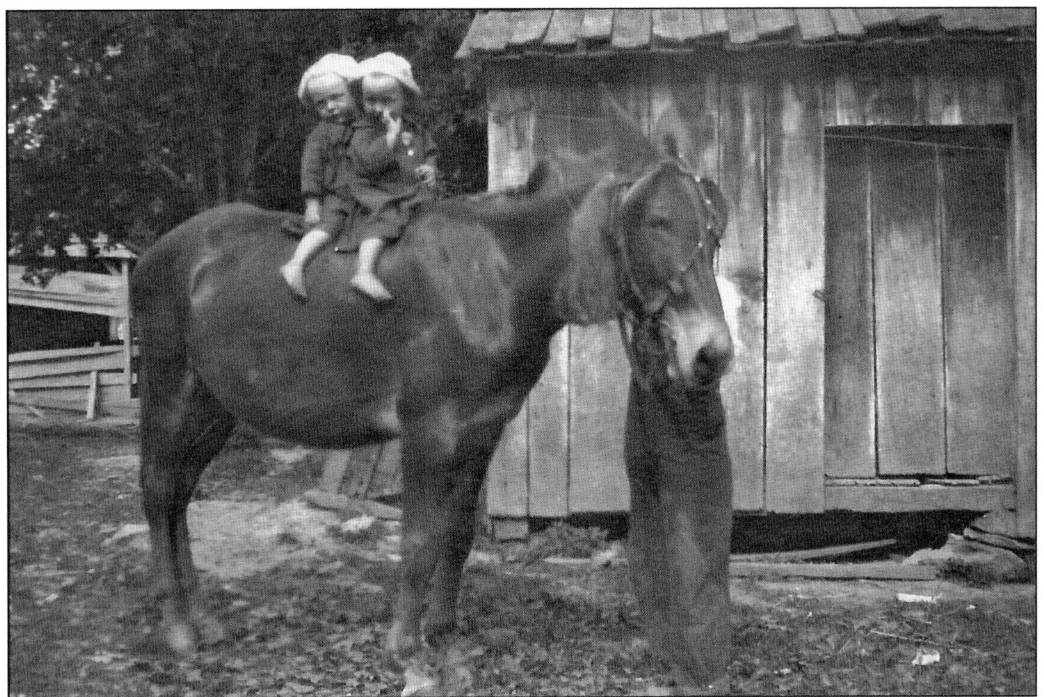

Ward and Walmer Gardner, the twin sons of Andrew and Nannie Quillen Gardner, are enjoying a ride on Kate, the mule. The boys' grandparents are Hiram and Matilda Smith Gardner, and Patten and Virginia Hart Quillen. (Courtesy of Elsie Gardner.)

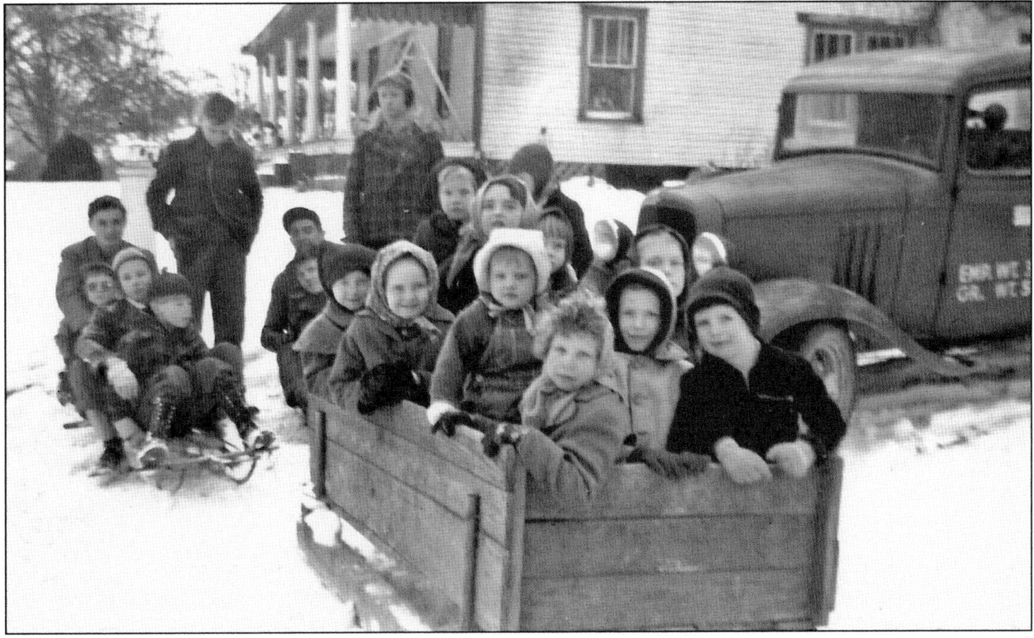

Shown is a homemade wooden sled that several of the children from the community enjoyed when there was snow on the ground. Included in the picture are Donnie Mann, Sandy Bralley, Elmer Curtis, Rose Smith, Carolyn Young, Jack Smith, Judy Curtis, Connie Curtis, Pat Bralley, Jane Mann, and Linda Mann. (Courtesy of Marianna Gardner.)

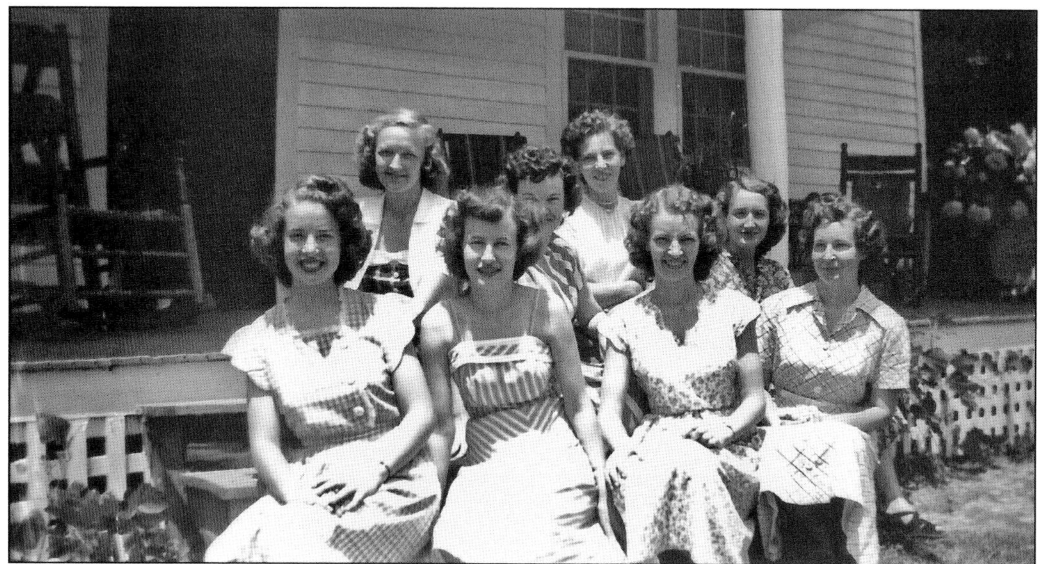

This picture includes the Maddux sisters and their sisters-in-law. Pictured from left to right are (first row) Wilma Sue Maddux Wilson, Clara Faye Maddux Woods, Juanita Maddux Bays, and Elsie Maddux Derting; (second row) Odis Maddux, Uva Maddux, Mary Maddux, and Lena Maddux. (Courtesy of Elsie Derting.)

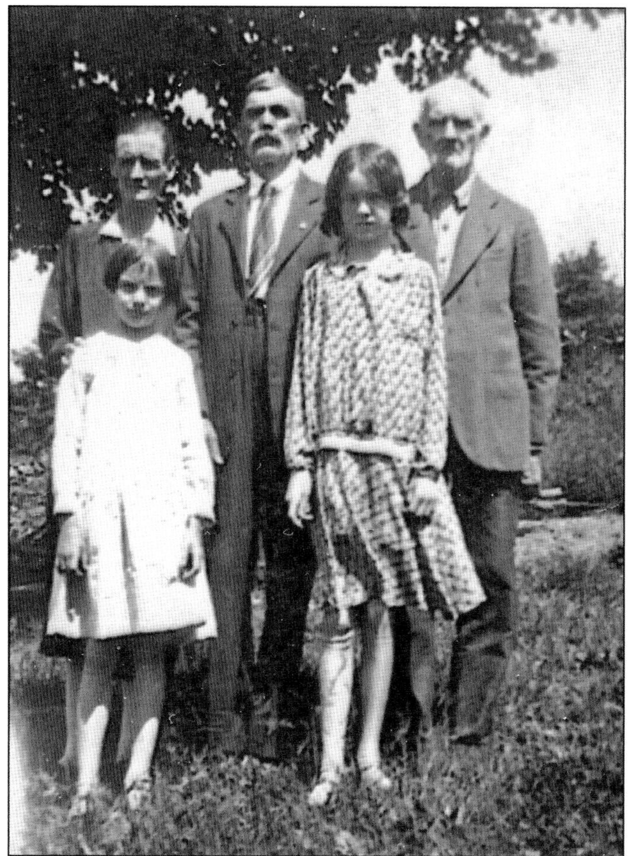

From left to right in the second row are Susie Godsey, Isaac Godsey, and John Hooker. The two girls in the front are unidentified. (Courtesy of Opal McMurray.)

Theta Lunsford is the daughter of Rendi Lunsford, whose family owned the Lunsford Mill. (Courtesy of Elsie Gardner.)

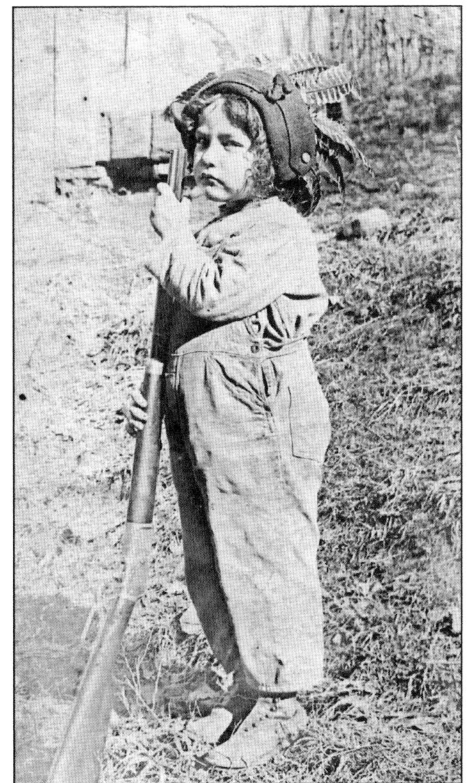

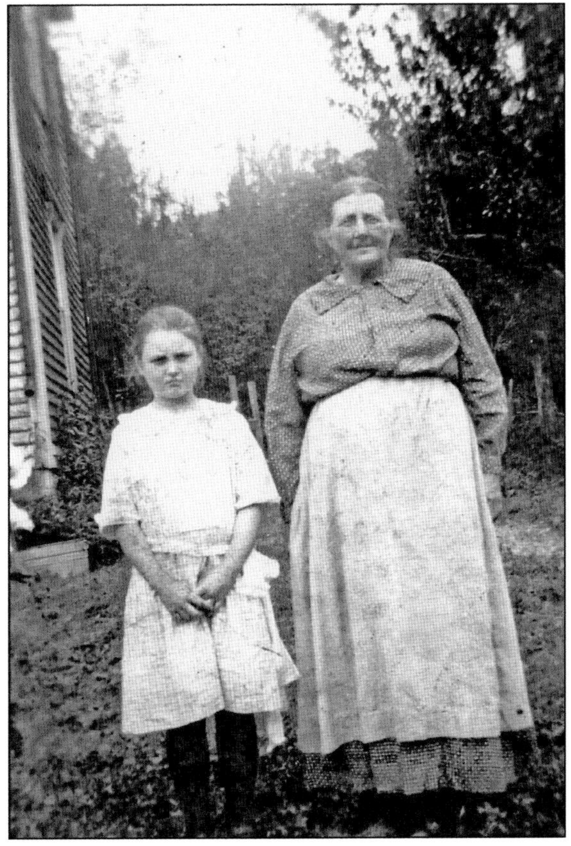

Pictured are Matilda Smith Gardner and her granddaughter, Elsie Gardner. Elsie's mother died when she was around five years old, and she and her siblings lived with their grandmother afterward. (Courtesy of Elsie Gardner.)

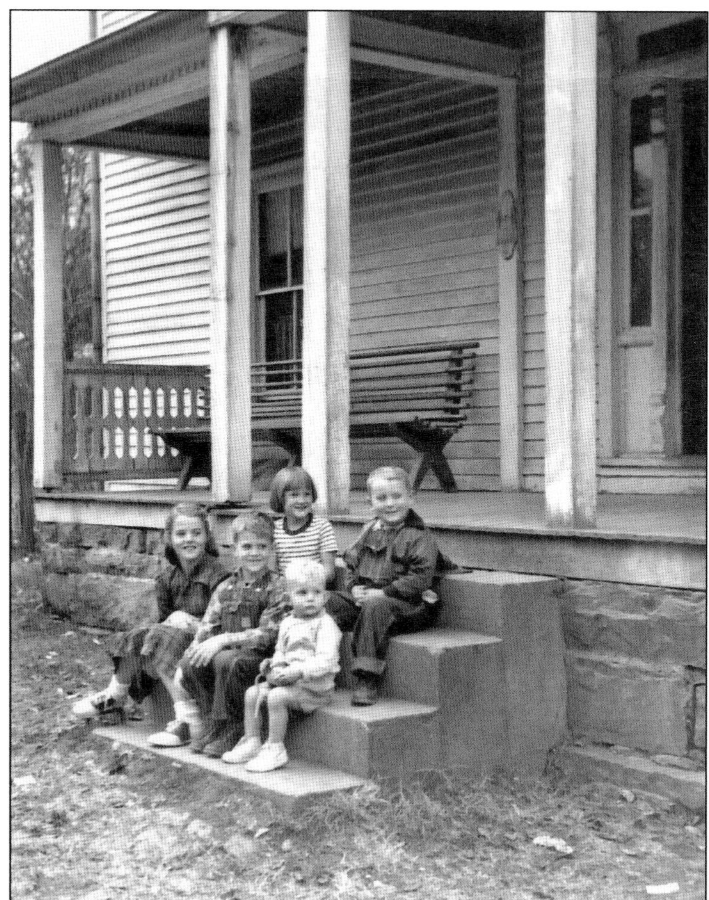

Shown from left to right are Gardner children (first row) Kathy, Rex, and Marvin; (second row) Jean and Ewell. They are sitting on the steps of the front porch of the home place of Hiram Gardner. (Courtesy of Marianna Gardner.)

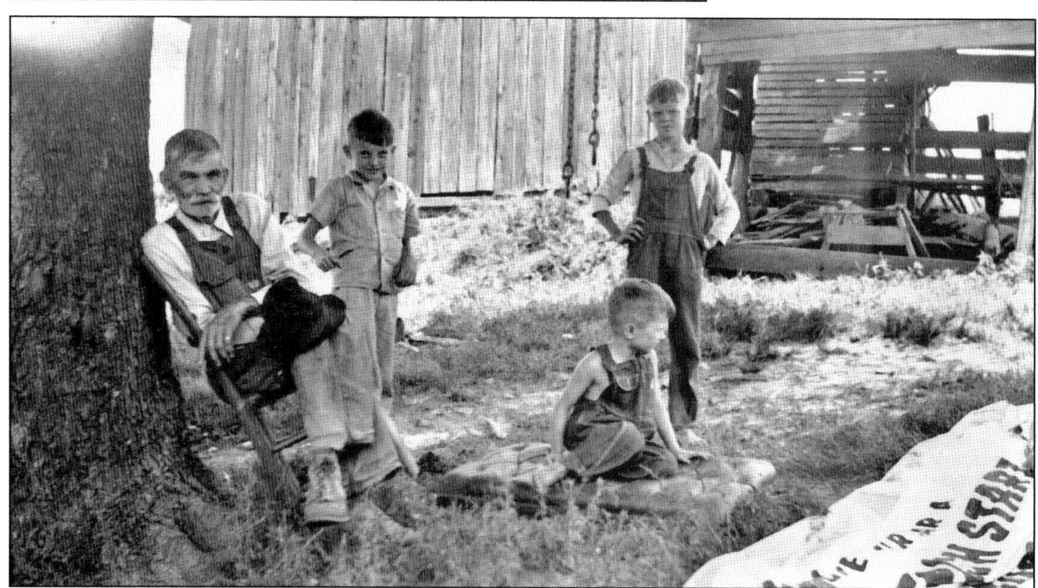

Around 1945, Isaac Godsey sits near the barn and watches three of his grandsons playing. From left to right are Jack ?, Doug McMurray, and Bobby ?. (Courtesy of Opal McMurray.)

Matilda Gardner is pictured with the old brown cow that Elsie Gardner learned to milk beginning when she was seven years old. Elsie is the granddaughter of Matilda Gardner. (Courtesy of Elsie Gardner.)

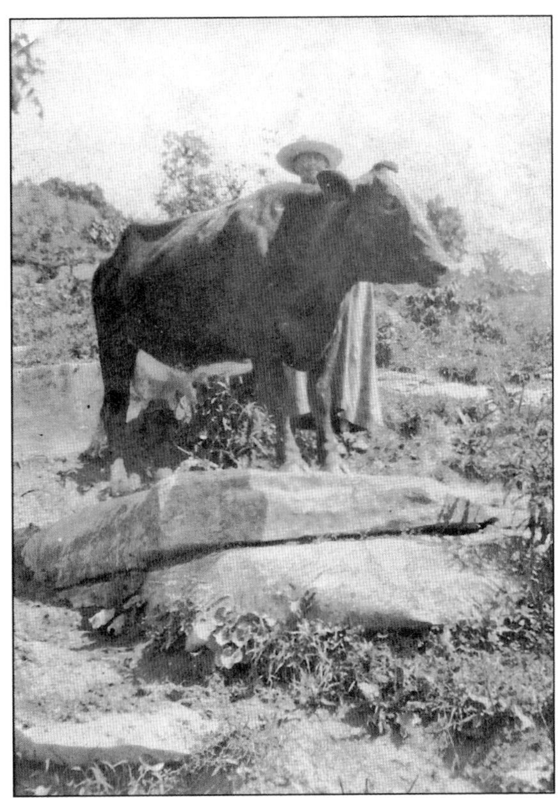

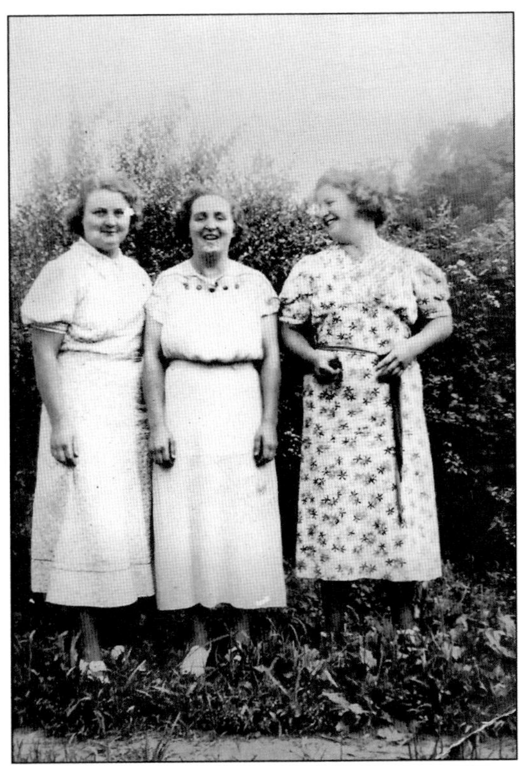

Pictured from left to right are Elsie, Thelma, and Sarah Gardner. Elsie went on to marry Clyde Gardner, and they had several children. She lived on the North Fork of the Holston River. (Courtesy of Elsie Gardner.)

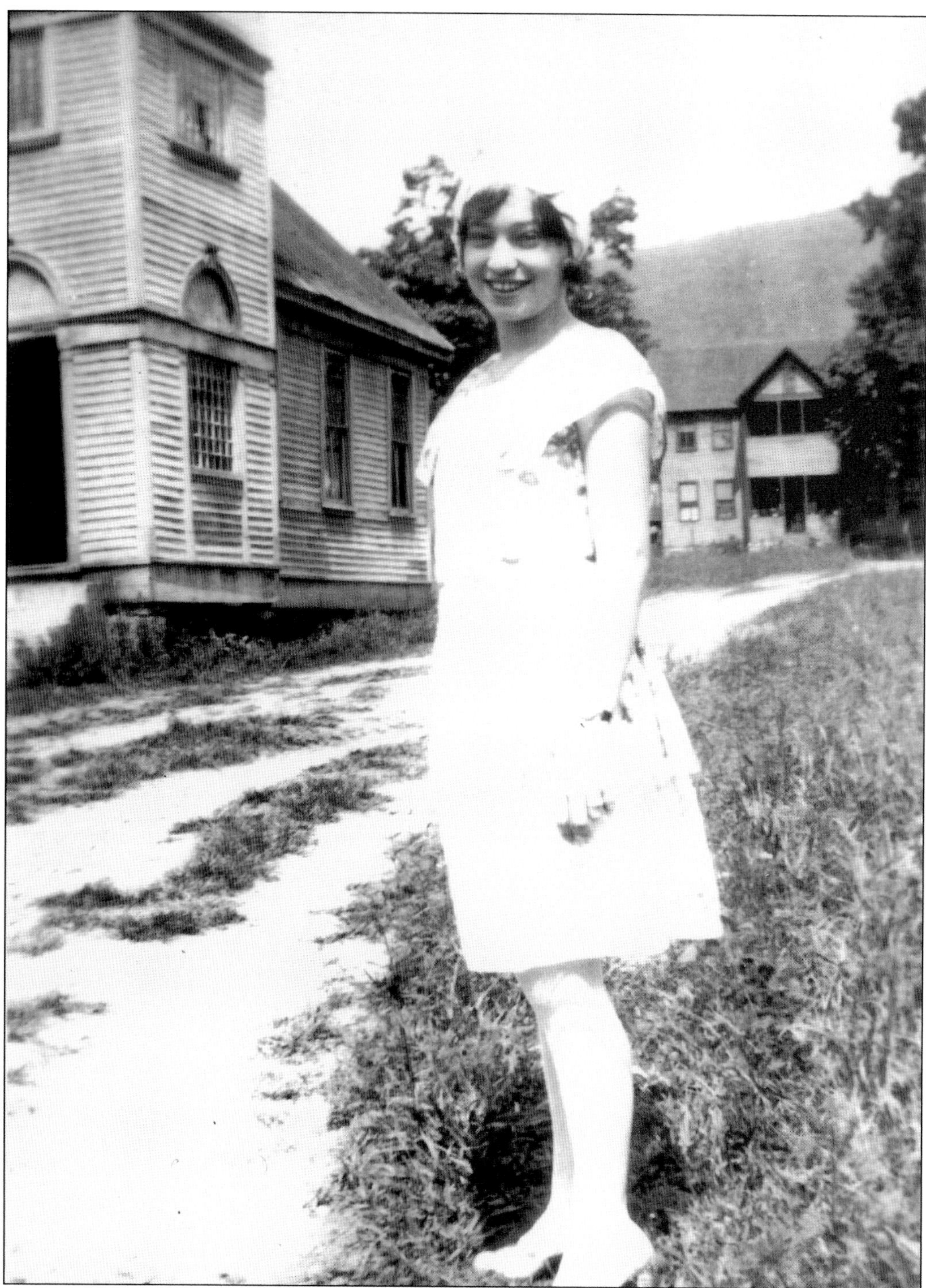

In a white dress, Sue Quillen Hall stands in front of the original Hilton Boarding School, the building to the right of her. Students from Nickelsville, Virginia, would come and board there to go to high school. To the left of her is the Methodist and Baptist churches building. The structure was used for both church services. (Courtesy of Marianna Gardner.)

Gertrude Godsey and Mattie Hooker play with a dog. Mattie was Isaac Godsey's sister. She married Billy Hooker, Susie Godsey's brother. (Courtesy of Opal McMurray.)

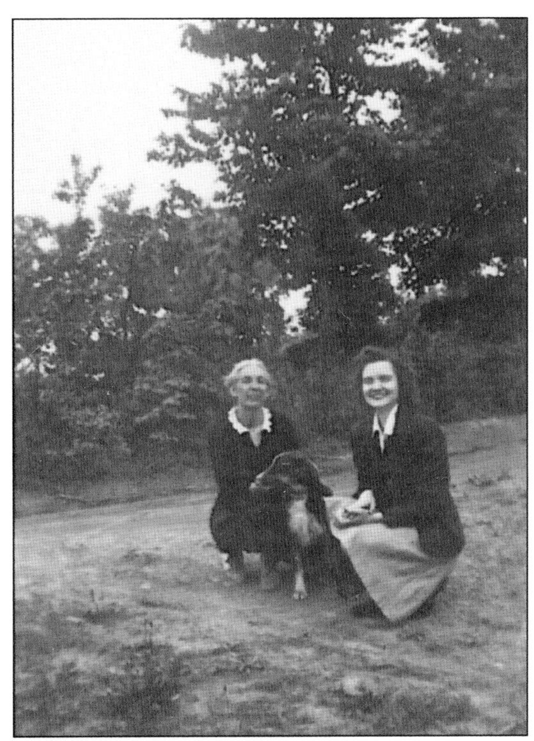

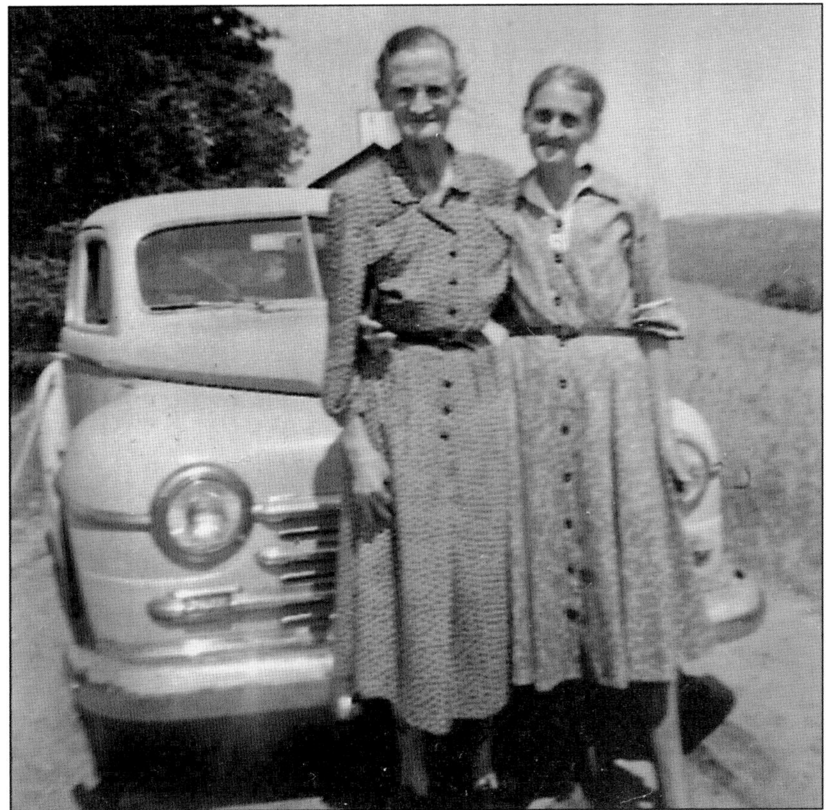

Pictured are Susie Godsey (left) and Ida Hensley. Hensley was a neighbor to the Godseys. She was married to Pat Hensley, and they had three children. (Courtesy of Opal McMurray.)

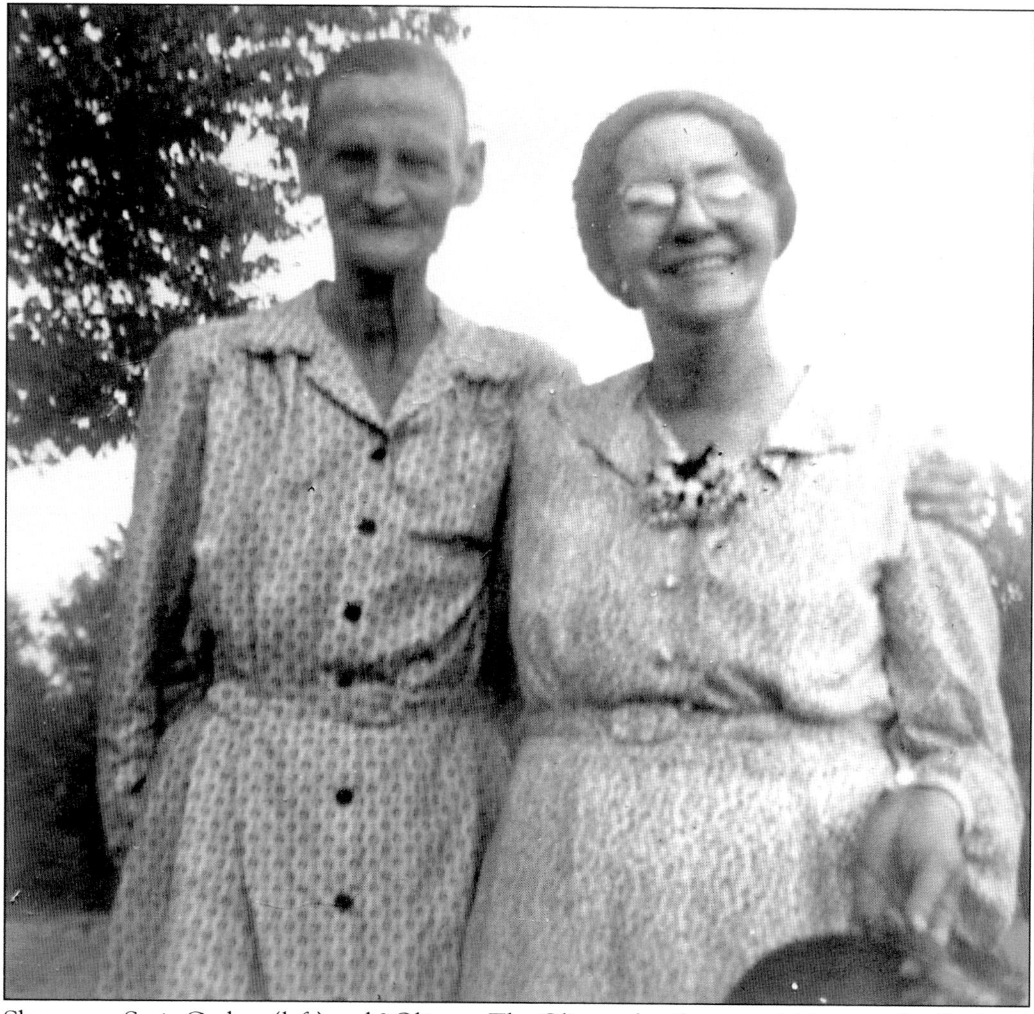

Shown are Susie Godsey (left) and ? Olinger. The Olinger family was neighbors to the Godseys. Ken Olinger had several children, including Willie Kate, Sylvia, Betty, Ruby, S. J., Carl, Clevey, and Lakey. Gordon and Cory Moody were more neighbors, and they had seven children. (Courtesy of Opal McMurray.)

Six

Ann Goode Cooper

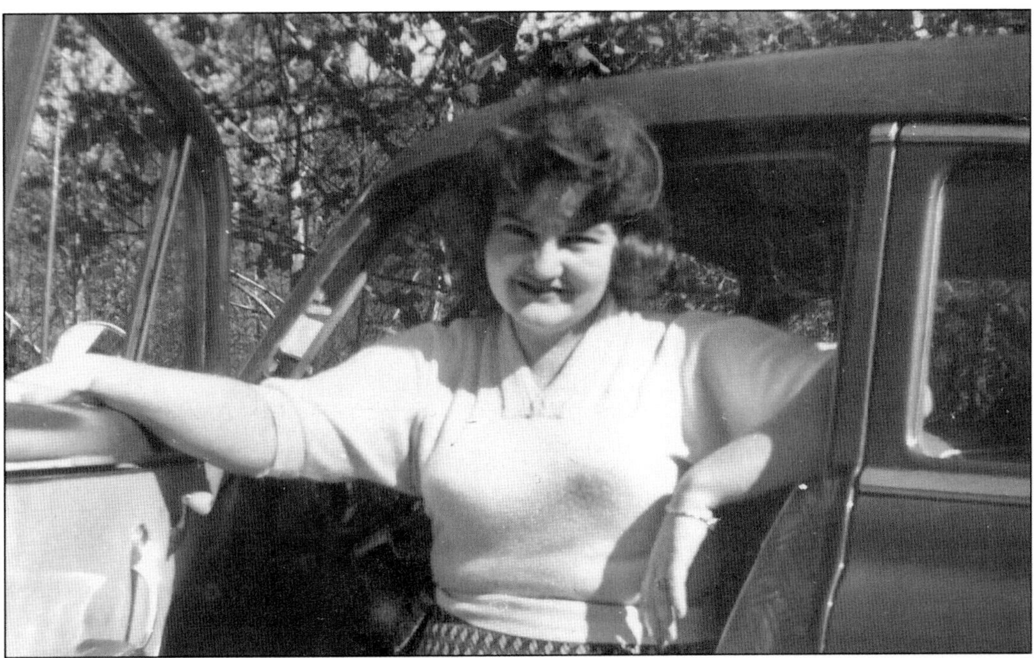

Ann Goode Cooper, pictured in 1957, is a local author and historian who still lives in her parents' home, where she was born. She married Ben Cooper, and they had one daughter, Hope. She has won several awards and has been invited to visit the Queen of England. (Courtesy of Ann Goode Cooper.)

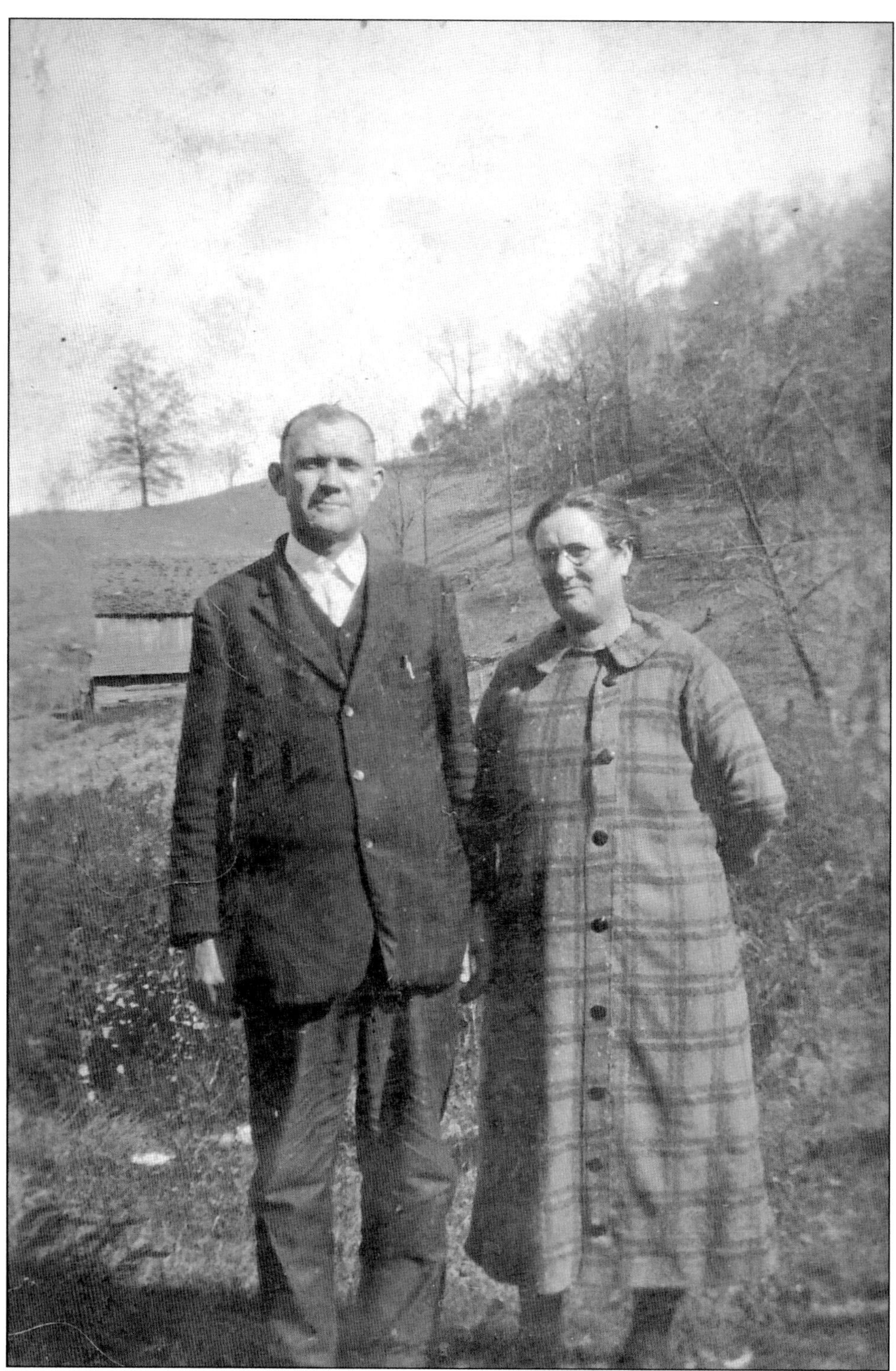

Pictured are Charlie and Cora Kilgore Bowlin. Cora was a teacher at the Saratoga School in Nickelsville, Virginia. The couple had three children: Claude, Lotus, and Bettie, and are the grandparents of Ann Goode Cooper. (Courtesy of Ann Goode Cooper.)

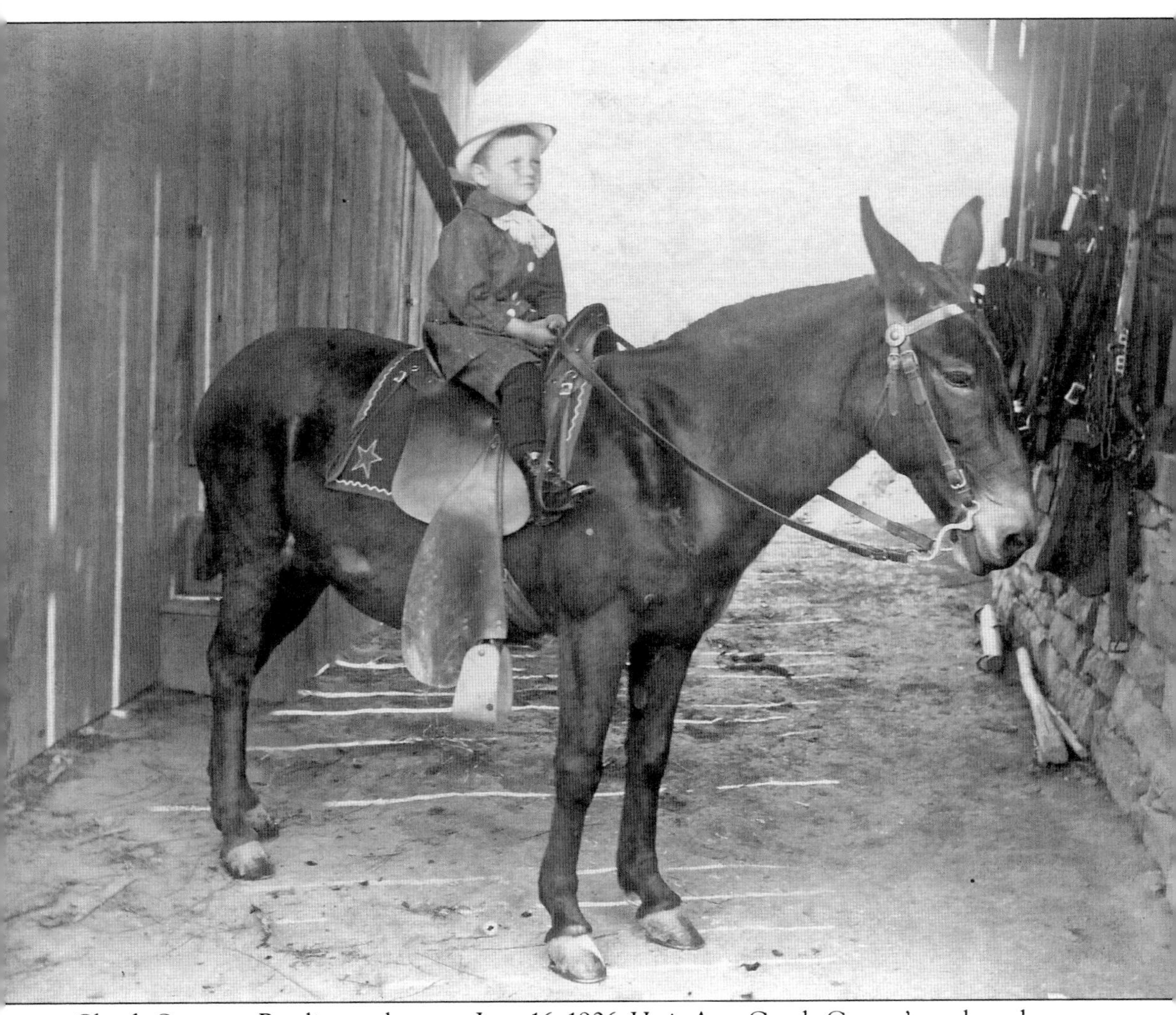

Claude Swanson Bowlin was born on June 16, 1906. He is Ann Goode Cooper's uncle and a son of Charles and Cora Kilgore Bowlin. He married Mary Good and spent most of his life farming for a living. (Courtesy of Ann Goode Cooper.)

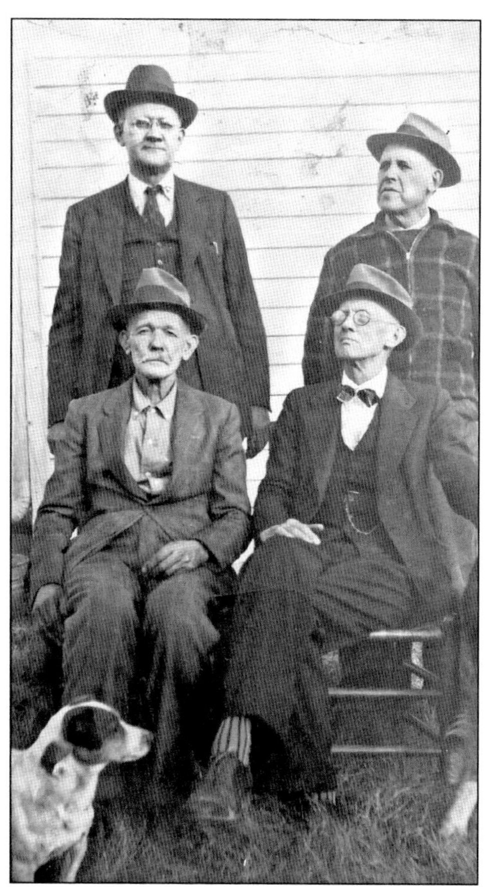

These are the four Bowlin brothers: (first row, left to right) Jim and Will "W. H." Bowlin; (second row, left to right) Charlie and John. All four brothers became professionals; Jim was a merchant, Charlie and John were both teachers, and Will was a lawyer. They are the sons of Billy and Sarah Dulaney Bowlin. (Courtesy of Ann Goode Cooper.)

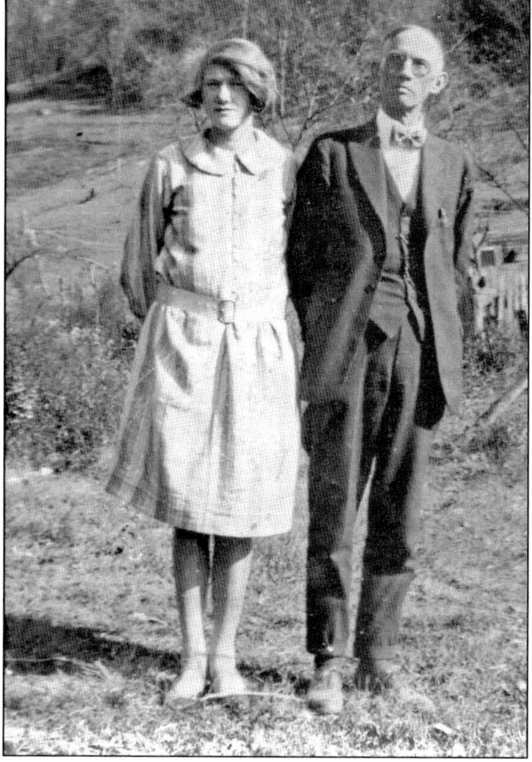

Pictured are lawyer Will Bowlin and his niece Lotus Osborne. Lotus was the daughter of Charlie and Cora Bowlin, and she married Gordon Osborne. Lotus died at a young age, and her son with Gordon, Charles Jackie, died in infancy. (Courtesy of Ann Goode Cooper.)

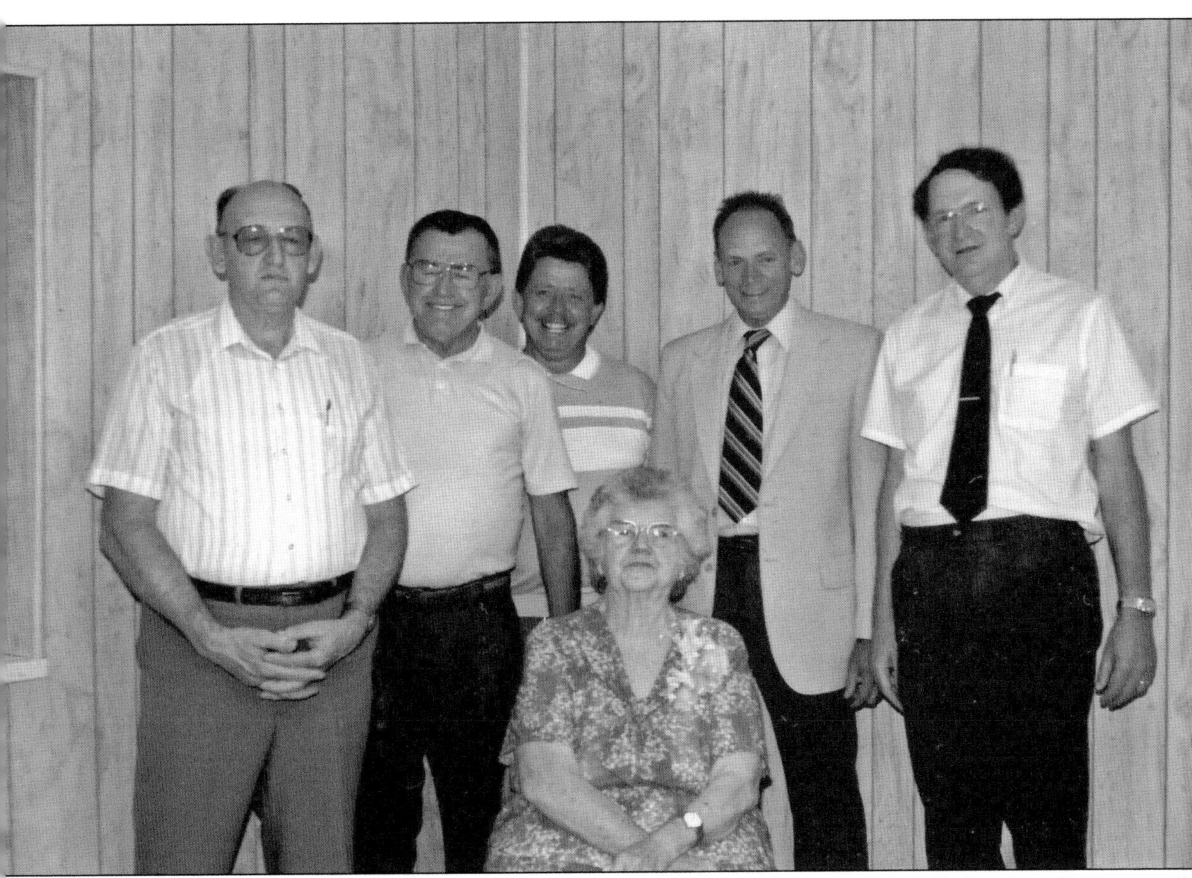

Pictured here are Bettie Bodwin Goode (seated) and five cousins (left to right): Billy Bowlin, C. T. Goode, Wayne Goode, Bayard Goode, and Johnny Bowlin. Billy Bowlin was the son of Claude and Mary Good Bowlin. He was the oldest of four sons and married Jeanette Bowlin, who now resides in Bristol. They had two daughters, Lisa and Karen. (Courtesy of Ann Goode Cooper.)

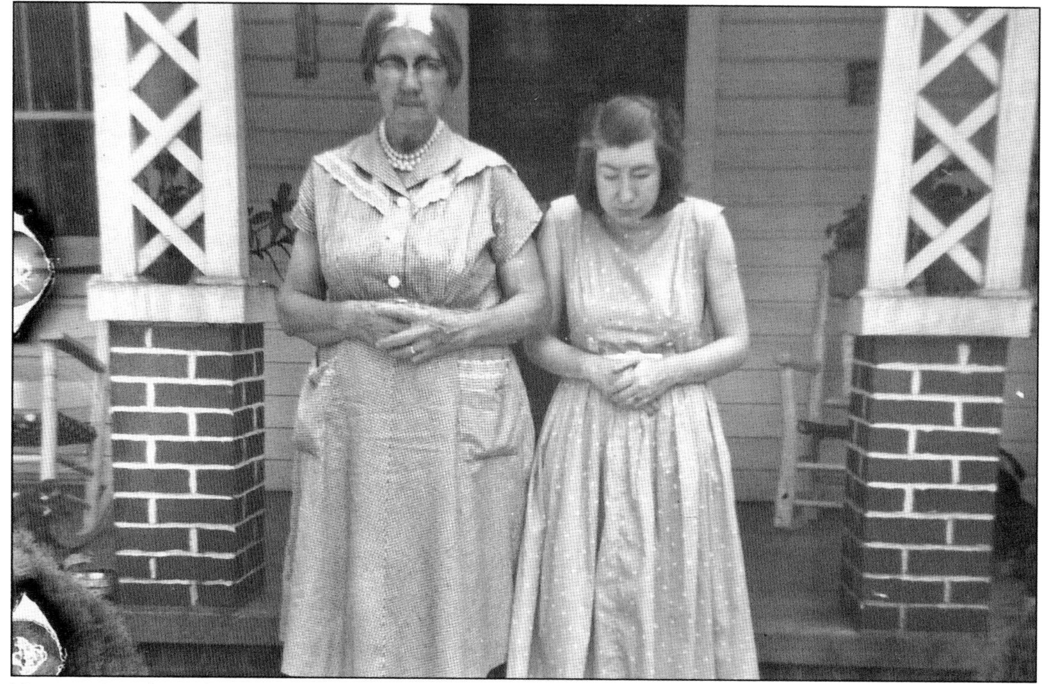

Nannie Smith and Virginia Smith are pictured around June 1960. Nannie Smith is the daughter of Thomas and Drucilla Larkey Goode. She married Clifton Smith, who owned the only sawmill in the area. They had one child, Virginia, who always lived at home with them. (Courtesy of Ann Goode Cooper.)

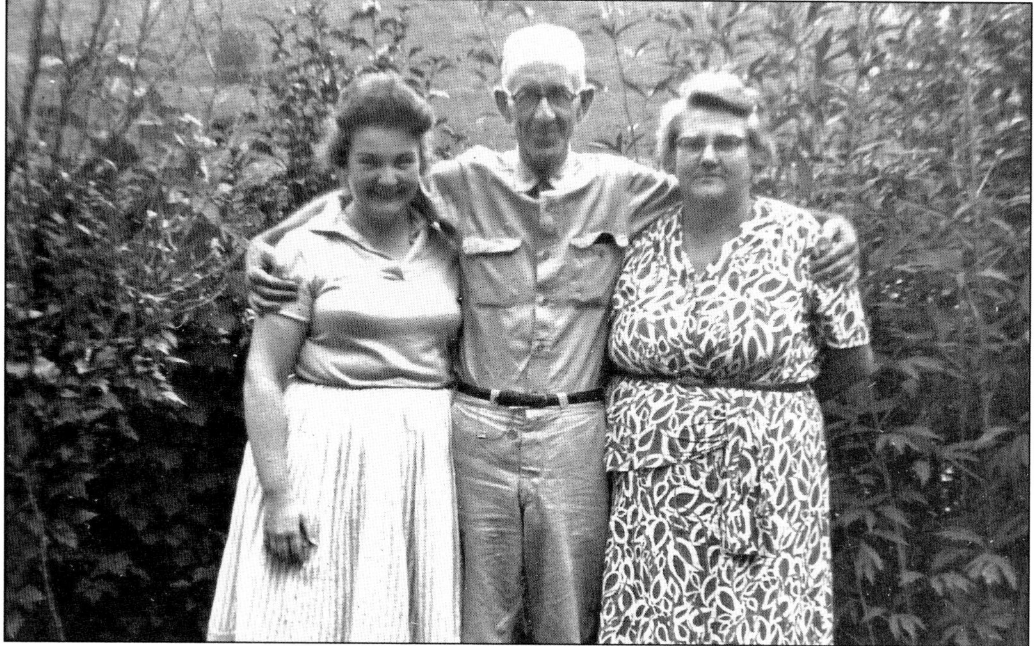

Ann Goode Cooper poses with her parents, George and Bettie Bowlin, in the summer of 1958. George Goode had five siblings, J. C., Pheobe, Nannie, Walker, and Mary. Bettie had two siblings, Claude and Lotus. (Courtesy of Ann Goode Cooper.)

William D. Bowlin, age 18 here, graduated from Hilton High School in May 1953. He never married, because his one true love died before their wedding day. He put all his effort into becoming an accomplished lawyer. (Courtesy of Ann Goode Cooper.)

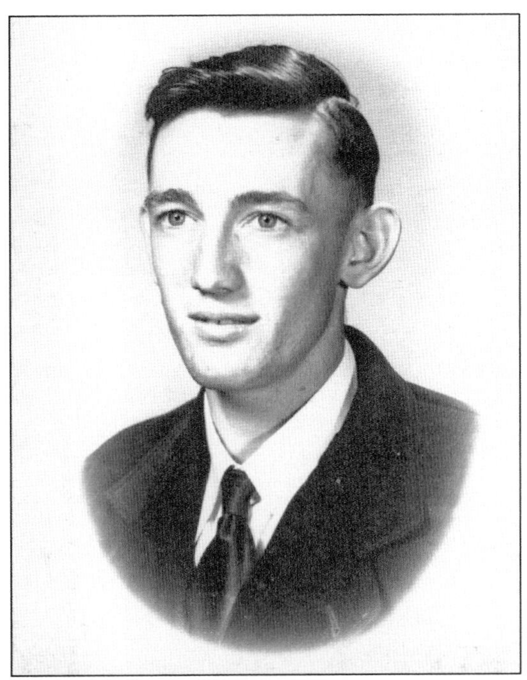

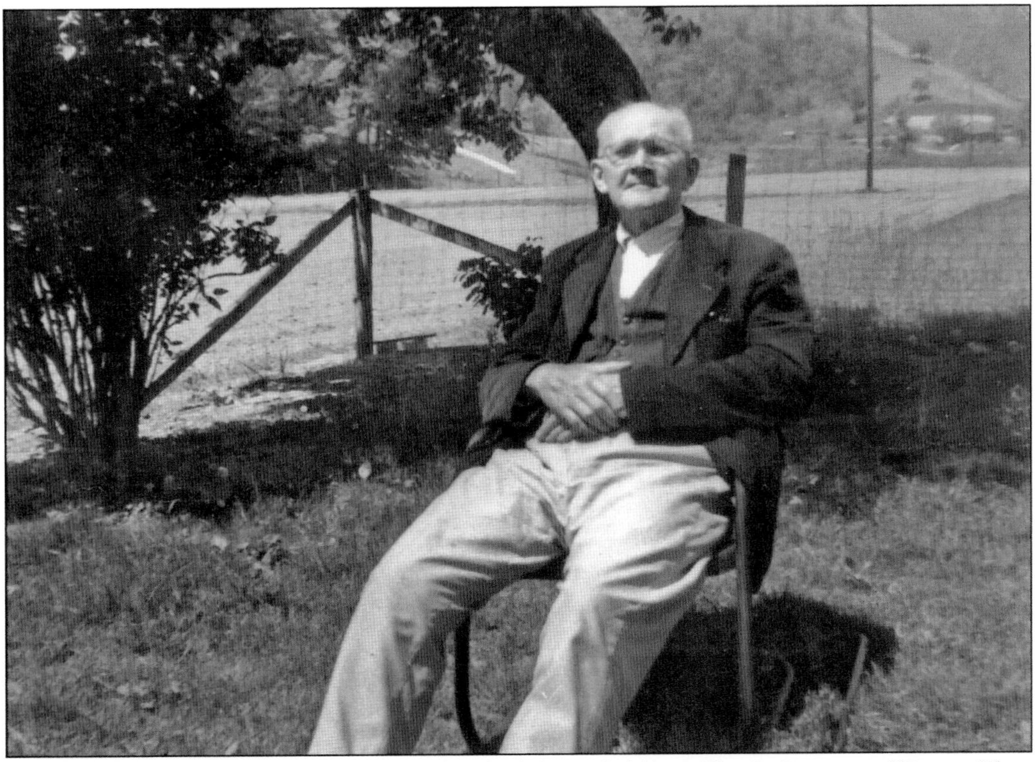

Charlie Bowlin married Corie Kilgore. They had three children: Claude, Lotus, and Bettie. They lived on the Bowlin home place, and he was a farmer. He was instrumental in the building and development of Beech Grove Primitive Baptist Church. He was the youngest child in his family. (Courtesy of Ann Goode Cooper.)

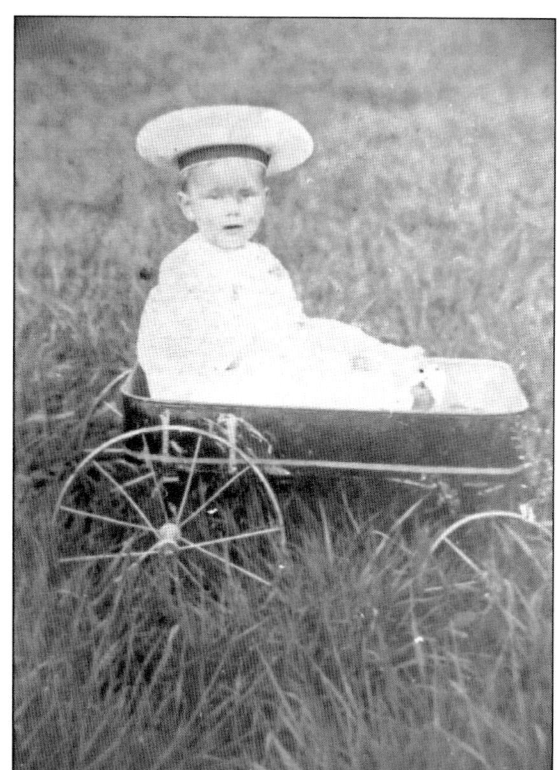

Claude Bowlin married Mary Good, and they had seven children. Claude spent most of his life farming. He was the son of Charles and Cora Kilgore Bowlin. (Courtesy of Ann Goode Cooper.)

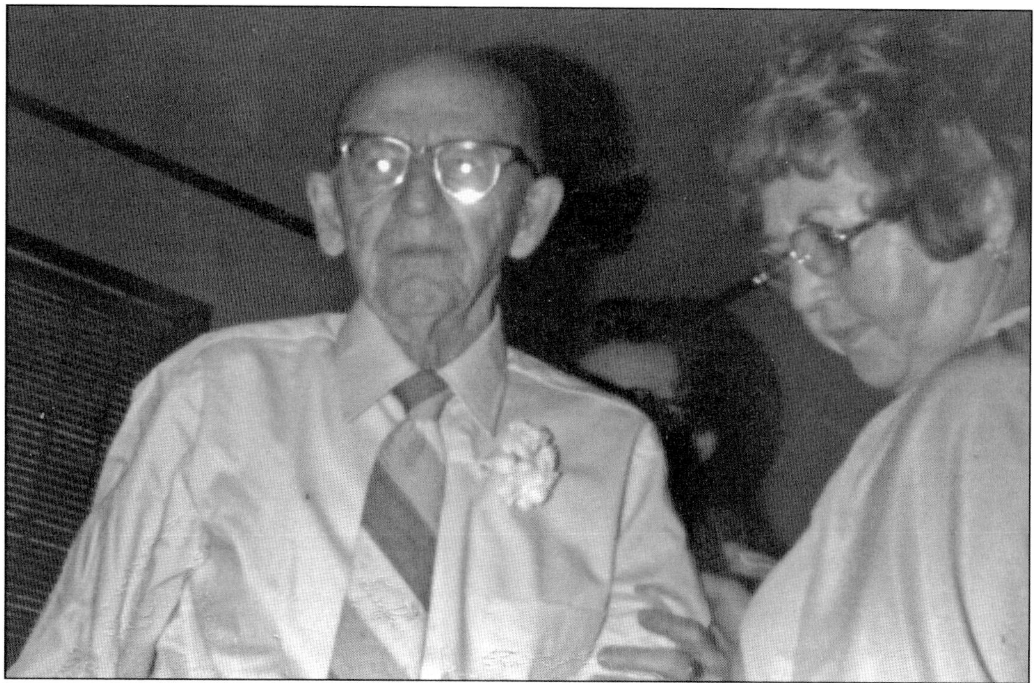

Shown are Jim "J. C." Goode and his daughter, Carmen. J. C. is Ann Goode Cooper's uncle and the son of Tom and Drucilla Good. He served in World War I and married Earlie Hunsucker. They have four children: Carmen, Elmer, C. T., and Dan. (Courtesy of Ann Goode Cooper.)

Seven

CARTERS

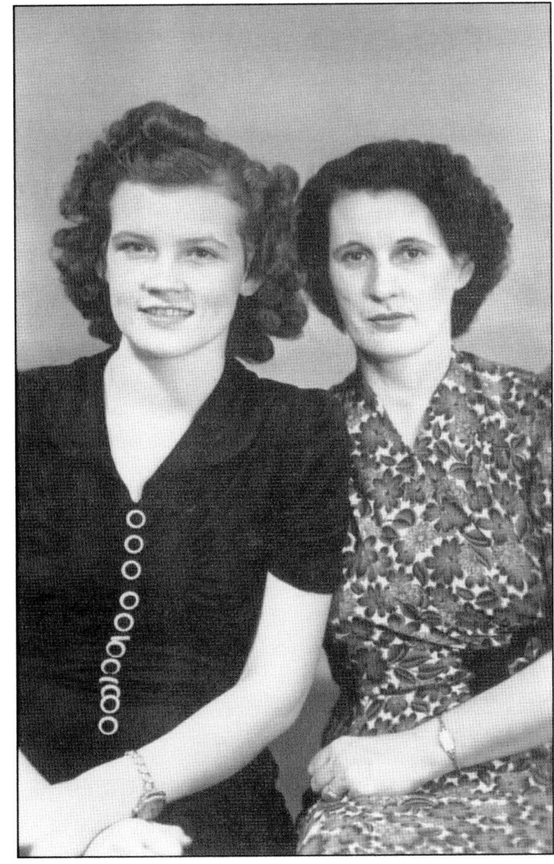

The two women shown here are Janette (left) and Sara Carter. Janette is the daughter of A. P. and Sara (Dougherty) Carter. Sara was born in 1898. Sara's mother passed away when she was only three years old. Janette started the Carter Fold in the 1970s. Janette married Jimmy Jett in 1940. (Courtesy of Rita Jett Forrester.)

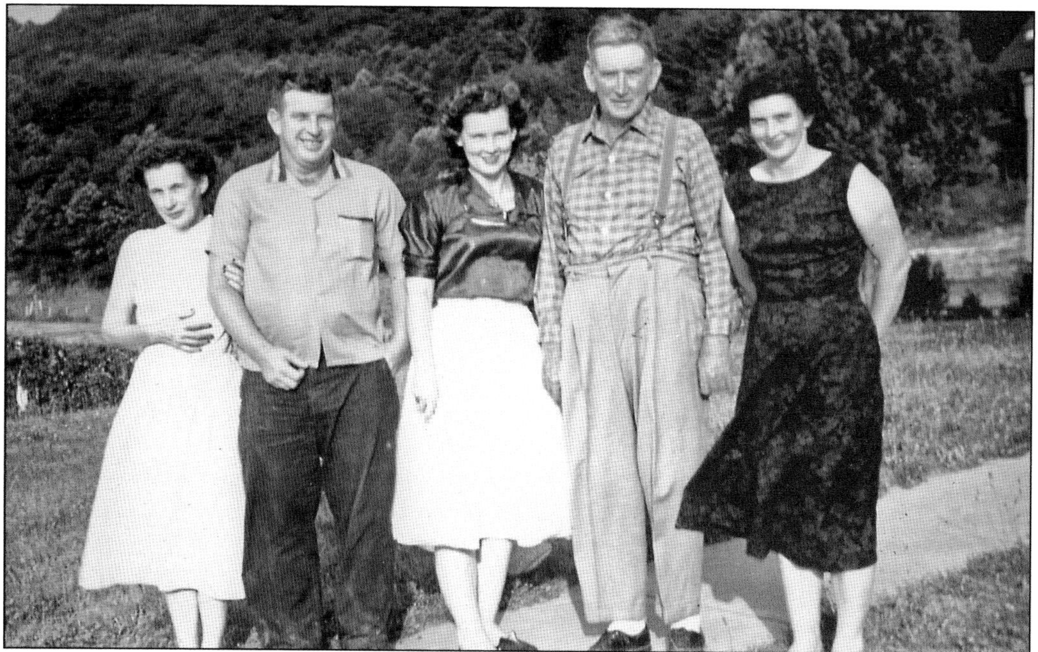

From left to right are Sara, Joe, Janette, A. P., and Gladys. Both Janette and Joe were regulars at the Carter Fold until their deaths. Janette first performed with the Original Carter Family sometime in the 1930s. Joe played guitar and sang at the Fold. Gladys took over the family farm from A. P. and helped her siblings Joe and Janette with the Carter Family Memorial Music Center. The family takes great pride in their musical heritage. (Courtesy of Rita Jett Forrester.)

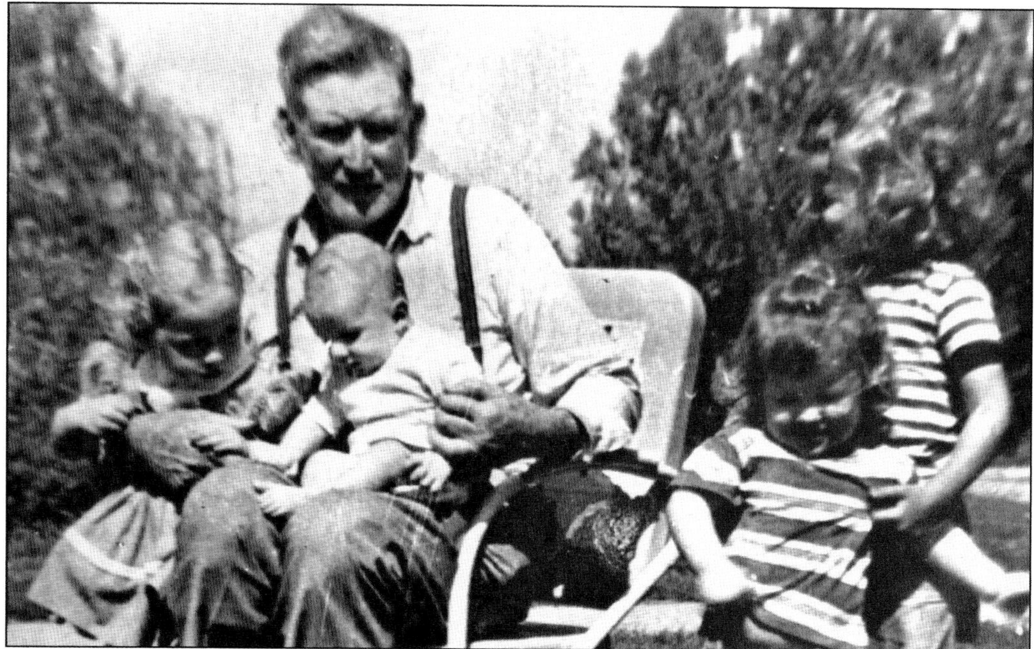

A. P. Carter, pictured with his grandchildren, was fond of his grandchildren and enjoyed spending time with them. Today the grandchildren are involved with carrying on the musical heritage of A. P. and the Original Carter Family. (Courtesy of Rita Jett Forrester.)

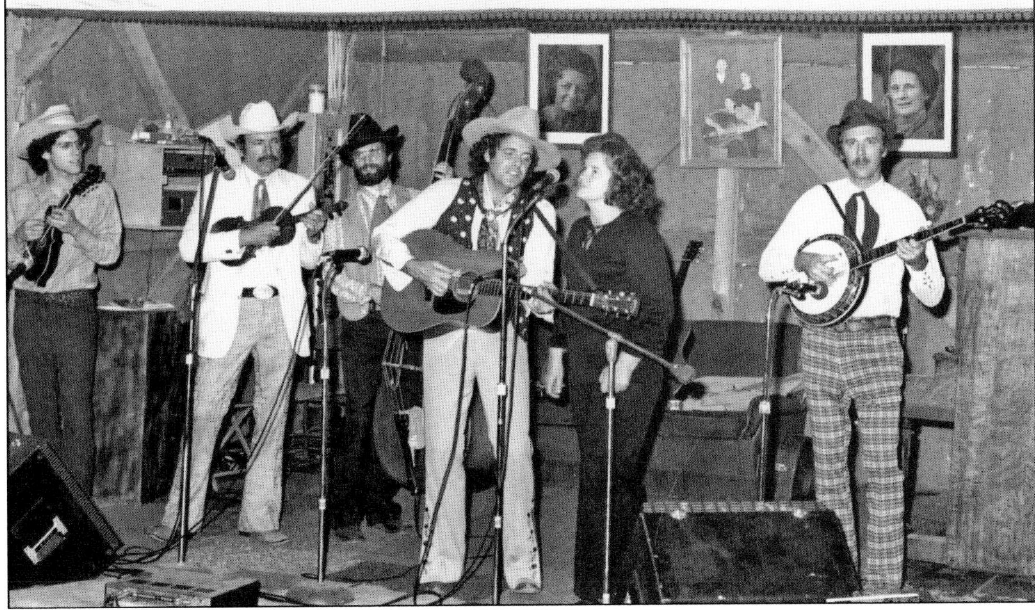

This is a group of singers at the Carter Fold. Musical performances are held each Saturday night at the Fold. Regional entertainers, as well as those who are internationally known, perform there. Music at the Fold is a family event, and no drinking is permitted. Each August, the Fold is the scene of a festival which lasts an entire weekend. (Courtesy of Rita Jett Forrester.)

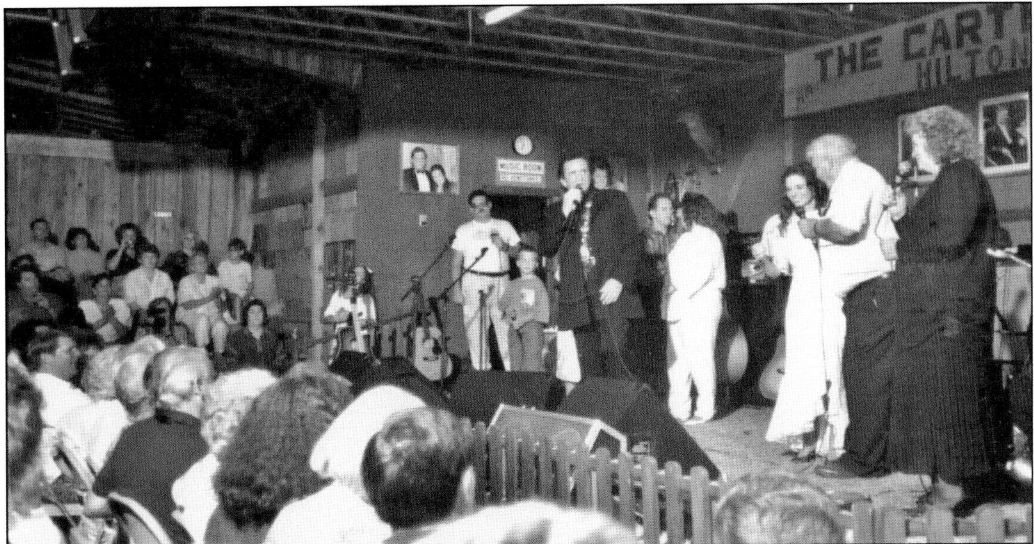

Center stage at the Carter Fold are Johnny Cash (with microphone), June Carter Cash (third from right), Joe Carter (second from right), and Janette Carter (far right). Johnny had met June Carter in 1955. They began performing together and were later married in 1968. The pair would visit the Hiltons area and perform on stage at the Fold. All four are now deceased, Johnny and June having passed away within months of each other. (Courtesy of Rita Jett Forrester.)

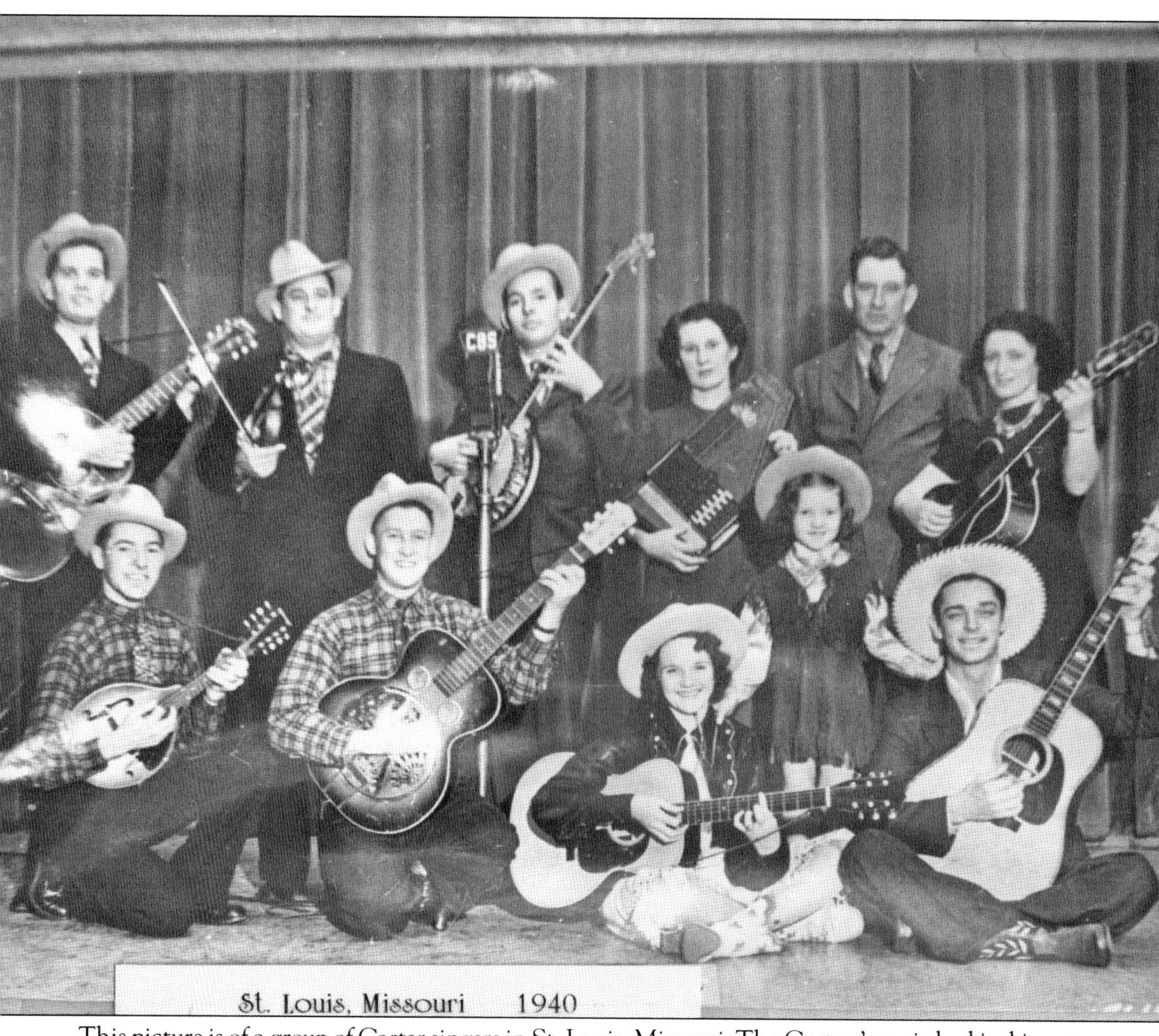

This picture is of a group of Carter singers in St. Louis, Missouri. The Carters' music had its biggest fans in Midwestern and Southern farming areas. People could relate to their songs, which were generally about life's hardships and its good times. (Courtesy of Rita Jett Forrester.)

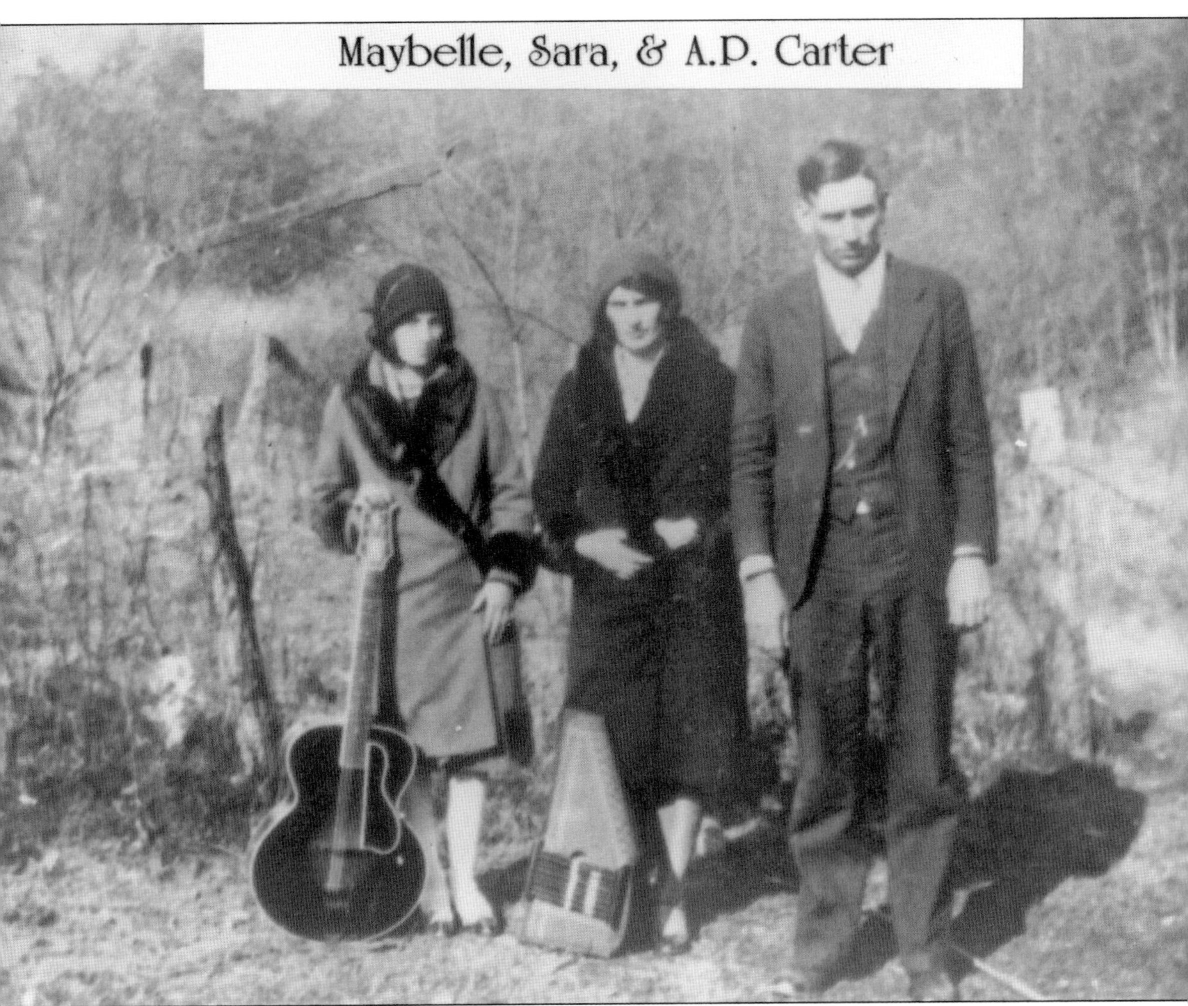

Maybelle, Sara, & A.P. Carter

This is an early snapshot of the Carter Family. The type of mass media that is available today was not possible back at the time when the Carter Family began touring. Radio, billboards, and posters, along with publicity photographs, were the only ways to advertise, but these methods were quite effective in their day. Even in the heart of the Great Depression, folks would manage to come to the performances in large numbers. (Courtesy of Rita Jett Forrester.)

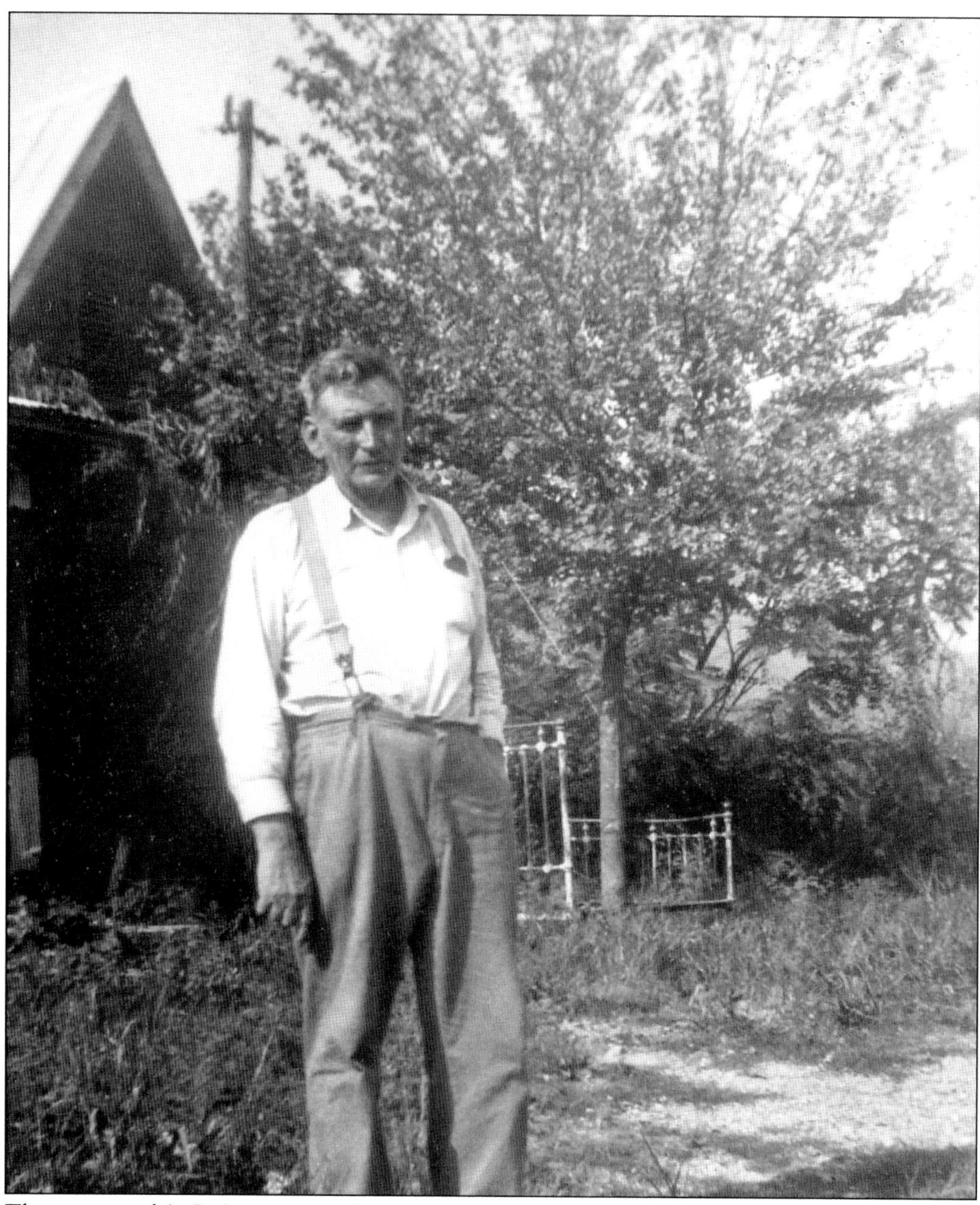

This picture of A. P. Carter was taken in 1950. A. P. was quite accessible to his neighbors. Most everyone knew him on a first-name basis, and many folks would come by his store to hear him sing. Though he was known worldwide for his impact on the music world, he remained the same person he had been before his fame. A. P. was well thought of by his neighbors. (Courtesy of Rita Jett Forrester.)

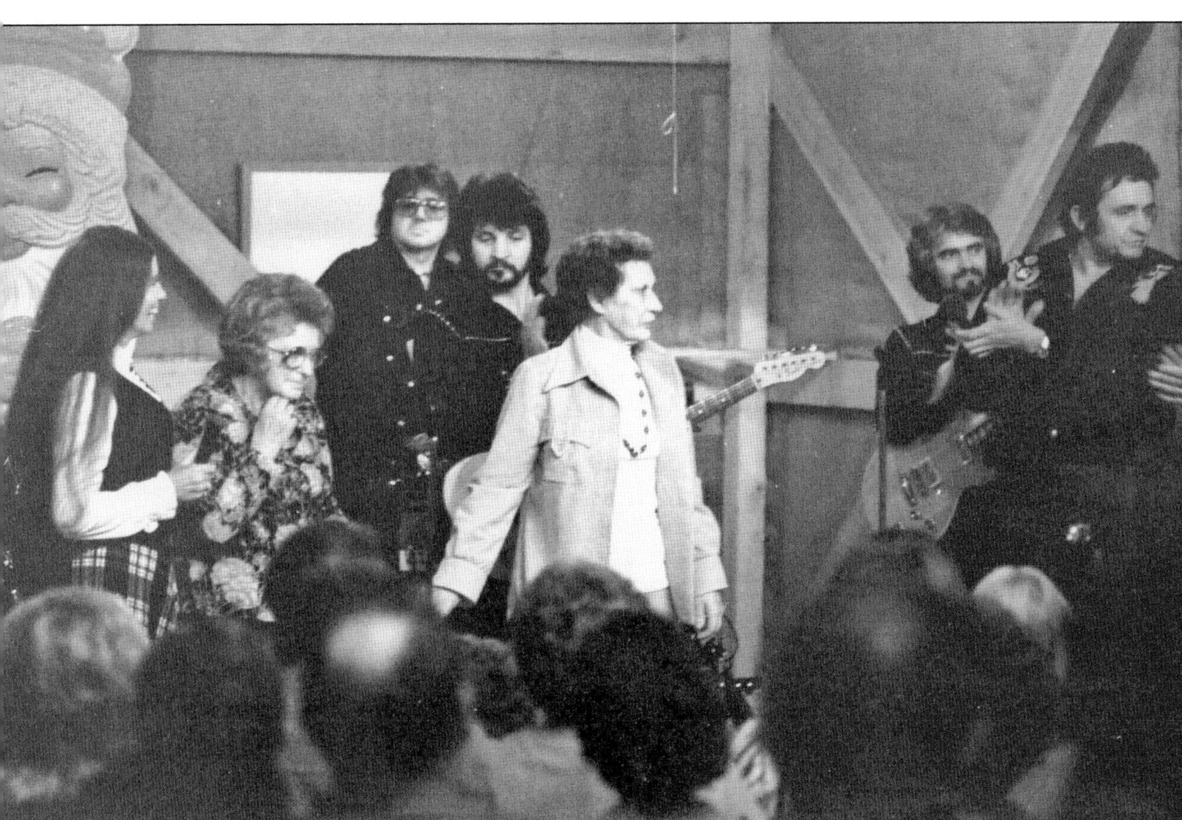

Pictured are June Carter Cash (far left), Maybelle Carter (glasses), Sara Carter (center, white shirt), and Johnny Cash (far right) on stage at the Carter Fold. These were good times, and everyone enjoyed the visits to the Fold by Johnny Cash. Any time that Johnny and June came to the Fold, it was quite an event for Hiltons. Such stars as Tom T. Hall and Marty Stuart have also been to the Fold. (Courtesy of Rita Jett Forrester.)

BIBLIOGRAPHY

www.carterfamilyfold.org

Davidson, Nannie Mae. *Scott County: Virginia and its people 1814–1991*. NC: Walsworth Publishing Company, 1991.

www.pbs.org.

Whitlock, Becky, ed. *Kingsport and the People of the Holston River Valleys*. Vol. I. TN: *Kingsport Times News* and Holston Valley Medical Center, 2005.

———. *Kingsport and the People of the Holston River Valleys*. Vol. II. TN: *Kingsport Times News* and Holston Valley Medical Center, 2007.

———. *Soldier Stories from East Tennessee and Southwest Virginia*. TN: *Kingsport Times News* and Eastman Credit Union, 2006.

INDEX